A FIGHTING CHANCE

THE MORAL USE OF NUCLEAR WEAPONS

JOSEPH P. MARTINO

A FIGHTING CHANCE

THE MORAL USE
OF NUCLEAR WEAPONS

Foreword by
Ambassador Edward L. Rowny
*Special Advisor to the
President and Secretary of State
for Arms Control Matters*

IGNATIUS PRESS   SAN FRANCISCO

Cover by Roxanne Mei Lum

DEDICATION

To Theresa, Tony, and Mike—
who will have to share the world
with nuclear-armed tyrants.

CONTENTS

PART THREE:

SOME STEPS TO TAKE

FOREWORD

In their pastoral letter on war and peace, the U.S. Catholic Bishops affirmed a nation's right to defend itself but stated that "We must find means of defending peoples that do not depend upon the threat of annihilation" (no. 221). Dr. Martino's comprehensive and closely reasoned study provides practical and moral guidelines for adopting defenses which meet the bishops' concerns.

In an approach reminiscent of Aquinas, Dr. Martino responds convincingly to the arguments of those who allege that nuclear war would violate every just war criterion on *ius ad bellum* and *ius in bello* grounds. I found particularly persuasive his thesis that if we follow the paths on which technology and our own human intelligence are leading us, it is possible over time to develop weapon systems and devise better strategies for employing them. In other words, should the need arise, we would be able to exercise command and control over the use of weapons which even more closely meet the criteria of discrimination, proportionality, and legitimate authority.

Dr. Martino's Christian approach to these complex issues enables him to offer us hope that we and our descendents may live in peace and freedom. He acknowledges as immoral some uses of force by the Allies in World War II and regrets that "the Catholic Church as such made little attempt to apply just war doctrine either to World War II or to the use of nuclear weapons since 1945". He insists that "reviving the distinction between defending ourselves and devastating the enemy is important from a moral standpoint." He holds that "it is our duty to demand that our Defence Department take Just War Doctrine into account when its officials plan to defend us." On this latter point, I can assure Dr. Martino that the United States Government *is* responding to the bishops' admonition that, "[I]n developing battle plans and weapon systems, . . . try to ensure that these are designed to reduce violence, destruction, suffering, and death to a minimum, keeping in mind especially non-combatants and other innocent persons" (no. 312). Moreover, while seeking to limit death and destruction should deterrence fail, the Administration is pursuing the Strategic Defense Initiative to see whether it is possible to have deterrence rest primarily on defensive systems, which threaten no one, rather than on offensive systems which depend upon the threat of retaliation. Dr. Martino is surely correct when he says, "It is crucial that we learn again to distinguish between preserving ourselves, with a defensive shield, and devastating the enemy."

While much of *A Fighting Chance* deals with *ius in bello* issues, Dr. Martino also brings a good deal of perceptive analysis to bear on *ius ad bellum* concerns. Indeed, his arguments are cogent as to what constitutes the moral use of nuclear weapons in a just war because he gives precedence to examining what constitutes legitimate cause for going to war. Dr. Martino reminds us, as do the American, French, and German bishops, that the United States and Soviet Union are not moral equals. "There *is* a moral difference between the U.S. and the USSR, and defending that difference is justified, even to the extent of using nuclear weapons in a discriminating and proportionate manner." This is not a consequentialist argument by any means. Rather it calls our attention to the care that must be exercised in reaching prudential judgments on the question of proportionality. We must do so with a correct understanding of why a war fought in defense of the values of our Judaeo-Christian heritage would be just.

My only argument with Dr. Martino's watershed study is his belief that all "arms controllers" hold a monolithic point of view. They do not. Those in the Reagan Administration responsible for developing and implementing arms control policies are the first ever to bring about a U.S.-Soviet agreement for actual reductions in nuclear weapons. They did so because they were the first to insist on reductions of weapons, not their codification at high levels. They were the first to insist that certain types of nuclear weapons are more dangerous than others and therefore their reductions should be given priority treatment in the interests of stability. They were also the first to demand that effective verification requires on site inspection to supplement the traditional "national technical means". Arms control efforts based on these principles can lead to good agreements which, by improving strategic stability, would reduce the risk of nuclear war.

Shortly after the U.S. Catholic Bishops approved their pastoral letter on war and peace, then Bishop John J. O'Connor, a member of the committee which drafted the letter, said that the bishops:

> . . . encourage our military planners and experts to accept the tremendous challenge that is theirs and to recognize it as a superb opportunity, namely, to do everything in their power to develop weapons systems and battle plans that will keep violence, destruction, suffering, and death to a minimum, even when war is justifiable.

Dr. Martino has accepted this challenge and met it magnificently. His book points us in the right direction and provides guideposts along the way. It is now up to us, who are greatly in his debt, to follow his lead.

Edward L. Rowny
Special Advisor to the President
and Secretary of State
for Arms Control Matters

PREFACE

The most devastating military threat facing the United States today is nuclear missile attack. Other forms of attack might be damaging: submarine warfare against our shipping industry, conventional attacks against our allies, even terrorism in our cities. But only nuclear attack threatens our immediate survival. Our policy, at least since the Soviet Union tested its first nuclear weapon, has been to deter nuclear attack through the threat of a counterattack on enemy cities. Deterrence then is the centerpiece of U.S. military policy.

However, the meaning of "deterrence" is unclear, and the idea of retaliating with nuclear weapons has been questioned on moral grounds. The U.S. Catholic bishops, in their pastoral letter *Challenge of Peace: God's Promise and Our Response* (1983),[1] gave deterrence only "strictly conditioned moral acceptance", and as of this writing have formed a committee to review whether the United States is indeed satisfying the conditions they specified as essential to their acceptance. The bishops of the United Methodist Church in 1986 issued a pastoral letter, "In Defense of Creation" which condemns nuclear weapons completely: "We say a clear and unconditioned No to nuclear war and to any use of nuclear weapons" (p. 13).

Despite the statements of these Christian leaders, it is my contention that a No to nuclear weapons is not an adequate moral doctrine for the times in which we live. On the contrary, it is mere moralistic posturing—a moral evasion. Moreover, I contend that this No is simply a continuation of our long-standing refusal to face the crucial issue of how to use nuclear weapons morally, in defense of justice and freedom.

In the following chapters I examine several popular "solutions" to the moral problems of nuclear weapons and show that these solutions create more serious moral problems than the ones they purport to solve. Next, I review the Just War Doctrine and apply it to the problems of nuclear warfare, not in the abstract but in today's world. Finally, I suggest some practical steps that may be taken to increase our ability to employ nuclear weapons in defense of important values while satisfying the criteria of the Just War Doctrine.

---

[1] Subsequent references to "the bishops' pastoral" or the "Challenge of Peace pastoral" refer to this document.

XIII

Some may note that I do not mention the subject of peacemaking, that is, of finding ways to reduce the likelihood of war by nonmilitary means. This is not because I don't consider it important—I do—but because the moral problems of peacemaking are sufficiently large to deserve their own treatment. Just to illustrate this point, consider the problem of "reducing tensions" with the USSR. It would be incredibly naïve not to recognize the totalitarian nature of Soviet society. The Soviet leaders have the sole power to make war. The Soviet people have no voice in how they are governed. Any attempt to improve relations with the Soviet people themselves would be seen by the Soviet government as a threat to its control, and would increase tensions. Any attempt to improve relations with the Soviet leadership would increase its totalitarian control by adding to the apparent legitimacy of its rule. The would-be peacemaker must find the morally correct balance between reducing tensions with those who can actually make war and ameliorating the conditions of an oppressed people.

The root of the problem, of course, is that peace cannot be attained directly. On the contrary, "peace is an enterprise of justice" (Is 32:17). Peacemaking must be first of all an effort to secure and expand the reign of justice. As such, it presents many moral problems which deserve full treatment in their own right. Hence I have chosen not to include this important issue, but to concentrate only on the equally important issue of the moral use of nuclear weapons.

In their Challenge of Peace pastoral, the Catholic bishops called for a dialogue on the moral problems of war and peace in the nuclear age. This dialogue cannot be restricted to professional theologians and pastors alone. Canon 212 of the *New Code of Canon Law* (1983) states, "[The faithful] have the right, indeed at times the duty, in keeping with their knowledge, competence and position, to manifest to the sacred Pastors their views on matters which concern the good of the Church. They have the right also to make their views known to others of Christ's faithful." As one who has spent nearly thirty-five years dealing with military applications of new technology, I hope this book will contribute to that dialogue, and to a resolution of the apparently conflicting requirements of morality and security.

ACKNOWLEDGMENTS

Permission to use the following quotations is gratefully acknowledged. Quotations from *The Button*, by Daniel Ford, are copyright 1985 by Daniel Ford. Reprinted with permission of Simon & Schuster, Inc. Quotations from *We Hold These Truths*, by John Courtney Murray, are used with permission of Sheed & Ward, 115 E. Armour Blvd., Kansas City, Mo. Quotations from "Why the Soviet Union Thinks It Could Fight and Win a Nuclear War" are reprinted from *Commentary*, July 1979, with permission of Richard Pipes, the copyright holder. All rights reserved. Quotations from Benjamin S. Lambeth's chapter in *The Future of Strategic Deterrence* are used with permission of Macmillan Press Ltd., London, England. Quotations from "The Challenge of Peace: Did the Bishops Help", by Mark Amstutz, are used with permission of *This World*. Quotations from "Bishops, Statesmen, and Other Strategists on the Bombing of Innocents", by Albert Wohlstetter, from *Commentary*, June 1983, are reprinted with the permission of the author and of *Commentary*. All rights reserved.

Portions of this book appeared, in somewhat different form, in the journal *This World*. Permission to reprint is gratefully acknowledged. In addition, portions of the manuscript were reviewed by Lawrence E. Beilenson, Joseph Coates, Sam Cohen, Michael J. Dunn, Lt. Gen. Daniel O. Graham, USA (Ret.), George W. Earley, Fr. James Heft, BG Albion W. Knight, USA (Ret.), Joseph Kunkel, Will Morrisey, Matthew D. Murphy, Rudolph Rummel, and Col. Raymond A. Shulstad, USAF. They contributed significantly to clarifying my ideas, for which I am deeply grateful. However, this does not necessarily mean they agree with all or even any part of those ideas. Moreover, they bear no responsibility for any remaining errors of omission or commission; such responsibility is solely mine.

PART ONE

THE MORAL PROBLEM

CHAPTER ONE

DETERRENCE AND/OR DEFENSE

Before the dawn of the nuclear age, the United States had drifted, as though sleepwalking, into making war on women, children, the sick, and the elderly. The firebombings of Dresden and Tokyo were the precursors of the atomic bombings of Hiroshima and Nagasaki, and they actually resulted in more deaths, a majority of which were women and children. Although during World War II a few voices raised moral objections to the policy of direct attacks on civilians, the moral issues were for the most part simply ignored. The general attitude was "if they want total war, we'll show 'em what total war is like."

This precedent of ignoring moral issues, set in the Second World War, continues to this day. In the four decades since 1945, most analyses of the morality of nuclear war have consisted of subterfuges to avoid the hard question of how to use nuclear weapons morally. We can see this in analyses of the United States' policy with regard to the use of nuclear weapons.

The official policy of the United States is deterrence of nuclear attack. Before trying to discuss this policy, some definitions are in order. In *Webster's New Twentieth Century Dictionary, Unabridged* second edition, we find:

> defend: (1) to fend or ward off; (4) to guard from attack; to protect by opposition or resistance; to prevent from being injured or destroyed.
> deter: to discourage or keep (a person) from doing something through anxiety, fear, doubt, etc.
> dissuade: (2) to turn (a person) aside (from a course, etc.) by giving reasons or motives.

By these definitions, a *defense* against attack could be said to *deter* the attack if it convinced the enemy that his attack would avail him nothing. In fact, historically there was no other way to deter an attack than by being capable of an effective defense.

However, the meaning of *deter*, as applied to modern warfare, no longer has a connection with any possible defense. As Kincade and Porro (1979) note, deterrence means "dissuasion of a potential adversary from initiating an attack or conflict, often by the *threat of unacceptable retaliatory damage*" (emphasis added). That is, an enemy may be deterred by means other than by defense. A threat of destruction may deter the enemy, even if the defender cannot protect himself from equivalent destruction.

As long ago as 1961, Glenn Snyder made this important distinction: "Deterrence means discouraging the enemy from taking military action by posing for him a prospect of cost and risk outweighing his prospective gain. Defense means reducing our own prospective costs and risks in the event that deterrence fails" (p. 1). He went on to point out that military forces capable of deterring may be different from those capable of defending.

Scowcroft (1984) attempted to maintain the same distinction, speaking of "deterrence by denial" (that is, denying the enemy victory or gain), and "deterrence by pain" (that is, inflicting damage on the enemy even if we cannot prevent the enemy from inflicting damage on us) (1984, p. 75).

The introduction of nuclear weapons has had the effect of separating deterrence from defense. Each can now exist without the other. We have the situation as described in the following figure. The figure is divided into four cells, each representing a possible combination of pure defense and pure deterrence.[1]

Deterrence

		Yes	No
Defense	Yes	Security	Shield but no sword Vulnerable to attrition and irrational attackers
	No	Vengeance from the grave Vulnerable to blackmail	Complete insecurity Vulnerable to blackmail

Figure 1. Combinations of deterrence and defense

If the defender has both defense, which reduces the amount of damage that can be done by an attack, and deterrence, which threatens the enemy with serious losses if he attacks, the defender enjoys security. This security may not be absolute, but the likelihood of attack can be greatly reduced. Only under extreme circumstances would an enemy be willing to undertake an attack.

If the defender has neither defense nor deterrence, as shown in the lower right cell, then he is in a position of complete insecurity. He is dependent solely on the goodwill of his adversary. Moreover, in this

---

[1] This analysis is based on an idea suggested by Michael J. Dunn.

situation he is highly vulnerable to blackmail. The mere suggestion that an attack might be forthcoming under certain circumstances will give the victim an incentive not to allow those circumstances to arise.

If the defender has defense but no deterrence, he is able to protect himself from damage (at least to a degree and for a time) but is still unlikely to dissuade an enemy from attacking. Like a gladiator with a shield but no sword, the defender will eventually be overwhelmed: the attacker can simply wear him down. Thus even a one-hundred-percent effective "pure defense" is not absolute assurance of security.

The situation of defense without deterrence can arise when the attacker is irrational. An Ayatollah Khomeini or a Ho Chi Minh, both of whom sent large numbers of teen-aged boys into combat, are examples of attackers who are irrational. The losses suffered by their troops, although high by the standards of the defender, were not unacceptable to them.

This situation emphasizes another distinction between defense and deterrence. There is some objectivity to defense. We can compare our defensive forces with the enemy's offensive forces and estimate whether we could be successful in defeating an attack. There is nothing objective with which to compare our deterrent forces. Deterrence exists only in the mind of the attacker. It does not matter what the *defender* thinks about the deterrent capabilities of his forces. Deterrence is subjective since it exists only to the extent that the *attacker* judges the cost of an attack to be unacceptable.

The final cell in the figure, deterrence but no defense, is the situation in which the United States today finds itself with regard to the Soviet Union.[2] It amounts to "vengeance from the grave": a threat to destroy the enemy after the enemy destroys the defender. It is a very brittle and risky situation. If deterrence fails, it fails in a catastrophic manner. Moreover, the defender in this situation finds himself vulnerable to blackmail from apparently irrational opponents. A Stalin, who made it clear he feared war less than the United States feared war, can put the defender in a position where one more concession seems a small price to pay to avoid catastrophe. The attacker in this situation can adopt the attitude described by Herman Kahn: "One of us has to be reasonable, and since it isn't going to be me, it had better be you." Unfortunately, the situation can become even more brittle if both sides become con-

---

[2] The degree to which the Soviet Union considers itself to have a deterrent but no defense is arguable. The Soviets are putting significant resources into missile defense, air defense, and civil defense, and their internal discussions clearly indicate they believe these will be effective. Their preparations will be discussed in more detail in subsequent chapters.

vinced that in a crisis the other will be "reasonable" and back down rather than risk catastrophe.

The intent of *nuclear* deterrence, then, is to dissuade the enemy from attacking, *even though the defender cannot realistically protect himself*. This is to be done through the threat of destroying the enemy *after the enemy attacks*, regardless of the strength of the attack. The idea is frequently expressed as "Since we cannot defend, we must deter."

The separation of deterrence from defense has led to two unfortunate intellectual consequences. First, the idea of defense as the blocking of an attack has been lost completely. Then, defense has been telescoped into deterrence. Despite the efforts of analysts such as Snyder and Scowcroft, the distinction between defense and deterrence has been obliterated. Just as deterrence was once subsumed by defense, today it is taken for granted that defense is subsumed by deterrence, and no other form of defense can exist. In both the popular imagination and the discussions of moralists, the idea of defense has been lost completely, and the idea of deterrence has been reduced to the idea of threatening to destroy the enemy after he has destroyed you.

A recent book, *Objections to Nuclear Defense: Philosophers on Deterrence*, illustrates this loss of a distinction. Every contributor to this collection of essays is a university professor of philosophy, yet none of these professional philosophers seems to notice the shift in meaning.

The extent to which this idea has permeated Catholic thinking about nuclear war is clearly shown by the statements of the Second Vatican Council, and of Pope John Paul II. In the Pastoral Constitution on the Church in the Modern World (1965) the Second Vatican Council wrote:

> Undoubtedly, armaments are not amassed merely for use in wartime. Since the defensive strength of any nation is thought to depend on its *capacity for immediate retaliation*, the stockpiling of arms which grows from year to year serves, in a way hitherto unthought of, as a deterrent to potential attackers (no. 81, in Abbot, 1966) (emphasis added).

Here the identification of defense with deterrence is quite clearly evident. Defense is to be viewed not as a means of blunting or halting an attack, but as "immediate retaliation" in kind.

John Paul II, in his "Message to U.N. Special Session 1982", stated:

> Many even think that such preparations constitute the way—even the only way—to safeguard peace in some fashion or at least to impede to the utmost in an efficacious way the outbreak of wars, especially major conflicts which might lead to the ultimate holocaust of humanity and the destruction of the civilization that man has constructed so laboriously over the centuries.

In this approach one can see the "philosophy of peace" which was pro-claimed in the ancient Roman principle: *Si vis pacem, para bellum*. [If you want peace, prepare for war.] Put in modern terms, this "philosophy" has the label of "deterrence" and one can find it in various guises of the search for a "balance of forces" which sometimes has been called, and not without reason, the "balance of terror" (no. 3).

However, this seems to be an unwarranted extension of the Roman principle quoted by His Holiness. The Romans meant that to have peace, a nation must be prepared to repel attack. They did not mean that to have peace a nation must be prepared to devastate the enemy nation after it had first been devastated by the enemy.

Historically, the meanings of words shift with time as people find the need to express changing ideas. Therefore I cannot fault those who use *defense* in its new meaning. However, this shifted meaning creates a problem. The telescoping of *defense* into *threat of vengeance* deprives us of an adequate vocabulary to discuss some important distinctions.

In the remainder of this book, I will attempt to adhere to a vocabulary that will maintain those necessary distinctions. *Defense* will mean the warding off of an attack, the countering of the enemy's attack, or reduc-ing the extent to which the enemy can achieve his objectives through the use of force. *Deterrence* will mean the threat of vengeance—destroying the enemy without regard to whether the enemy will, or already has, destroyed the defender. *Dissuasion* will mean the discour-aging effect on the enemy of *either* deterrence or defense. Later on, it will be important to distinguish between *defense* as simply warding off an attack, and *defense* as destroying the enemy's means of attack. The latter will be described as *counterforce*. In addition, it will be important to distinguish between nonhuman targets with economic or political value, and the enemy population itself. Attacks on the former will be called *countervalue*; attacks on the latter (that is, the kinds of attacks threatened to achieve *deterrence*) will be called *countercity* or *counterpopu-lation*.

Why is it important to have a vocabulary for discussing these distinc-tions? Because the inability to discuss them means we are faced with moral problems, not just semantic ones.

The telescoping of meaning, which sees defense only as pure deter-rence, is part of the reason why the last four decades have seen a contin-uous refusal to face the hard moral questions which must be answered with regard to nuclear weapons. I will take several chapters to examine the subterfuges which people have used to avoid facing these moral questions. First, however, it is important to understand how the prob-lem arose in the first place. The next chapter will review the history of *strategic bombardment*, particularly how it led to noncombatants being considered legitimate targets, and eventually led to the idea of deterrence replacing defense.

REFERENCES

Abbot, Walter M., ed. *The Documents of Vatican II*. New York: America Press, 1966.

Blake, Nigel, and Kay Pole, eds. *Objections to Nuclear Defense: Philosophers on Deterrence*. Boston: Routledge & Kegan Paul, Ltd., 1984.

Kincade, W. H., and J. D. Porro. *Negotiating Security: An Arms Control Primer*. Washington, D.C.: Carnegie End. 1979.

Scowcroft, Brent. "Understanding the U.S. Strategic Arsenal". In *Nuclear Arms: Ethics, Strategy, Politics*, edited by R. James Woolsey. San Francisco: ICS Press, 1984.

Snyder, Glenn H. *Deterrence & Defense*. Princeton: Princeton University Press, 1961.

CHAPTER TWO

PRE-ATOMIC DETERRENCE: A BRIEF HISTORY OF STRATEGIC BOMBARDMENT

For military analysts as well as moralists, the advent of nuclear weapons brought something new to the scene. Everyone said the world was a different place after Hiroshima. As Bernard Brodie put it:

> People often speak of atomic explosives as the most portentous military invention "since gunpowder". But such a comparison inflates the importance of even so epoch-making an event as the introduction of gunpowder (Brodie, 1959, p. 147).

It may be true that the problems we face after Hiroshima are unprecedented. It is worth remembering, however, that prior to Hiroshima many people *perceived* that they faced problems very much like those of today. The validity of their perceptions is not relevant here. What is important is that we can learn something from how they reacted to their perceptions. As George Quester put it:

> [T]he major strategic complications imposed by bomber aircraft actually appeared long before 1945, [and] they arose early in the twentieth century with the introduction of aircraft systems that first led governments to *assume* the bomb-delivery capabilities that only now exist. Throughout this period the bomber was considered as a weapon that facilitated rapid infliction of great pain on civilian populations, and as one that might impose greater losses on the military forces of a defended territory than on the invading forces. . . . It matters little, for our analytical purposes, that these capacities of air weaponry were thus enormously and persistently exaggerated from 1900 to 1945 (we now also probably retrospectively underrate these capacities). Exaggerated or not, these early estimates of *punishing* or *disabling* capabilities were premises on which a series of policy decisions were made in this period—decisions, therefore, responding to problems remarkably similar to those that we face today. Modern terms such as "deterrence", "tacit agreement", or "balance of terror" show up often in the literature, coupled with descriptions of war scenarios every bit as awesome as a nuclear holocaust; sophisticated strategic analyses also appear (1966, p. 1).

Before 1914 it was already believed that bomber attacks against military installations and population centers would be a feature of aerial warfare. An illustration of how British leaders perceived the threat of

9

German air attacks on England is given in a letter written in September
of 1914 by Winston Churchill, then First Sea Lord (by a quirk of inter-
service politics, aerial defense of Great Britain was the responsibility of
the Royal Navy):

> There can be no question of defending London by artillery against aerial
> attack. It is quite impossible to cover so vast an area; and if London, why
> not every other city? Defence against aircraft by guns is limited abso-
> lutely to points of military value. . . .
>
> Far more important than London are the vulnerable points in the Med-
> way and at Dover and Portsmouth. Oil-tanks, power-houses, lockgates,
> magazines, airship sheds, all require to have their aerial guns increased in
> number. . . .
>
> But, after all, the great defence against aerial menace is to attack the
> enemy's aircraft as near as possible to their port of departure. Director of
> Air Division has already received direction on this. The principle is as
> follows:—
>
> (a) A strong oversea force of aeroplanes to deny the French and Bel-
> gian coasts to the enemy's aircraft, and to attack all Zeppelins and air
> bases or temporary air bases which it may be sought to establish, and
> which are in reach (Quester, 1966, p. 16).

Several points in this strategic analysis are worth noting. First, it was
assumed that a *point defense* of military installations would be possible,
whereas an *area defense* of a large city would not be. Second, however, it
was assumed that even though the Germans might attack London, the
natural target for German attack would instead be military installations.
Therefore the defense of these installations was more important than
defense of the cities. Third, the most effective defense of either military
installations or cities would be to intercept the attacking air forces well
away from their targets, as near to their bases as possible, and even to
attack the bases themselves.[1]

In his letter, Churchill had outlined a concept which would inspire
every theoretician and practitioner of air warfare for the next two gen-
erations. Historically, armies had sought ways to get around the enemy
forces immediately facing them to reach those things in the rear—
supply depots, armories, main roads—which were crucial to the enemy's prosecution of the war, but which were not themselves militarily

---

[1] This principle was a long-standing British naval tradition. As early as 1587, when the
Spanish Armada was being prepared, Sir Francis Drake argued that the best way to use
the British fleet was to attack the Armada in its harbors rather than waiting for it to arrive
off the English coast. He led a raid on Cadiz which was referred to as "singeing the king of
Spain's beard". The attack resulted in the burning of twenty-four Spanish ships and the
capture of a treasure ship.

"tough". The object was to concentrate one's strength on the enemy's weak spots; to *turn his flank*; to bypass his strength and cut it off from its sources of supply. That way his army withered on the vine; it wasn't necessary to meet it head-on and defeat it. The technological conquest of the air opened a *third flank*. Instead of trying to bypass the enemy's main strength on the ground, one could go over it, out of reach of ground-based forces.

But of course both sides could exploit the new medium. Just as the attacker tried to turn this new flank, the defender tried to strengthen it, with both antiaircraft artillery and defending aircraft. For the next six decades, attackers sought higher speed and higher altitude, to turn this third flank successfully, while defenders sought to extend their defenses, both ground-based artillery (later missiles) and aircraft, high enough to *wall out* the attackers. By the 1970s, both attack and defense had essentially reached the outer limits of the atmosphere. Aircraft could no longer fly above the reach of the defender's missiles. The attackers had to fight their way through, just as ground forces did.

But in 1914 that development was still a long way off. In pursuit of the policy described in his letter, Churchill sent his bombers to raid the zeppelin sheds at Düsseldorf, Cologne, Friedrichshafen, and Cuxhaven. These would now be called *counterforce attacks*. They were also *preemptive attacks,* since although they were launched after the outbreak of war, there had as yet been no zeppelin attacks on England proper (although there had been zeppelin attacks on Paris).

Thus at the outset of the war, both sides assumed that strategic air forces should be used against the other side's military targets, and that counterforce attacks were an important element of aerial warfare. How well did the reality match these assumptions?

Through 1914 to the spring of 1915, zeppelin attacks on England avoided London. British strategic attacks were limited to counterforce attacks. French aircraft bombed targets in the Rhineland, but attempted to concentrate on military industry. By then, however, it had become clear to everyone that the accuracy of aerial bombardment was not good enough to single out military targets for attack. Bombing attacks on factories inevitably led to casualties in nearby urban areas. So the weight of the attacks was shifted to area bombardment of cities in hopes of destroying civilian morale and shortening the war. Thus military leaders' high prewar expectations of the effectiveness of aerial attacks on military targets were not realized. Conversely, these leaders' low prewar expectations about defense were also proven wrong. British defenses against zeppelins turned out to be so good that the Germans ceased the attacks by the end of 1916.

Nevertheless, the attacks had important effects. German air attacks on Great Britain delivered 155 tons of bombs, killing 500 people and wounding 1200. These numbers seem small, but the psychological shock to the London populace was strong enough to cause extensive absenteeism in munitions factories and to result in British airmen being assaulted on the streets by civilians who felt they weren't being adequately defended (Quester, 1966, p. 28). The attacks targeted directly at urban areas actually resulted in some fifty casualties per ton of bombs.

These figures should be compared with the Blitz of 1939–1945, in which the Germans dropped 67,000 tons of bombs, killing 58,000 and injuring 88,000, for a death rate of slightly under one person per ton of bombs. The Allied bombing of Germany delivered 1,500,000 tons of bombs, killing 300,000 and injuring 700,000, leading to one death per five tons of bombs. The air attacks on Japan delivered 160,000 tons of bombs (nonatomic), killing 225,000 and wounding 640,000, for a death rate by conventional bombing of just over one death per ton of bombs.

The official British view of the effectiveness of city-bombing can be seen in a committee report prepared under the direction of Lt. Gen. Jan C. Smuts, which was presented to the British War Cabinet in August of 1917. It argued for the establishment of a separate Air Ministry, and by implication for an independent Air Force, separate from the Army and Navy. This recommendation was adopted. The committee's words, however, were prophetic.

> As far as can at present be foreseen there is absolutely no limit to the scale of its [air power's] future independent war use. And the day may not be far off when aerial operations with their devastation of enemy lands and destruction of industrial and populous centers on a vast scale may become the principal operations of war, to which the older forms of military and naval operations may become secondary and subordinate (quoted in Brodie, 1959, p. 71).

The British viewed the end of World War I as a narrow escape. It was perceived that if the Germans had possessed a truly adequate air force, with hundreds of aircraft capable of delivering thousands of tons of bombs, the results would have been catastrophic. General J. F. C. Fuller published an apocalyptic vision of future aerial warfare based on this view:

> I believe that, in future warfare, great cities, such as London, will be attacked from the air, and that a fleet of 500 aeroplanes each carrying 500 ten-pound bombs, of, let us suppose, mustard gas, might cause 200,000 minor casualties and throw the whole city into panic within half an hour of their arrival. Picture, if you can, what the result will be: London for

several days will be one vast raving Bedlam, the hospitals will be stormed, traffic will cease, the homeless will shriek for help, the city will be in pandemonium. What of the government at Westminster? It will be swept away by an avalanche of terror. Then will the enemy dictate his terms, which will be grasped at like a straw by a drowning man. Thus may a war be won in forty-eight hours and the losses of the winning side may be actually nil (Fuller [1923], p. 150, quoted in Quester, 1966, p. 157).

Nor was there any hope of defense. Prime Minister Stanley Baldwin, in 1932, painted this grim picture:

[I]n the next war you will find that any town which is within reach of an aerodrome can be bombed within the first five minutes of war from the air, to an extent which was inconceivable in the last war, and the question will be whose morale will be shattered quickest by that preliminary bombing? I think it is well also for the man in the street to realize that there is no power on earth that can protect him from being bombed. Whatever people may tell him, the bomber will always get through. . . . The only defence is in offence, which means that you have to kill more women and children more quickly than the enemy if you want to save yourselves (Baldwin, 1932, cols 631–38).

Of course, Baldwin's publicly stated beliefs were colored by his opposition to increased military appropriations. In his opinion, there was no point in spending money on defense, since no defense was possible. However, none of the advocates of increased military spending attempted to refute his views.

Thus, official and public perceptions of aerial warfare were much like today's perceptions of nuclear warfare, and the prescriptions were the same. Since you couldn't defend yourself and you couldn't wipe out the enemy air force quickly enough by counterforce attacks, your only recourse was to engage in *city-busting* on a vast scale in the hope that the enemy would give up before your own people did. One analyst described the situation in words that have a strangely modern sound:

It would be a balance of terrors—for that is what the balance of power, loaded with bombs, should truly be called. In the end one group must strike (Griffin [1938], p. 75, quoted in Quester, 1966, p. 89).

Despite the perception by both government officials and the public at large that future aerial warfare would be nothing more than a city-busting contest, the professionals in the air forces had different views. In both England and the United States, professionals believed that with modern technology, bombing accuracy would be good enough to make precision attacks on military targets feasible, including precision attacks on factories producing military supplies. Both the Royal Air Force (RAF) and the U.S. Army Air Corps prepared to carry out precision bombardment of factories, railroad depots, and similar targets. They spoke confidently of destroying the enemy's ability to wage war.

When war finally came, how did things turn out? As was the case with World War I, the results were different from the initial expectations.

The first failure of expectations was that civilian populations did not panic under aerial bombardment. In both Germany and England, the civilian populations underwent suffering of a kind that hadn't been seen since the siege warfare of the Middle Ages, and they did it without breaking. Brodie notes that while bombing attacks on Germany did seriously depress civilian morale, this had no effect on the government or on the Germans' ability to continue the war (Brodie, 1959, pp. 131–32).

Second, defense turned out to be more effective than expected (this was a repeat of World War I—once more, people failed to learn from history). Both the German and British air forces found that daylight attacks were too costly; the defenses were too good. Both soon shifted to night attacks.

This led to a third failure of expectations as the accuracy of bombing declined dramatically. Despite the prewar talk of targeting military installations and defense plants, both sides shifted to area bombardment of cities. Although the actual policy changed months before the declared policy did, eventually both sides claimed they were targeting the enemy's *will* to fight rather than his *ability* to fight. The war would be ended when the enemy's will cracked under the strain.

At the end of 1941 the United States entered the war and began a slow buildup of bomber forces in England. At the outset the U.S. bomber forces continued to proclaim their prewar belief that precision bombardment was the most effective use of strategic bombers. This required bombing in daylight, because radar wasn't then accurate enough for precision night bombing. But again, the strength of air defense was underestimated. Daylight raids suffered heavy losses. However, the U.S. bomber forces didn't switch to night attacks. Instead they took advantage of technological improvements in aircraft engines and aerodynamics and employed long-range fighter aircraft as escorts. By the middle of 1944 the number of bombers and escort fighters available rose to the point that heavy attacks could be mounted. The number of tons of bombs delivered per month jumped from 41,000 in February 1944 (already more than twice the average for 1943, despite the cloudy winter weather) to 145,000 in July 1944; remained above 80,000 throughout the winter of 1944–1945; and jumped again to over 200,000 in March of

1945. These attacks were directed at factories and similar installations, with reasonably good results. While many bombs missed the intended targets and killed civilians, a great many of them did hit the intended targets, and the escort fighters saw to it that most of the bombers got home safely. As Brodie notes, "vulnerable areas when chosen consistently as the bull's-eyes were invariably destroyed" (Brodie, 1959, p. 125).[2]

After some fumbling in selection of targets for attack, the U.S. bomber forces concentrated on three target systems: aircraft factories, the oil industry, and the railroads. Within eight months, from the middle of 1944 to early 1945, these attacks essentially brought the German economy to a halt.

Spaatz quotes several sources to illustrate the effectiveness of strategic bombing against German targets. The U.S. Strategic Bombing Survey came to the overall judgment, "Allied air power was decisive in the war in Western Europe" (quoted in Spaatz, 1946, p. 393).

Lieutenant General Linnarz, commander of the German Twenty-sixth Panzer Division, stated to his Allied interrogators:

> The basic conception of winning a war through strategic air power is sound. . . . It is obvious that in the future the first strategic objective in war cannot be the destruction of the armies in the field but the destruction of the enemy's resources and war arsenals. Without these, the armies in the field are doomed to defeat. . . . In the future war [the decisive striking force] could conceivably be a type of perfected V-bomb (quoted in Spaatz, 1946, p. 393).

Albert Speer, who had served as Reich Minister for Armaments and War Production, said under interrogation:

> The planned assaults on the chemical industry (synthetic oil) which began on May 12, 1944, caused the first serious shortages of indispensable basic products. . . . [T]his type of attack was the most decisive factor in hastening the end of the war. . . . The attacks on the synthetic oil industry would have suffered, without the impact of purely military events, to render Germany defenseless. . . . From 1944 onward, vital key industries were transferred to caves and other underground installations. Production was hindered not so much by these dispersals as by the shattering of transport and communication facilities. Consequently it can be said in

---

[2] In no small measure the success of U.S. bombers was due not only to technology but to the efforts of General Curtis LeMay, who drilled his aircrews in precision formation flying and accurate navigation. He thus made it possible to exploit the aircraft and bombsights to their full potential.

conclusion that a bomb load is more effective if it is dropped upon economic targets than if it is expended upon towns and cities (quoted in Spaatz, 1946, p. 394).

That is, bombs were more effective if delivered against countervalue rather than counterpopulation targets.

Thus after more than forty years, the claims of the pioneers of aerial warfare were vindicated. Air forces could concentrate their attacks on targets of military significance, and they could destroy an enemy's ability to fight. Then, a strange thing happened on the way to victory.

In Europe, by early 1945, these precision targets were all destroyed. The German rail system had largely stopped operating, and the oil refineries were burned out. But the bombers weren't grounded despite the lack of strategic targets. Nor were they switched to attacks on German military formations. Instead, U.S. and British air forces continued to bomb the cities. One such attack, a daylong bombardment of Dresden employing both high explosive and incendiary bombs, resulted in over 135,000 casualties among not only its normal residents but the large numbers of refugees who had fled the advancing Russian armies. A majority of the casualties, of course, were women and children.

On the other side of the world, the United States was waging a strategic bombing campaign against Japan. The B-29 aircraft was technologically superior to the B-17s and B-24s used in Europe, and its bombing radar represented a technological breakthrough. It was actually good enough for reasonably precise bombing at night. The B-29 force initially began attacking factories and military installations in daylight, with disappointingly little success.

The problem was twofold. The B-29s bombed from 30,000 feet to avoid Japanese air defenses. This meant that the high winds prevailing over the Japanese islands had six miles of altitude in which to push the bombs off course. The inevitable result was that bombing accuracy was poor. Moreover, the major Japanese factories were supported by an enormous network of small shops and home-assembly operations dispersed throughout the residential areas of their cities. There was no way the B-29s could target these individual assembly shops.

General Curtis LeMay, by then commander of the B-29 forces operating out of bases in the Pacific, was under extreme pressure from General Arnold, commanding general of the Army Air Forces, to get results quickly. He made two changes in bombing policy. The first was to shift the force to low-altitude night attacks against Japan. The second was to use the lower altitude, not to achieve precision, but instead to shift the attacks from the bombing of specific industrial or military point-targets to area bombing of Japanese cities, using incendiary bombs. In the highly combustible Japanese cities, the results can only be described as apocalyptic. One single raid on Tokyo produced 100,000 casualties.

However, the switch to area bombing was not absolutely necessary. The Japanese could not disperse their petroleum industry nor their railroads, which the war in Europe had already demonstrated could be attacked successfully and with enormous impact on the enemy's war effort. Thus, despite superior technology, U.S. bomber forces in the Pacific abandoned the approach that had been found successful in Europe and returned to the city-busting the British and German air forces had resorted to only because their technology was inadequate to carry out their original intentions.

Then came the atomic bomb. Once city-busting had become acceptable and the civilian population was assumed to be the proper target for strategic bombing, it was natural to drop the atomic bombs on cities.

Batchelder describes the process by which the decision to drop the first atomic bomb on Japan was reached and the process by which a target was selected. President Harry Truman decided to drop the bomb on a "military target", by which was meant not a fortification or an army encampment, but *a city engaged in military production* (Batchelder, 1962, p. 90). The civilians who worked in the defense plants were considered legitimate military targets. Those who worked in other types of plants, and the wives, children, and aged parents of all the workers, were simply left out of consideration.

As Batchelder put it (1962, p. 158):

> [T]he primary reason that demonstration of the atomic bomb on a purely military target was not attempted apparently is that it was never considered. And the reason it was never considered is that the distinction between attack on a military target (in which civilians might incidentally suffer injury and death) and attack on a city (in which military objectives would be damaged as a result of direct attack upon the fabric of civil life) was lost.

Another indication of the extent to which city-busting had become acceptable is the following quote from Dr. Vannevar Bush, head of the Office of Scientific Research and Development during World War II. In testimony to Congress in late 1945, opposing the development of intercontinental missiles, he said:

> The people who have been writing these things that annoy me have been talking about a 3,000-mile, high-angle rocket shot from one continent to another carrying an atomic bomb, and so directed as to be a *precise weapon which would land on a certain target such as this city* (quoted in Clarke, 1962, p. 9, emphasis added).

Bush asserted that an ICBM would be technically infeasible for "a long period to come". In this he was quite wrong; the United States deployed its first ICBM within seventeen years, and could have done so sooner had not negative predictions such as Bush's retarded the effort. The important point, however, is that Bush was reflecting both official and public opinion that a city as a whole was a target, and that *precision* meant hitting the city itself, rather than hitting a specific installation within it.

Thus the lessons of World War II seemed to be that cities were appropriate targets for nuclear weapons, and that there was no defense against nuclear attack. Even one bomber getting through would mean that the city would be devastated. The only way to prevent devastation was to be able to threaten it in retaliation: to replace defense by deterrence.

As Martin points out, this replacement of defense by deterrence dates back to the beginning of the nuclear age:

> The idea that deterrence was the appropriate strategic motif for a nuclear world burgeoned very early in the nuclear age. . . . The source of the idea lay in the notion that, defence being thought impossible, only the threat of retaliation could afford security. That this retaliation was always assumed to be of "counter-value", city-destroying kind seems to have been the result more of the technologically determined incapacity of strategic air forces to attempt anything else for most of World War II than of any rational effort to relate atomic weapons to the psycho-political requirements of deterrence (1981, p. 60–61).

[Note that Martin uses *countervalue* in a sense different from that which I have defined. His meaning is expressed by my term *countercity*.]

This change from the idea of defense to the idea of deterrence through threats of counterpopulation attacks actually came quite rapidly. Spector notes that the American public came out of World War II having abandoned the principles which animated its original opposition to the Axis forces.

> American opposition to the Japanese conquest of China rested largely on revulsion against Japanese use of airpower on civilian targets. Yet the United States itself initiated an unprecedented campaign of aerial bombardment against Japan (1981).

That is, the change came during the course of the war itself.

During the years between the world wars there was a use of airpower that is not, strictly speaking, part of the history of strategic bombardment. Nevertheless, in its own way it was a precursor of the use of airpower in World War II and is worth mentioning. This was what came to be called *Air Control*. The Royal Air Force was assigned responsibility for maintaining order in British-controlled territory in the Near East—Iraq, Aden, and the Trans-Jordan—and on the Indian frontier with Afghanistan.

Prior to the institution of Air Control, the conventional method of controlling primitive tribes in British-administered territory was the use of ground troops. Slessor (1957, p. 54) notes that between 1895 and 1925 there were fifty ground expeditions mounted to take reprisals for attacks by primitive tribesmen in Waziristan alone. One of these expeditions, in 1919–20, cost the British 1800 dead, 3675 wounded, and 40,000 sick from local diseases.

Air Control meant bombing and strafing the villages of the tribesmen responsible for the "trouble". Slessor points out that the intent was not to destroy the village, but (in the words of the RAF War Manual) to interrupt "the normal life of the enemy people to such an extent that a continuance of hostilities becomes intolerable". These air attacks were much cheaper for the British, both in monetary cost and in lives, than were the more traditional ground expeditions. Shooting at tribesmen who were not personally responsible for the misbehavior being punished was justified, in the words of the India Office, by "the time-honoured method of enforcing on a tribal community responsibility for the acts of its individual members" (Slessor, 1957, p. 54–55).

The procedure was to notify the tribe in question what it had done wrong and what was required of it (payment of fines, return of stolen goods or livestock, etc.). If the tribe refused these terms, then it was ordered out of its territory and warned that "any village, house, palm grove or cultivation was liable to be bombed without further warning by day or night and that all personnel or livestock seen moving in the area were liable to be attacked from the air" (Slessor, 1957, p. 63).

Slessor goes to great pains to make clear that warnings were always given; that in fact very few casualties resulted; and that the results were much less costly for both the British and the tribes being controlled than use of ground expeditions would have been. He rejects the charges of those (primarily in the British Army) who opposed Air Control and described it as "indiscriminate bombing". He points out that bombing of villages was strictly controlled by the Political Officers responsible for the territory in question, whereas those same villages could be shelled by artillery, with no warning at all, on the authority of an army officer commanding a punitive expedition, with equal or greater loss of life. Moreover, if the tribe actually stayed outside the proscribed area, there was no bombing at all.

Despite Slessor's protestations about the relative humaneness of Air Control as compared with punitive ground expeditions, the fact remains that Air Control represented a deliberate policy of attacks upon civilians, including civilians who had no part in the behavior that elicited the punishment. As such, it was a forerunner of the city-busting attacks of World War II.

The point of this excursion into history is to show how the word *deterrence* has come to mean threatening the enemy's noncombatants. For over forty years, air power strategists had thought in the same terms as any other military leaders: find the enemy's weak spots and concentrate your forces on them. For those same forty years they had been frustrated by the inadequate technology they had to work with. In two world wars they resorted to city-busting because their weapons weren't good enough to do what they wanted to do. Finally, in 1944 they had their hands on technology that was good enough, and they demonstrated that their ideas had been right all along. Then, in 1945, another piece of technology made city-busting even easier than it had been in the two world wars, and these strategists completely lost sight of their original intentions. What is worse, so did the political leaders of their nations.

REFERENCES

Baldwin, Prime Minister Stanley. United Kingdom. House of Commons. *Debates,* November 10, 1932, cols. 631–38. Quoted in Quester, 1966, p. 67.

Batchelder, Robert C. *The Irreversible Decision.* Boston: Houghton Mifflin, 1962.

Brodie, Bernard. *Strategy in the Missile Age.* Princeton: Princeton University Press, 1959.

Clarke, Arthur C. *Profiles of the Future.* New York: Harper & Row, 1962.

Fuller, J. F. C. *Reformation of War.* London: Hutchinson and Co., 1923.

Griffin, Jonathan. *Glass Houses and Modern War.* London: Chatto and Windus, 1938.

Martin, Laurence. "The Determinants of Change: Deterrence and Technology". In *The Future of Strategic Deterrence,* by Christopher Bertram. Hamden, CT: Archon Books, 1981.

Quester, George H. *Deterrence before Hiroshima.* New York: John Wiley & Sons, 1966.

Slessor, Sir John. *The Central Blue*. New York: Frederick A Praeger Publishers, 1957.

Spaatz, Carl. "Strategic Air Power": *Foreign Affairs* (April 1946), pp. 385–96.

Spector, Ronald H. *Eagle against the Sun: The American War with Japan*. New York: The Free Press, 1985.

CHAPTER THREE

THE END OF STRATEGY

The advent of the atomic bomb, which made city-busting even easier than it had been in the two world wars, had another important effect beyond the acceptance of civilians as legitimate targets. This was the apparently complete disappearance of strategy.

Karl von Clausewitz had captured the essence of war as seen by modern Western society: "War is a continuation of policy by other means" (1953, p. 16). The purpose of a war is not found within itself, but only in the policy objectives that the war is intended to achieve. Policy prescribes ends; war is only a means. "War may have its own grammar, but not its own logic."

Within the grammar of war are both strategy and tactics. According to Clausewitz, tactics consists of arranging and conducting individual engagements (battles); strategy is the combing of these individual engagements to obtain the object of the war (1953, p. 62). That is, tactics consists of sequences of actions taken to win a battle, where *winning* means to achieve the goals of the strategy which called for a battle at that time and place. Strategy, in turn, involves a sequence of battles to achieve the goals of the policy that called for a war at that time with that adversary.

In the immediate aftermath of World War II and the atomic bomb, the whole concept of strategy seemed headed for oblivion. On a single day in August 1944 the Germans had launched 101 buzz bombs against London. Of these, ninety-seven were shot down by the defense, while four got through. Had those four carried atomic bombs instead of high explosive warheads, London would have been destroyed. Thus if the whole city is a target and enough atomic bombs can be launched at it, the city will inevitably be destroyed. Given these premises, it apparently made no sense to identify specific targets for bombardment on the basis of their contribution to the enemy's war effort.

This revolution in military thinking can be illustrated by an instructor's statement to my class at the Air Force's Squadron Officer School, in 1957: "We used to target the enemy's weaknesses. Now we target the enemy's strengths." That is, in the pre-atomic era, bomber strategists talked of finding the enemy's weak spots and concentrating on them, just as did ground and naval strategists. Part of the problem in Europe during World War II had been learning what the enemy's weak spots were, and how they could best be attacked. That's why it took so long

to focus on transportation and petroleum. Once the atomic bomb became available, this approach of husbanding one's forces and utilizing
them efficiently no longer seemed necessary. Why waste time finding
the weak links in the enemy's war machine when with one bomb you
can take out a whole city and *all* the factories in it?

General Curtis LeMay, Commander in Chief of Strategic Air Command (CINCSAC), was a firm believer in this view. His SAC Emergency War Plan 1-49 called for the delivery of the entire stockpile of 133
atomic bombs on seventy Soviet cities within a thirty-day period (Kaplan, 1983, p. 44). Cohen quotes LeMay as saying (1985, p. 38): "When
we kill enough of them [Russians], they'll stop fighting."

LeMay thus brought to the issue of atomic-bomb targeting the same
attitude he had brought to attacks upon Japanese cities during World
War II. The War Department had originally proposed that U.S. bombing attacks upon Japan follow the pattern applied in Germany: precision
daylight attacks upon war industries. As related in the preceding chapter, cloudy weather, which made it difficult to find the targets with visual bombsights, and high winds, which scattered the bombs during
their fall, made these attacks ineffective. LeMay then, upon his own initiative (but with the support of his subordinate commanders) ordered
low-level night attacks upon Japanese cities, using incendiary bombs. If
he couldn't destroy the targets individually, he would destroy them
collectively, along with the cities themselves. As far as he was concerned, the war would be over when all Japanese cities were burned out
(Kaplan, 1983, p. 43; Batchelder, 1962, pp. 182–84).[1]

This attitude continued to dominate U.S. military thinking. As the
number of atomic bombs available grew, so did the plan for delivering
them quickly. By 1962, the Joint Strategic Target Plan called for delivering 1459 nuclear weapons, totaling 2164 megatons, against 654 tar-

[1] Ironically, LeMay's attempt to destroy the factories by burning down the cities was
being proven ineffective at the same time he was proceeding with it. The Strategic Bombing Survey in Germany was learning that obliteration bombing attacks on German cities
had been very ineffective in disrupting production when compared with the direct attacks
on defense plants. In Hamburg, the Survey found that destruction of nonessential
businesses such as restaurants released workers for the munitions factories. After the
surrender of Japan, the Survey found that obliteration bombing had been somewhat
more effective there since the small shops which supported the aircraft and munitions
industries had actually been burned out along with the workers' homes. However, the
Survey also found that in many cases these shops were being shut down by the submarine
blockade, which made it impossible to obtain the raw materials they needed (Batchelder,
1962, pp. 182–84). Thus, if a target system can be destroyed by more than one means, it
is imprudent to destroy it twice, since that means additional risks to one's own forces for
no additional gain. Moreover, when two or more methods of destroying the same target
system are available, the attacker has the option of choosing the one that causes the fewest
casualties, either among his own forces or among enemy civilians.

gets as quickly as possible at the outset of a war. The single targeting plan included targets in the Soviet Union, mainland China, and Eastern Europe. There was no provision for omitting Chinese targets if China didn't happen to join the Soviet Union in the war against us (Kaplan, 1983, p. 271–72).

With the adoption of this policy of *nuclear spasm*, military strategy, in Clausewitz's sense of rationally ordering military actions to support national policy, simply disappeared. Tactics was the only consideration: how to get the bombers through the enemy's defenses. Bernard Brodie summarized the situation as "Strategy hits a dead end".

When ICBMs arrived on the scene after 1957, even tactics disappeared, since there seemed to be no defense against missiles. Once launched, they always got through. Thus by the 1960s we were faced with the apparent paradox of military activity devoid of both strategy and tactics. Warfare was reduced to two choices: destroy the enemy before he destroyed you, or destroy the enemy after he destroyed you. Warfare lost any rational content, such as protection against attack. The strongest military forces existed only to threaten the enemy with devastation, and thereby "deter" him from devastating you.

The use of nuclear weapons against cities was de facto U.S. policy in the early postwar years. It finally became declaratory policy when Secretary of State Dulles announced the doctrine of massive retaliation on January 12, 1954, in a speech to the Council on Foreign Relations:

> The basic decision was to depend primarily upon a great capacity to retaliate, instantly, by means and at places of our own choosing. . . . That permits of a selection of military means instead of a multiplication of means. As a result, it is now possible to get, and share, more basic security at less cost.

An attack on one of our European (and later Asian) allies would be met with a nuclear response, which might be aimed at the instigators of the attack, instead of a conventional response aimed at the proxies immediately responsible for the attack. Nuclear weapons were the deterrent that would preserve what was called the *Free World* by holding Soviet (and later Chinese) cities hostage for the good behavior of their otherwise unstoppable armies.

Secretary Dulles' doctrine of *massive retaliation,* however, came too late. It was announced only after the Soviet Union had tested its first atomic bomb. Thus massive retaliation was a game that two could play. The two-sided nature of nuclear deterrence led to the nuclear planner's nightmare: a situation in which both sides effectively got off a first strike, with one side launching its weapons but with the other side getting warning and launching its undamaged forces before the attacker's weapons arrived. Each side would suffer the full weight of the other's strongest possible attack.

However, not everyone agreed that the situation was a potential nightmare. As early as 1955, Winston Churchill foresaw that within a few years both the United States and the Soviet Union would reach the point of being able to inflict serious damage on each other. Churchill thought we could take comfort in this prospect of mutual deterrence, saying:

> It does not follow, however, that the risk of war will then be greater. Indeed, it is arguable that it will be less, for both sides will realize that global war would result in mutual annihilation. . . . After a certain point has been passed, it may be said, the worse things get, the better (Ikle, 1970, p. 119).

Ultimately, of course, the problem was that when war meant the devastation of both attacker and attacked, there was no meaningful policy which could be achieved by war. Without policy, strategy and tactics were inherently impossible.

This issue was addressed, although from a very parochial perspective, by Robert McNamara, who became Secretary of Defense after the Kennedy election victory in 1960. Enthoven and Smith relate that the new administration found the Air Force and the Navy each generating *requirements* for large numbers of missiles and bombers, without regard for the forces already existing or planned by the other service.

> Without some measure of total needs and capabilities, there was no effective way of appraising our strategic posture. . . .
> If the threat of a few bombs was really enough to deter the Soviets, and if we didn't care how we performed should deterrence fail, the strategic mission could have been done for about a third of what was being spent at the time. Without a *theory of requirements,* what we were getting was the worst of both worlds; we were paying for a first-strike posture, but settling for a minimum-deterrence capability (Enthoven and Smith, 1971, p. 171)[2] (emphasis added).

While there was certainly much to criticize in the approach taken by the two branches of service to the problem of determining nuclear strat-

---

[2] The phrase "theory of requirements" used by Enthoven and Smith is itself very telling. They, like Mr. McNamara, were looking for a theory that would tell them "how much is enough". They wanted this theory to be quantitative, like the theories of economics and the management sciences, from which they drew their inspiration. It never occurred to them that Karl von Clausewitz had provided a "theory of requirements" over a century and a quarter earlier and that it was qualitative, not quantitative. Had someone proposed it to them, they would undoubtedly have dismissed it on the grounds that the concept of *strategy* had been made obsolete by nuclear weapons.

egy, the services could have countered legitimately (had they thought of it) that they had never been given the policy guidance they had a right to expect from their country's elected leaders. Unfortunately, the new administration chose not to provide policy guidance either. Instead, the McNamara Defense Department attempted to determine "How much destruction would be enough to deter the Soviets?"

It turned out that when plotted, a graph of Soviet casualties versus the number of megatons delivered rose steeply at first and then flattened out. That is, it had a sharp *knee* in it at 25 percent of the Soviet population and 50 percent of Soviet industrial capacity. The reason is quite simple. The population of the Soviet Union is mostly rural. The Soviet Union has only a few large cities. After wiping out these few large cities with a few large bombs, the attacker then finds that he is reduced to bombing small cities and hamlets. From that point on, it takes a lot more megatons to kill only a few more people.

Secretary McNamara picked the knee of the curve, the point where killing stops being cheap and starts being expensive, as his basis for deciding how much was enough. He announced that if the United States retained the capability to commit this much destruction even after the Soviet Union had delivered a first strike against the U.S. missile and bomber forces, then the Soviet Union would be deterred from making that first strike. This was called *assured destruction*. Once this point was settled (by fiat, without public debate in the United States, and without determining if that would indeed be enough to deter the Soviets), the only question became one of achieving assured-destruction capability at minimum cost.

But as noted above, deterrence had already become a two-sided affair. If we wanted to maintain an assured-destruction capability against the Soviets, then it seemed only natural to McNamara that the Soviets would want to maintain an assured-destruction capability against us too. This raised a problem. If we took steps to reduce the damage that a Soviet attack could do to us (these were known as *damage-limiting* actions), the Soviets would feel that their deterrent capability was weakened and *strengthen their assured-destruction forces*. This would mean we had to increase our assured-destruction forces to offset the increased losses from their first strike and retain the ability to destroy 50 percent of their industry in a second strike.

The logic of this situation appeared obvious. Defense was impossible, and if we were so foolish as to attempt it, the only result would be to raise the cost of maintaining an assured-destruction force. By this logic, both we and the Soviets would be better off if neither side were defended and both sides maintained only the minimum strategic forces needed to maintain an assured-destruction capability. The idea of mutual deterrence was finally formalized in the concept of Mutual Assured Destruction (MAD), embodied in the ABM Treaty, SALT I, and SALT II. The idea was that both sides would be safe so long as each side's civilian population was hostage to the other.[3]

President Jimmy Carter was making this point when he said, in his 1979 State of the Union address:

> Just one of our relatively invulnerable Poseidon submarines—comprising less than two percent of our total nuclear force of submarines, aircraft and land-based missiles—carries enough warheads to destroy every large and medium-sized city in the Soviet Union.

Since we had such a capability, we were, in President Carter's view, completely safe from attack by the Soviet Union.

What about the morality of deliberately targeting enemy civilians, and only as a vengeance measure, after millions of your own civilians have been killed? The advocates of MAD ignored this question. Their view was that if the threat were horrible enough, it would never have to be carried out, and the moral questions could be ignored. They attempted to will the moral questions out of existence by the fervency of their faith in the efficacy of deterrence.

As Brodie described it, the situation was one in which

> . . . there are some things which we want very much (for example, national integrity and independence) and which we do not know how to defend against external menace except by threatening certain actions which do risk national suicide. We justify or rationalize this posture on the ground that our threats will suffice to hold the menace in check and will not be challenged (Brodie, 1959, p. 306).

One important consequence of MAD has already been mentioned in Chapter I. The situation is very brittle. If we make nuclear war horrifying in an attempt to assure it won't happen, we have also assured that it will be extremely horrible if it does happen. It seems very imprudent to take a course of action that, if it fails, is certain to fail in the worst possible way. This ought to be of particular concern to those who believe that so long as nuclear weapons exist, nuclear war is inevitable. If they really believe that, they should be working to minimize its horrors when it happens, instead of maximizing them in what, by their own beliefs, is a futile attempt to prevent it.

---

[3] Enthoven and Smith present an insider's view of how the "assured destruction" position was reached, in their chapter "Nuclear Strategy and Forces". Speed reproduces the graphs of damage vs. delivered megatonnage (1979, p. 25), as does Kaplan (1983, p. 318).

However, even more important than the issue of prudence is the issue of morality. As the consequences of MAD became clear, people began to question the morality of threatening "vengeance from the grave". In the next chapter we will look at their criticisms.

REFERENCES

Batchelder, Robert C. *The Irreversible Decision*. Boston: Houghton Mifflin Co., 1962.

Brodie, Bernard. *Strategy in the Missile Age*. Princeton: Princeton University Press, 1959.

Clausewitz, Karl von. *On War*. Translated by O. J. Mathijs Jolles. Washington, D.C.: Combat Forces Press, 1953.

Cohen, Sam. *We CAN Prevent World War III*. Ottawa, Ill.: Jameson Books, 1985.

Enthoven, Alain C., and K. Wayne Smith. *How Much Is Enough?* New York: Harper & Row, 1971.

Ikle, Fred C. *Every War Must End*. New York: Columbia University Press, 1970.

Kaplan, Fred. *The Wizards of Armageddon*. New York: Simon & Schuster, 1983.

Speed, Roger D. *Strategic Deterrence in the 1980s*. Stanford, Calif.: Hoover Institution Press, 1979.

CHAPTER FOUR

THE REACTION TO VENGEANCE

Even from the beginning of the nuclear age there have been voices questioning the morality of a policy of city-busting. When city-busting become a two-sided threat, even more voices were added.

Fred Ikle attempted to show that the neutral-sounding language used to discuss mutual deterrence really was a cover-up for something horrible:

> The language in which the strategy of deterrence is being discussed tends to obscure the fact that this strategy is based on a scheme of totally unprecedented cruelty. Various abstractions and metaphors—which remain necessarily (and fortunately) untested by reality—help to insulate the design against the wrath of the innocents who are its target. Owing to these metaphors, a scheme that would have been rejected as abhorrent in the Dark Ages by kings and the common people alike, appears to reflect the humane ideals of modern civilization:
>
> *"Mutual" deterrence* ("mutual" sounds like an arrangement that distributes benefits evenly)
> *will be "stable"* (that is, of unfailing continuity)
> *if both "sides"* (and later three "sides")
> *maintain nuclear capabilities so that a "potential aggressor"* (as if all wars started because somebody so decided)
> *must expect that his attack would lead to a nuclear "exchange"* ("exchange" as with commodities in foreign trade?)
> *resulting in the "assured" destruction* ("assured" seems to convey comfortable certitude)
> *of "his" cities* (are the cities to be destroyed necessarily the property of those who would start a nuclear war?)
>
> (Ikle, 1970, p. 129).

However, Ikle's argument is only indirectly a moral one. It attempts to expose a coverup of something frightful but does not say in so many words that the frightful thing is actually immoral. Others made more direct appeals to morality.

From the beginning these appeals focused directly on the act that lies at the heart of deterrence: attacking cities and civilians with atomic bombs. They provided an answer to the moral question, "Is it licit to destroy cities with atomic bombs in retaliation for a like attack?"

Pope Pius XII, in his address to the World Medical Association on September 30, 1954, condemned attacks upon civilians with the following words:

It would no longer be a question of "defense" against injustice and necessary "protection" of legitimate possessions, but of the annihilation, pure and simple, of all human life within the affected area. That is not lawful on any title.

The Second Vatican Council reiterated long-standing Catholic teaching regarding attacks on noncombatants (Pastoral Constitution on the Church in the Modern World, 1965, no. 80):

Any act of war aimed indiscriminately at the destruction of entire cities or of extensive areas along with their population is a crime against God and man himself. It merits unequivocal and unhesitating condemnation.

This is an extremely strong statement: It is even stronger than the Council's reference to abortion as an "unspeakable crime", and is the Council's *only* use of the word *condemn*.

In their Challenge of Peace pastoral, the American Catholic bishops wrote (1983, II. A. 1):

Under no circumstances may nuclear weapons or other instruments of mass slaughter be used for the purpose of destroying population centers or other predominantly civilian targets. Retaliatory action which would indiscriminately and disproportionately take many wholly innocent lives, lives of people who are in no way responsible for reckless actions of their government, must also be condemned.

Protestants likewise condemned the use of atomic bombs against cities. Reinhold Niebuhr wrote in 1950:

Thus we have come into the tragic position of developing a form of destruction which, if used by our enemies against us, would mean our physical annihilation, and if used by us against our enemies, would result in our moral annihilation (quoted in Davidson, 1983, p. 43).

Dr. Godfrey, Archbishop of Westminster, said in his Easter Sermon in 1958:

Nobody can subscribe to the thesis that it would ever be morally lawful to use indiscriminate nuclear weapons on centres of population which are predominantly civilian (quoted in Stein, 1961, p. 115).

Paul Ramsey, a Protestant theologian, wrote:

If it is unjust for an enemy to destroy our society, the fact that he does or tries to do so first cannot make it any less of an injustice for us to destroy his (quoted in Davidson, 1983, p. 46).

Philosopher Michael Walzer presented a view from the Natural Law tradition rather than from a religious viewpoint when he wrote:

Atomic war was death, indeed, indiscriminate and total, and after Hiroshima, the first task of political leaders everywhere was to prevent its recurrence. The means they adopted is the promise of a reprisal in kind. Against the threat of an immoral attack, they have put the threat of an immoral response. This is the basic form of nuclear deterrence (quoted in Davidson, 1983, p. 49).

Theodore Roszak, writing from within the Just War tradition, concluded that neither nuclear attacks on cities, nor nuclear attacks aimed at military targets, could be justified, because of the high civilian casualties which would result (1963, pp. 101ff.).

This universal condemnation of direct attacks on cities left unanswered another moral question, "Is it licit to *threaten* to destroy cities with atomic bombs as a means of deterring such an attack?"

Some moralists argued that not only is it immoral to use nuclear weapons to attack cities, it is immoral to *intend* to use them to attack cities.

The American Catholic bishops, in their 1976 pastoral letter *To Live in Christ Jesus,* said:

Not only is it wrong to attack civilian populations, but it is also wrong to threaten to attack them as part of a strategy of deterrence (quoted in Castelli, 1983, p. 22).

In their Challenge of Peace pastoral, the bishops expanded upon this position (1983, I.B.2):

No *use* of nuclear weapons which would violate the principles of discrimination or proportionality may be *intended* in a strategy of deterrence. The moral demands of Catholic teaching require absolute willingness not to intend or to do moral evil even to save our own lives or the lives of those we love (emphasis in original).

In this statement, the bishops came as close to condemning a policy of deterrence as they could without actually contradicting Pope John Paul II, who had already stated several times that deterrence was morally acceptable as long as it was based on balance rather than being an end in itself and as long as it was an interim step toward nuclear disarmament. Some typical papal statements include the following. In his address to UNESCO in 1980, he said (no. 21):

Up to the present, we are told that nuclear arms are a force of dissuasion which have prevented the eruption of a major war. And that is probably true. Still, we must ask if it will always be this way.

Speaking to the U.N. Special Session in 1982, he said (no. 8):

> In current conditions "deterrence" based on balance, certainly not as an end in itself but as a step on the way toward a progressive disarmament, may still be judged morally acceptable. Nonetheless in order to ensure peace, it is indispensable not to be satisfied with this minimum which is always susceptible to the real danger of explosion.

In a 1982 letter to an international seminar on nuclear conflict, he wrote:

> You can more easily ascertain that the logic of nuclear deterrence cannot be considered a final goal or an appropriate and secure means for safeguarding international peace.

Ultimately, the American bishops accepted deterrence conditionally. They rejected it as a permanent solution, however. In their Challenge of Peace pastoral, the bishops wrote (I.B.3):

> Deterrence is not an adequate strategy as a long-term basis for peace; it is a transitional strategy justifiable only in conjunction with resolute determination to pursue arms control and disarmament.

The bishops further limited their acceptance of deterrence in the following words:

> These considerations . . . lead us to a strictly conditioned moral acceptance of nuclear deterrence. We cannot consider it adequate as a long-term basis for peace (1983, no. 186).

One of the conditions they attached to their acceptance was that "nuclear deterrence should be used as a step on the way toward progressive disarmament".[1]

---

[1] There is a serious flaw in the bishops' conditioned acceptance of deterrence: namely, they provide statesmen and voters no criteria by which to judge whether *progressive disarmament* is being achieved at a morally acceptable rate. This flaw is compounded by the bishops' decision to have a committee determine whether the U.S. government is actually meeting the conditions under which the Bishops will accept deterrence. Whatever conclusion this committee reaches, it will be completely arbitrary, since the bishops initially provided no criteria by which to judge. The rationale for the conclusion can only amount to "because we say so".

Nor is the requirement for progressive disarmament compatible with the realities of the world. Suppose you are attempting in good faith to negotiate disarmament, but you are dealing with an opponent who demands terms that you consider unfair; terms that would leave him much better armed than you. Suppose you refuse to accept those terms. Are you then making the progress the bishops call for? And if not, are you then obliged to dismantle your deterrent with no reciprocal concessions from your opponent? The bishops' "condition" could be read to say that in the face of an intransigent and aggressive opponent, your only moral option is to disarm.

This demand by the bishops, which lays an ill-defined burden on statesmen and which ignores reality, is unfortunately all too typical of the kind of thinking which pervades much of the purportedly moral analysis of nuclear deterrence.

Within the Catholic Church, the Second Vatican Council had already set the tone for this uneasy acceptance of deterrence (Pastoral Constitution on the Church in the Modern World, 1965, no. 81):

Undoubtedly, armaments are not amassed merely for use in wartime. Since the defensive strength of any nation is thought to depend on its capacity for immediate retaliation, the stockpiling of arms which grows from year to year serves, in a way hitherto unthought of, as a deterrent to potential attackers. Many people look upon this as the most effective way known at the present time for maintaining some sort of peace among nations. Whatever one may think of this form of deterrent, people are convinced that the arms race, which quite a few countries have entered, is no infallible way of maintaining real peace and that the resulting so-called balance of power is no sure genuine path to achieving it.

Not all, however, were willing to make even this much of a concession on deterrence. For some, the licitness of even the threat of retaliatory attacks against cities had to be denied.

Gerald Dworkin, for instance, argued that it would be immoral to threaten an act (nuclear bombardment of cities) that would be immoral to carry out. Therefore a policy of deterrence would be immoral (1985).

Father Richard McSorley, S.J., put it even more simply: "It's a sin to build a nuclear weapon." He went on to argue that our willingness to use nuclear weapons is "the taproot of violence in our society" (1976, p. 13).

John Cardinal Krol, in his 1979 testimony to the Senate Foreign Relations Committee regarding SALT II, said:

The moral judgment of this statement is that not only the use of strategic nuclear weapons, but *the declared intent to use them involved in our deterrence policy is wrong* (emphasis added).

He went on to say that only the hope of eliminating nuclear weapons entirely allows Catholics to tolerate their possession while disarmament negotiations are taking place. In the absence of this hope of complete elimination, he said, both use and possession would be condemned.

The Episcopal House of Bishops, in 1982, issued a pastoral letter that stated:

. . . the United States has never disavowed a policy of deterrence that intends the use of nuclear weapons in a massive first-strike against whole cities and land areas should it serve the national interest in warfare. . . . We ask, how can this policy be squared with a free nation's commitment to justice when it intends the calculated killing of millions of human beings who themselves are not on trial? We hold such an intention to be evil.

Catholic Archbishop Raymond J. Hunthausen spoke out against the Trident submarines based near his Sea city of Seattle. These submarines provide the portion of our deterrent forces that is currently most secure against destruction in an enemy first strike. Castelli quotes him as saying:

> I was moved to speak out against Trident, because it is being based here. We must take special responsibility for what is in our own back yard. And when crimes are being prepared in our own name, we must speak plainly. I say with deep consciousness of these words that Trident is the Auschwitz of Puget Sound (1983, p. 28).

Bishop Raymond Lucker, of New Ulm, Minnesota, wrote in his diocesan newspaper:

> Nuclear weapons may not be used for attack or for first strike. They may not be used in defense. They may not be threatened to be used. Therefore it seems to me that even to possess them is wrong (Castelli, 1983, p. 37).

Walter Stein, in his introduction to a 1961 collection of essays by Catholic philosophers, stated their collective views as follows:

> . . . there is now no *moral* alternative to an unconditional renunciation of "the deterrent": this is the central submission of this book (p. 23) (emphasis in original).

Bishop Leroy J. Matthieson of Amarillo, location of the Pantex nuclear weapons plant, said:

> Nuclear weapons . . . are immoral; and if that's true, then it's immoral for us to build, assemble, deploy, and threaten to use them (quoted in Spaeth, 1982, p. 7).

Where do these conflicting opinions, for and against the morality of deterrence, leave us? They simply confirm that as of today, there are no convincing answers to the moral questions regarding use or even possession of nuclear weapons. When one considers that for more than forty years nuclear weapons have been the mainstay of U.S. military power, this situation is tragic. Surely we should have been able to obtain satisfactory answers before this.

Why haven't the answers been forthcoming? In part, because most of the moral analysis of nuclear weapons has been simplistic and superficial. Moral analysts have tended to look only at the two extreme alternatives—either all-out nuclear war or complete nuclear disarmament—and have denied that other alternatives existed. Both of these alternatives appeared to pose insuperable moral problems. Therefore too many moralists have sought ways to evade the problem: to have deterrence without immorality, or to make disarmament appear better than deterrence.

In the next several chapters, we will examine some of these evasions, to show that any attempt to evade the real but difficult moral questions presents the evader with even more thorny moral issues than the ones he attempts to evade.

REFERENCES

Castelli, Jim. *The Bishops and the Bomb*. New York: Image Books, 1983.

Davidson, Major (Chaplain) Donald L., U.S. Army. *Nuclear Weapons and the American Churches*. Boulder, Colo.: Westview Press, 1983.

Dworkin, Gerald. "Nuclear Intentions". In *Nuclear Deterrence: Ethics and Strategy*, edited by Russell Hardin et. al. Chicago: University of Chicago Press, 1985.

Hardin, Russell, et. al., eds. *Nuclear Deterrence: Ethics and Strategy*. Chicago: University of Chicago Press, 1985.

Ikle, Fred C. *Every War Must End*. New York: Columbia University Press, 1970.

McSorley, Richard J. "It's a Sin to Build a Nuclear Weapon". *U.S. Catholic* (October 1976), pp. 12–13.

Roszak, Theodore. "A Just War Analysis of Two Types of Deterrence". *Ethics*. No. 75 (January 1963), pp. 100–9. (Reprinted in Hardin, et al.)

Spaeth, Robert L. "Disarmament and the Catholic Bishops". *This World* (Summer 1982), pp. 5–17.

Stein, Walter, ed. *Nuclear Weapons: A Catholic Response*. New York: Sheed and Ward, 1961.

CHAPTER FIVE

RETALIATION AS THREAT ONLY

When it appeared that the Catholic bishops might go so far as to reject deterrence by condemning the *intent* to use nuclear weapons against cities, some writers asserted that the bishops were stating the issue incorrectly. They argued that a policy of deterrence didn't mean we *intended* to destroy cities. It meant we *threatened* to destroy cities. We *intended* to deter attack.

Spaeth objected to the argument that "condemns nuclear deterrence as immoral because nuclear war is immoral". He wrote:

> What is absent from this argument is an adequate understanding of the morally defensible functions of a nuclear deterrent. The argument depends on the assumption that a nuclear deterrent is essentially a design or plan to use the weapons. . . . The facts, however, can be understood the other way around; the nuclear deterrent force of the United States is intended to prevent a nuclear war from occurring. . . . If this [force] could prevent nuclear war between the two superpowers, certainly the deployment of a nuclear deterrence force by the United States would be morally defensible, for the primary moral aim—prevention of an unjustified war—would be achieved without any intention of any sort of engaging in such a war (1982, p. 14).

Amstutz summarizes the position the Catholic bishops took in their Challenge of Peace pastoral as follows (1985, p. 30):

> The [pastoral] letter affirms deterrence but calls into question the traditional means used to implement such a policy . . . the letter states that the strategy of assured destruction is wrong because it fails to protect noncombatants from direct attack; but it also affirms that the shift towards counterforce/limited-nuclear-war options is wrong because it increases the possibility of nuclear conflict. The fundamental principles of the pastoral letter are thus contradictory: nuclear war is wrong; deterrence is morally satisfactory; but the means to sustain deterrence are immoral.

He goes on to state:

> The major conceptual weakness here is the failure to treat deterrence differently from war. . . . Those who believe threats and actions are morally identical generally ignore the ambiguity involved in the different levels of intention inherent in deterrence. . . . Deterrence does not require the certainty of retaliation. All that is required is the certainty of uncertainty of retaliation.

36

He concludes:

> The fundamental argument of the Bishops is based on the application of moral criteria of just war to deterrence. But just war is about war, not about deterrence.

Unfortunately, this debate about the moral question "Is it licit to threaten to destroy cities in retaliation even though it would be immoral to actually do it?" is wasted effort. The question itself leads to a dead end. Even if the question were to be answered in the affirmative, treating the threat to carry out an immoral act as morally acceptable simply amounts to a more subtle way of ignoring the basic moral issues. It provides no moral guidance on what to do if deterrence fails.

The threat of destroying cities in retaliation can be pure bluff in that if deterrence fails, we do nothing; or it can represent "deterrence, but . . ." in that if deterrence fails we do something else instead. The pure bluff will be treated in the next chapter. Here I want to examine the "deterrence, but . . ." position.

Suppose deterrence fails. Do we retaliate on the enemy cities anyway, simply because we threatened it? In that case, we have not only threatened an immoral act, we have actually carried it out. Thus even if we are satisfied that the threat itself was moral, we have crossed the line into immorality by executing the threat.[1]

Moreover, this response to a failure of deterrence presents some practical problems. Suppose the enemy initiates war with a disarming attack that scrupulously avoids or minimizes our civilian casualties while destroying a significant segment of our missile and bomber forces. He might then warn us that if we attack his cities with what remains of our weakened nuclear forces, he will attack our cities. That is, even though we have failed to deter his attack, the enemy may attempt intrawar deterrence of our counterattack. Retaliation against his cities, while threatened before the war as a deterrent measure, might seem a very foolish thing to do once deterrence has failed—not to mention a very wicked thing.

The idea of "deterrence, but . . ." is an attempt to get around this problem. This is the idea that while we may threaten massive retaliation in order to deter an attack, if deterrence fails we may want to do something else instead. This is obviously true, but not helpful. It provides neither practical nor moral guidance about what to do once deterrence

---

[1] Kenny presents an excellent analysis of this issue (1985, pp. 52–56). Responding to the idea of someone saying that should deterrence fail, the only thing to do is carry out the threat, Kenny offers: "If he says that and means it, then I can only tell him, quite soberly, that he is a man with murder in his heart."

has failed. If the thing we do instead is more effective than retaliating against the enemy's cities, why didn't we threaten it in the first place, instead of threatening retaliation? If it's less effective, is it worth doing? In any case, there is likely to be very little time for thinking once deterrence has failed, especially if the nation's top leadership has been annihilated, and the acting president has been elevated from several steps down the ladder of succession. If no one had thought of a better idea in peacetime, it is unlikely anyone will think of one once deterrence fails.

This, ultimately, is the major deficiency of the debate over the morality of threatening an immoral act. Should deterrence fail, we will need alternatives to retaliation. The time to think of alternatives is before deterrence has failed. The debate over the morality of threatening an immoral act is a distraction from searching for alternatives to retaliation on cities, alternatives which are both moral and of practical, war-fighting value. If we can think of some moral and practical alternatives, we can threaten with them instead of threatening an immoral retaliation. To a great extent the debate over the morality of threatening an immoral act is an attempt to evade thinking about how to use nuclear weapons morally.

REFERENCES

Amstutz, Mark R. "The Challenge of Peace: Did the Bishops Help?".
    This World (Spring/Summer 1985), pp. 22–35.
Castelli, Jim. The Bishops and the Bomb. New York: Image Books, 1983.
Kenny, Anthony. The Logic of Deterrence. Chicago: University of Chicago Press, 1985.
Spaeth, Robert L. "Disarmament and the Catholic Bishops". This World (Summer 1982), pp. 5–17.

CHAPTER SIX

THE BLUFF

An extreme form of "deterrence, but . . ." is the bluff. Under this scheme, we would threaten nuclear retaliation but would secretly decide in advance that if deterrence failed, we would not only not carry out the threat, but would make no use of nuclear weapons at all. The usual argument given in favor of adopting the bluff is that "the enemy could never be sure we're only bluffing; he wouldn't dare take the chance". This neatly bypasses the issue of whether it is moral to threaten something that would be immoral to do without ever planning to carry out the threat.

The difficulty is that the bluff poses some moral problems of its own. A bluff is simply a lie. If the bluff is to deter, however, the enemy must believe it. Presumably we can ignore the issue of deceiving the enemy, since the enemy has no right to the truth anyway. If the bluff is to be effective, though, the following groups, who do have a right to the truth, must also be deceived:

1. The citizens who voted for the bluffing president, perhaps in preference to a candidate who honestly stated that he would not retaliate;

2. The legislators who appropriated money for the weapons that the bluffing president has no intention of using, perhaps in the belief they were strengthening the nation's defenses;

3. The taxpayers who paid for the weapons that the bluffing president has no intention of using, believing they were paying to defend themselves against aggression;

4. Allies who accepted the validity of our threat, and who sided with us instead of settling for the best terms they could get from the enemy.

Clearly, deceiving this large number of people poses moral problems. The American Catholic bishops in their Challenge of Peace pastoral implicitly recommended a policy of bluffing when they accepted deterrence as temporarily acceptable, even though they rejected both nuclear retaliation on cities and nuclear attacks on the enemy's military forces. James Turner Johnson commented on this as follows:

> Behind the bishops' judgment in this matter lies a fundamental confusion—the belief that somehow deterrence can be separated from use in war. It is difficult to see how this belief arose, but common sense

suggests that no threat will deter another's act if he judges it is only a threat. Deterrence by threat alone depends on the ability to lie convincingly. Thus we are left with the conclusion that the American Catholic bishops would have Christian statesmen systematically and convincingly lie in order to achieve nuclear deterrence—a strange bit of moral advice for Christians (1983, p. 11).

However, even ignoring the problem of lying, the bluff doesn't avoid moral problems. As Nye put it:

> Even if a president intends to bluff, but keeps the intention secret, the forces must be trained and his successor(s) named. By the death of the president, or accident, the threat may actually be carried out. While a bluff might salve the president's conscience, it doesn't solve the moral dilemmas faced by his subordinates (1986, pp. 53–54).

Moreover, there is no way a bluffing president can enforce this same policy on his successors, except by sabotaging the armed forces to such an extent that his successor cannot possibly rebuild them in any reasonable time. However, this sabotage is likely to be detected by the enemy, undermining the effectiveness of the bluff and inviting nuclear blackmail or actual attack. In any case, this sabotage would be a violation of the president's oath of office.

Finally, there is a fifth group that would have to be deceived by the bluff, a group that is almost always overlooked by those who advocate the bluff as a way out of the moral dilemma of deterrence: the members of the armed forces.

From the perspective of the one in uniform, the distinction between only threatening an immoral act and carrying it out is a meaningless one. He must constantly train to carry out the threat and be constantly prepared to carry it out if ordered. To say to him "It would be immoral to carry it out, but you must prepare for it as though you intended to carry it out in order to gain the deterrent effect" is absurd on the face of it. America has always found enough people with the courage and competence we need in our armed forces who were willing to spend a lifetime gaining and maintaining proficiency in skills they hoped they would never have to use. America will find very few people with that courage and competence willing to spend a lifetime maintaining proficiency in skills that they knew were never intended to be used because using them would be a monstrous crime. They simply could not maintain the sham necessary to carry out the bluff.

Of course, it might be objected that the national leadership could deceive the troops as well. It could lead them to think retaliation was the real policy, even though the leadership was secretly determined not to retaliate. This still poses a problem. Under such circumstances, people who consider retaliation on cities to be immoral will not enter the services, or at least not the relevant branches. This means that the people who are careerists, and who will eventually be promoted to the top of those branches, will be people who have spent their lives preparing to do—and who are willing to do—something that the rest of the country considers immoral. Is that really the kind of military leadership we want?

The root of the problem is that the superficially attractive idea of the bluff treats the military as though they were robots. Not only does this denigrate their humanity and their citizenship, but it creates a structure of perverse incentives that drives out of the services the morally sensitive people the services ought to be trying to attract—people who will take moral considerations into account in waging the nation's wars.[1]

In short, the advocates of bluffing want to have it both ways. They want to have a clear conscience while enjoying the benefits of the threat of an immoral act. However, their attempt to evade the moral issues of nuclear war runs head-on into another set of moral issues that collectively are even worse than the ones they attempt to avoid.

REFERENCES

Johnson, James Turner. Letter to the editor. *Commentary* (December 1983), p. 11.

Nye, Joseph S., Jr. *Nuclear Ethics*. New York: The Free Press, 1986.

[1] The same problems as described here will arise with regard to the armed forces in the "deterrence, but . . ." situation described in the preceding chapter. However, in that situation the problems may be ameliorated if the troops are equipped and trained for other strategies in addition to retaliation against cities.

CHAPTER SEVEN

UNILATERAL NUCLEAR DISARMAMENT

Some who saw how difficult the moral problems of nuclear weapons were sought to escape them another way. They called for unilateral nuclear disarmament. While this group included many traditional pacifists, it also included many who objected not to non-nuclear weapons, but only to nuclear ones. Some of these unilateralists argued that if we disarmed, the Soviets would either cease to fear us and disarm themselves or be shamed into following our moral leadership. Others argued that it didn't matter whether the Soviets followed our moral leadership or not, we had to do what was moral regardless of what the Soviets did.

Henry Wallace was one of the first public figures to call for nuclear disarmament, in 1946. However, he was rapidly followed by many others.

Among those arguing for unilateral disarmament regardless of what the Soviets did was Victor Gollancz, noted British publisher and prominent Christian layman. In *The Devil's Repertoire*, he argued for the unilateralist position, stated in unequivocal terms:

> Let it be clear, finally, what the policy advocated *is*. Unilateral nuclear disarmament . . . the determination never to use nuclear weapons, and never to contemplate or threaten their use, whatever the circumstances that may exist or may conceivably arise; so to determine irrespective of what other people or peoples may do, threaten to do, or be suspected . . . of intending to do; together with an unambiguous statement to this effect, and a patent destruction of such nuclear weapons as may already exist. . . . Advocates of unilateralism . . . can never admit reservations or talk of "necessary safeguards": to do so would be to contradict themselves. . . . The world of absoluteness is one world and the world of safeguards is another: and any compromise between them is by their very natures impossible (1959, p. 35) (emphasis in original).

Another advocate of unilateral disarmament was Bertrand Russell, who openly advocated the "better Red than dead" view. Russell was at least consistent in his own way. Before the Soviet Union developed its atomic bomb, he advocated a "preventive war", to eliminate the Soviet threat while it could still be done easily. Once preventive war was no longer possible, he advocated surrender as the only way to avoid worldwide destruction.

In 1961, R. A. Markus, a lay Catholic scholar, wrote that "in any actual circumstances we can envisage, the use of H-bombs is morally inadmissable." He then went on to argue that even possession of these bombs is evil, since possession implies intent to use them, at least under some circumstances. He drew the logical conclusion from this position:

> . . . since we are thus obliged to renounce nuclear weapons, irrespective of what the other side may do, and since without these weapons we could not, in the last resort, be militarily successful, Western governments should be pressed to face up to the problem of *non-violent resistance* (emphasis in original).

More recently, Robert Goodin has made the same argument: if we abandon our nuclear weapons, the Soviets will not attack us with theirs, and we and the world will be safe from nuclear war (1985).

While the calls for unilateral disarmament without regard to consequences go back to 1946, Catholic bishops did not add their voices to the others until much more recently.

Archbishop Raymond Hunthausen of Seattle argued for unilateral disarmament in a 1981 speech:

> As followers of Christ, we need to take up our cross in the nuclear age. I believe that one obvious meaning of the cross is unilateral disarmament. Jesus' acceptance of the cross rather than the sword raised in his defense is the Gospel's statement of unilateral disarmament. We are called to follow. Our security as people of faith lies not in demonic weapons which threaten all life on earth. Our security is in a loving, caring God. We must dismantle our weapons of terror and place our reliance on God. . . . I am told by some that unilateral disarmament in the face of atheistic communism is insane. . . . I find myself observing that nuclear armament by anyone is itself atheistic and anything but sane (quoted in Hollenbach, 1983, p. 67, and Castelli, 1983, p. 28).

In December of 1981, Bishop Roger Mahony of the diocese of Stockton, California, issued a pastoral letter, *Becoming A Church of Peace Advocacy*, in which he advocated nuclear pacifism:

> Today I add my voice to the growing chorus of Catholic protests against the arms race because I believe the current arms policy of our nation, as well as of the Soviet Union, has long since exceeded the bounds of justice and moral legitimacy . . . any use of nuclear weapons, and by implication, any intention to use them, is always morally—and gravely—a serious evil. No Catholic can ever support or cooperate with the planning or executing of policies to use, or which by implication intend to use, nuclear weapons even in a defensive posture . . . (reprinted in Lefever and Hunt, 1982, p. 279).

The argument of the unilateralists is simple. Nuclear weapons cannot be used morally, therefore the only moral thing to do is get rid of them.

The problem with this argument is that there are moral consequences to getting rid of them.

The French Catholic bishops, in their pastoral letter *Winning the Peace*, (1983, no. 9) pointed out the dangers of unilateral disarmament:

> [U]nilateral disarmament can even provoke the aggression of one's neighbors by feeding the temptation to seize a prey which is all too ready for the taking: "After all, it would be much better for us to become their captives. We would be slaves, undoubtedly, but we would be alive", declare the fellow countrymen of Judith, terrorized by the extortions of Holofernes—which their defeatism encouraged (Judith 7:27). In a world where one man still preys upon another, to change oneself into a lamb could be to provoke the wolf.

In short, unilateral disarmament creates a moral hazard in that it provides an increased incentive for someone to commit an evil act he might otherwise be less likely to commit.[1]

Nor is this argument against unilateral disarmament simply a "consequentialist" one. It involves Catholic doctrine regarding the responsibilities of the State.

Pope Leo XIII was quoted with approval by Pope John XXIII in the latter's encyclical *Pacem in Terris*:

> . . . the safety of the commonwealth is not only the first law, but is a government's whole reason for existence.

Pope Pius XII, in the aftermath of World War II, which included the use of two nuclear weapons, wrote:

> *A people threatened with an unjust aggression, or already its victim, may not remain passively indifferent, if it would think and act as befits a Christian. . . .* Among (the) goods (of humanity) some are of such importance for society, that it is perfectly lawful to defend them against unjust aggression. *Their defense is even an obligation for the nations as a whole, who have a duty not to abandon a nation that is attacked* (Christmas message, 1948, emphasis in original).

---

[1] Even if one were to accept that the Soviet Union is not an aggressive nation, one still has to reckon with the fact that war breaks out only when nations disagree about their relative strengths; war ends when they reach agreement about relative strengths. There are many places in the world today where peace is uneasy but exists because both sides believe their strengths are equal, and neither has an advantage. If either side thought it had an advantage, the uneasy peace would end. This stable equilibrium would end as soon as the United States disarmed unilaterally, and many wars would break out. One can list several such hot spots: Korea, the Middle East, Europe, and South America. One need only note the violence that broke out when the United States withdrew support from the Shah of Iran and from Somoza in Nicaragua to recognize the potential for much greater outbreaks of violence should the current balance be dismantled unilaterally.

Despite the nuclear pacifism voiced by several of their number, the American Catholic bishops, in their Challenge of Peace pastoral, rejected the pacifist position. Instead, they stated:

> The moral duty today is to prevent nuclear war *and* to protect and preserve those key values of justice, freedom, and independence which are necessary for personal dignity and national integrity.

That is, defense of certain values is of equal importance to preventing the slaughter of innocents.

Thomas Mangieri summarized Catholic doctrine regarding the duties of the State as follows:

> A "pacifist state" is, by established Catholic social philosophy, a contradiction in terms. Its very *raison d'être*, due to the reality of a sinful world and the precepts of the natural law, requires it "to bear the sword" and be a "terror to the evil works" (1983, p. 20).

The bishops recognized this when, in their Challenge of Peace pastoral, they said (1983, no. 75):

> The council and the popes have stated clearly that governments threatened by armed, unjust aggression must defend their people. This includes defense by armed force if necessary as a last resort.

The position of the Catholic Church on this point then is quite clear: for a nation to fail to resist evil is itself evil. One doesn't escape sin by abjuring resistance.

Some have argued for passive resistance as a means of resisting evil, citing such figures as Mohandas Gandhi and Martin Luther King, Jr. This idea was promoted over a quarter of a century ago by Markus, in the quote given above. The Catholic bishops, in their Challenge of Peace pastoral, said (1983, no. 222):

> There have been significant instances in which people have successfully resisted oppression without recourse to arms. . . . The heroic Danes who would not turn Jews over to the Nazis and the Norwegians who would not teach Nazi propaganda in schools serve as inspiring examples in the history of non-violence.

The bishops also referred favorably to Sharp's studies of nonviolent resistance (1973).[2]

---

[2] Anyone who reads Sharp's books in conjunction with, say, *Murder of a Gentle Land*, or the books by Conquest, Fisher, or Nekrich, can only be struck with wonderment at the utter unreality, the total lack of awareness of what has happened in the world in this century alone, shown by those who think that passive resistance is going to have any effect at all on a determined aggressor. Moreover, as Bond has shown, many of Sharp's examples are actually misleading and do not support his points (1985, *passim*). Bond also shows that

The thing that must be kept in mind about passive resistance is that it has never worked against a tyrant. The heroic resistance of the Danes and Norwegians never amounted to more than a pinprick to the Nazis. Indeed, without the Normandy invasion, the Nazis might well still be in Norway and Denmark. Had Mohandas Gandhi or Martin Luther King, Jr. been up against the Soviet government, instead of the democratic governments they did face, they would have ended up in a labor camp and eventually an unmarked grave, not in the history books.

To those who argue we could expel an invader by nonresistance, one simply needs to point to the Soviet Union itself. Why haven't the Soviet people been able to get rid of their own government by such means? The fate of the Helsinki Watch committees is instructive. The Soviet Union signed a formal treaty (the Helsinki Accords) in which it agreed to certain solemn commitments. In effect we ratified their conquest of Eastern Europe, and in return they promised to treat their conquered subjects decently. Soviet citizens set up committees to observe and report on the Soviet government's adherence to its solemn commitments. The Helsinki Watch committees were smashed—their members sent to jail, to psychiatric prisons or to labor camps—just as all earlier dissident groups were smashed, and the Soviet government goes merrily on its way ignoring its solemn commitments. The Accords were signed on July 29, 1975. Already by January 1977 the Associated Press reported:

> The Soviet Union has convicted at least ninety dissidents since signing the supposedly liberating 1975 Helsinki Accords. . . . At least fifteen sane persons have been declared insane and sent to institutions.

It is easy to imagine Politburo members getting together and laughing themselves nearly to death at the naïvete of anyone who thinks that Gandhian measures will get rid of an invading Soviet army, just as they must be laughing hilariously at anyone who is naïve enough to think they would really take the Helsinki Accords seriously.

When nothing else is left, of course, passive resistance is still worth trying. The failure of the Helsinki Watch committees is tragic, but their heroism is inspiring. However, the ultimate objection against rejecting armed resistance and depending upon passive resistance alone is not simply that it is impractical, but that it is immoral. Mangieri says:

> Such advice assumes that passive resistance is inherently morally superior to active resistance, which, in Catholic theories of politics, is an erro-

---

the single most important factor on those occasions when nonviolence succeeded was that it took place within a democratic system. None of Sharp's cases shows ultimate success against an undemocratic system.

neous assertion. The bishops approvingly put before us the spectacle of a government which, as a matter of policy, throws its own people on the mercies of an invader, a course of action which is flatly immoral according to established Catholic doctrine (1983, p. 21).

A hypothetical unilateralist might respond to this argument by saying: "I agree that the State has a moral obligation to defend its citizens, not to surrender them. However, it must do so by moral means. It is meaningless to talk of carrying out a moral duty by means as immoral as nuclear weapons, which will kill millions of innocent people."

This is a fair argument, and it must be addressed. In a later chapter we will deal with the morality of killing innocent people in war, nuclear or conventional. At this point we need to examine the consequences that innocent people would suffer as a result of unilateral nuclear disarmament.

Let us assume that the United States dismantles its nuclear weapons. Would the Soviet Union be shamed enough by this moral action to dismantle its own forces? Its record in the past certainly does not encourage one to believe it will. Moreover, Soviet dissident Vladimir Bukovsky provides a reason why it would not:

> [W]hat would happen if the West were to disarm unilaterally? Could the Soviets follow suit? Certainly not. It would mean the rapid disintegration of their empire and a general collapse of their power (1982, p. 201).

Since it is incredibly naïve to think the Soviets will disarm, the virtually certain consequence of our nuclear disarmament would be our surrender. Markus and Hunthausen have drawn this as the logical outcome of unilateral nuclear disarmament, and expressed their willingness to accept it.

Our nuclear disarmament, before or even after surrender, might well lead to nuclear strikes against the United States by the Soviets. After all, what would there be to restrain them? The purpose of these strikes might be to destroy any facilities that would enable us to regain a nuclear capability. Or the purpose might be to destroy our conventional capability to resist their armies, turning their occupation into an administrative landing instead of an invasion. Or the purpose might be to cow us to such an extent that they wouldn't even need to bother occupying; they could count on us to police ourselves on their behalf, as the Poles do now. Thus one of the first consequences of unilateral nuclear disarmament might very well be the deaths of large numbers of innocent people in nuclear explosions.

Beyond this is the matter of the consequences of an occupation. The Soviet Union has demonstrated in the past that it knows how to deal with potentially "untrustworthy" peoples. Under Stalin a famine was deliberately engineered in Ukraine, with the specific purpose of eliminating people who did not fit the desires of the Soviet Union. This was preceded by a *dekulakization* campaign, which eliminated the more prosperous peasants.[3] Using Soviet census figures (even though they are known to be falsified in an attempt to hide the magnitude of the catastrophe), Conquest estimates some eleven to twelve million dead in these campaigns (Novak, 1984, p. 7; Conquest, 1968, *passim*). The bulk of these unnatural deaths were women and children; by any reasonable standard they would be held innocent. This was out of a total of 31.2 million Ukrainians counted in the 1926 census. Moreover, these numbers of deaths are an underestimate, because they do not include Volga Germans or others in the Southwestern USSR, where similar campaigns took place. Applying the same proportion of deaths to the current American population of 238 million, *Ukrainizing* the United States would result in over ninety-one million deaths. One has to ask, could a nuclear war be worse?

Other nationalities besides Ukrainians died in large numbers as the Soviet government deported them from their homelands to Siberia. Nekrich estimates that among the Chechens, Kalmyks, Ingush, Karachai, and Balkars, 220,000 died during the post-World War II deportations, out of a 1939 population of 743,000 (1978, p. 138). Fisher quotes letters and testimony from both victims of the deportations and defecting members of the NKVD (the Soviet secret police, since redesignated as the KGB) who describe the ill-treatment of the deportees. Death rates among the deportees exceeded 17 percent in the first year alone, of those who actually made it to their new "homes". Conquest lists estimates of death rates as high as 50 percent during the movement of the peoples (1970, passim). Moreover, these deaths were not from an engineered famine but simply from relocation. The alleged justification was collaboration with the occupying German army, but as Nekrich demonstrates, the charges were essentially trumped up, and in any case the deportations took place after the Germans were driven out, when even collaborators no longer posed a threat.

An unsigned article on Captive Nations Week in *The New American* for July 14, 1986, mentions an NKVD report for June 13, 1941 that tells of 11,102 Estonians, 16,255 Latvians, and 21,114 Lithuanians—a total of 48,471 people—loaded into 871 freight cars and sent off to Siberia on that one day alone. No information on deaths is available, but the sur-

---

[3] The term *kulak* originally meant the village moneylender, an easy person to agitate against. The Soviet government extended the meaning to include all prosperous people, and invented the term *sub-kulak* to include anyone else who was to be disposed of.

vival rate was probably even lower than that of the nationalities that were deported later. This report, for which we evidently have the occupying Nazi army to thank, gives us only a glimpse of the horrors that may one day be revealed if the Soviet government's archives are ever made accessible.

We must not overlook the Katyn massacre of 10,000 Polish officers who were killed in 1940 and buried in mass graves (for details see Heller and Nekrich, 1985, pp. 403–7). In addition, the occupying Soviets sent 200,000 Polish soldiers to internment camps in 1940. What would these two figures imply for the roughly two million military personnel now on active duty for the United States? Additional Polish civilians numbering in the hundreds of thousands were sent to labor camps in USSR. For both soldiers and civilians sent to labor camps, the death rates were staggering. Reports from the few survivors, however, are not sufficiently complete to allow precise estimates of the total deaths.

Finally, we need to look at the labor camps themselves. It is not sufficient to say these were originated by Stalin and ended with his death. As Conquest points out, labor camps were established as early as mid-1918, under Lenin, even though "the decrees legalizing them were passed in September 1918 and April 1919" (1968, p. 334). He goes on to state that the first true death camp was established in 1921, again well before Stalin's day. Moreover, these camps still exist, under Stalin's successors. Soviet General Peter Grigorenko warned the Crimean Tatars, in a speech on March 17, 1968:

> You think you have only to deal with honest people. This is not the case. What was done to your nation was not done by Stalin alone. And his accomplices are not only alive but holding responsible office (quoted in Conquest, 1968, p. 201).

It is particularly noteworthy that despite the *de-Stalinization* campaign under Khrushchev, none of these wrongs was righted or even acknowledged.

In these camps the survival rate, even from the beginning, was low. Conquest reports that around 1930, the average lifetime in a camp was two years (1968, passim). Heller and Nekrich state that:

> Most of those arrested in 1937 and 1938 were unable to survive the harsh conditions in the camps for more than two or three years. It is true that the Soviet concentration camps did not have gas chambers or crematoriums like the Nazi death camps. Mass extermination was organized in a more primitive way, due to technical backwardness. People were simply shot, starved to death, or killed off by disease, brutal treatment, or unendurably demanding labor (1985, p. 319).

Solzhenitsyn, describing the much less severe camps in which he was imprisoned, reports that many prisoners did not survive even a ten-year term. Large numbers of prisoners simply died before their terms were up (1973).

Exact numbers of persons now in the labor camps are hard to come by, but estimates of the current Gulag population include some half a million Vietnamese who were sent by their government to pay off, through their labor, the Vietnam War debts incurred for purchase of Soviet weapons. After unilateral disarmament, how many Americans would be sent to the Soviet Union for such reparations? How many would be sent to camps in the Dakotas, Alaska, or Hudson Bay? And how many would survive?

Of course, after unilateral disarmament, the United States might not actually be occupied by the Soviet Union. Instead, such an occupation might be administered by communists of some other nationality. Therefore it is worth mentioning that the Cambodian communist Pol Pot was responsible for the deaths of something like a quarter to a third of the people in his country after his victory. The Marxist-Leninist government of Ethiopia has engaged in massive relocations of "untrustworthy" people, just as the Soviets did, to eliminate rebels. It has forcibly relocated over 500,000 of its own people from rebel provinces, with death rates in the relocation camps of around 20 percent, matching the Soviet precedent. Current estimates are that over a million Ethiopians have died either from famine or relocation, and over two million are in exile.[4] The Marxist-Leninists ruling Nicaragua also followed the Soviet example of deporting "untrustworthy" nationalities, removing several thousand Miskito Indians from the coastal areas to the interior. The only reason the death rate in that case didn't match the Soviet precedent is that many of the Miskitos escaped to Honduras, where they survived in refugee camps. Finally, we mustn't forget the Chinese (some estimates place the number at sixty million) who died in the Cultural Revolution. Nor the effects of the Chinese occupation of Tibet. Accurate figures are again hard to come by, but the best estimates seem to agree that a quarter of the population of Tibet has died at the hands of the Chinese occupiers.

All these estimates are of course only approximate. The communists themselves may not even know how many people have died unnatural deaths through deportations, labor camps, death camps, and engi-

---

[4] Where would Americans go into exile once the United States had unilaterally disarmed? Would Canada or Mexico accept large numbers of refugees, especially if the Soviet Union demanded their return? Where would our boat people go? Cuba? Once there is no longer a place for refugees to go, the death rate would most likely be even higher.

neered famines. It is a hopeless task to attempt to estimate the number without even such records as the communists kept.

The point, though, is that unilateral disarmament would simply extend the system of deliberate killing to most of the rest of the world. As Nye put it:

> [U]nilateral disarmament would impose a risk of harm on innocent people in this country. Steps that seriously weaken deterrence merely shift risks among innocent people, and may raise risks to all (1986, p. 108).

We have overwhelming evidence that when you surrender to the communists, that doesn't mean the war is over. The war continues—but the surrendering side is disarmed. Bertrand Russell's choice of "Red or dead" turns out to be a false one. Under a Stalin, under Ethiopia's Mengistu or under Cambodia's Pol Pot, you could very well end up being both.

The terrible irony though, is that by taking the step of unilateral disarmament—a step that would result in the deaths' of millions of innocent people—we may not even succeed in escaping nuclear war. Every empire in history has collapsed eventually. Many have collapsed in civil war over the issue of succession to leadership, including Alexander's Macedonian empire, the Roman empire, Mohammed's Moslem empire, and several Chinese empires. Dare we believe that if civil war eventually broke out in a worldwide Soviet empire, the contenders would refrain from using the nuclear weapons in their possession? Unilateral disarmament may therefore be an almost certain recipe for eventual nuclear war.

The unilateralist may respond: "It is true that unilateral disarmament might result in the deaths of millions of innocents. But at least we wouldn't be responsible for those deaths. The other side would. Morally, it is better to suffer injustice than inflict it."

This attitude on the part of those advocating unilateral nuclear disarmament is really the key issue. Unilateral nuclear disarmament is simply another scheme to avoid the hard moral questions. If we "opt out of the nuclear arms race", as the British unilateralists phrase it, then we don't have to make decisions about nuclear weapons, and we can avoid the moral questions of how and when to use them. If we surrender to a tyranny, the unilateralist assumes we are no longer morally responsible for what happens.

As with all attempts to escape moral questions, however, this approach simply means that we would face a sharper set of moral questions later. The Second Vatican Council recognized that surrender to tyranny was not the way to achieve peace.

Peace is not merely the absence of war. . . . Nor is it brought about by dictatorship. Instead, it is rightly and appropriately called "an enterprise of justice" (Is 32:17) (*Gaudium et Spes,* 1965, no. 78).

The American Catholic bishops made the same point in their Challenge of Peace pastoral:

Justice is always the foundation of peace. In history, efforts to pursue both peace and justice are at times in tension, and the struggle for justice may threaten certain forms of peace (1983, no. 60).

Moreover, they noted that Saint Augustine had said:

War and conquest are a sad necessity in the eyes of men of principle, yet it would be still more unfortunate if wrongdoers should dominate just men (1983, no. 81, n. 31).

Basil Cardinal Hume of England stated:

Although nothing could ever justify the use of nuclear arms as weapons of massive and indiscriminate slaughter, yet to abandon them without adequate safeguards may help to destabilize the existing situation and may dramatically increase the risk of nuclear war (1983, no. 6).

Cardinal Charles Journet wrote in his essay, "The Conscience of a Christian About Nuclear Arms", in 1964:

If the noncommunist bloc unilaterally disarmed, it would give the world to the Soviet Empire and would betray all the holy values, temporal and spiritual, which we ought to defend; this would be the evil of betrayal. . . . [If] the Christians succeed in imposing unilateral disarmament upon their bloc, the Soviets, by the threat of war, would hold the world in their hands. . . . We face the moral risk of seeing our freedom destroyed if the moralists confine their condemnations only to things in the abstract and if they refuse to face up to actual conditions (quoted in Schlafly, 1981).

The root of the problem is the unilateralist's false dichotomy: inflict injustice or suffer it; use nuclear weapons unjustly or surrender and see the conquerors commit injustice. This dichotomy is false because it ignores any alternatives to the extreme positions. Indeed, the whole point of the unilateralist is to ignore alternatives to the extremes. Thus the attempt to avoid the moral questions about the use of nuclear weapons by giving them up and surrendering brings on a moral responsibility for the triumph of injustice, when that triumph might have been prevented.

REFERENCES

Barron, John, and Anthony Paul. *Murder of a Gentle Land*. New York: Reader's Digest Press, 1977.

Bond, Douglas G. "Alternative to Violence: An Empirical Study of Nonviolent Direct Action". Ph.D. dissertation, University of Hawaii, Honolulu. May, 1985.

Bukovsky, Vladimir. "The Soviet Role in the Peace Movement", in Lefever and Hunt.

Castelli, Jim. *The Bishops and the Bomb*. New York: Image Books, 1983.

Conquest, Robert. *The Great Terror*. New York: Macmillan Co., 1968.

Conquest, Robert. *The Nation Killers*. New York: Macmillan Co., 1970.

Fisher, Alan W. *Crimean Tatars*. Stanford, Calif.: Hoover Institution Press, 1978.

Gollancz, Victor. *The Devil's Repertoire*. Garden City: Doubleday & Co., 1959.

Goodin, Robert E. "Nuclear Disarmament as a Moral Certainty". In *Nuclear Deterrence: Ethics and Strategy*, edited by Russell Hardin, et al. Chicago: University of Chicago Press, 1985.

Heller, Mikhail, and Aleksandr M. Nekrich. *Utopia in Power*. New York: Summit Books, 1985 (translation of the 1982 Russian language edition by Phyllis B. Carlos).

Hollenbach, David, S. J., *Nuclear Ethics*. New York: Paulist Press, 1983.

Lefever, Ernest W., and E. Stephen Hunt, eds. *The Apocalyptic Premise*. Washington, D.C.: Ethics and Public Policy Center, 1982.

Mangieri, Thomas P. *Nuclear War, Peace, and Catholicism*. Front Royal, Va.: Christendom Publications, 1983.

Markus, R. A. "Conscience and Deterrence". In *Nuclear Weapons: A Catholic Response*, edited by Walter Stein. New York: Sheed and Ward, 1961.

Nekrich, Aleksandr M. *The Punished Peoples*. Translated by George Saunders. New York: W. W. Norton & Co., 1978.

Novak, Michael, ed. *The Man-Made Famine in Ukraine*. Washington: American Enterprise Institute, 1984.

Nye, Joseph S., Jr. *Nuclear Ethics*. New York: The Free Press, 1986.

Schall, James V., ed. *Out of Justice Peace and Winning the Peace* [Bishops' Pastoral Letters]. San Francisco: Ignatius Press, 1984 (collection of the German and French bishops' pastoral letters [both 1983], and letter [1983] of Basil Cardinal Hume, primate of England).

Schlafly, Phyllis. "The Immorality of Disarmament". *Our Sunday Visitor* (November 6, 1981).

Sharp, Gene. *The Politics of Nonviolent Action* (3 volumes). Boston: Porter Sargent Publishers, 1973.

Solzhenitsyn, Aleksandr I. *The Gulag Archipelago*. New York: Harper & Row, 1973.

Stein, Walter. *Nuclear Weapons: A Catholic Response*. New York: Sheed and Ward, 1961.

CHAPTER EIGHT

MUTUAL DISARMAMENT

Some who wish to escape the moral problems of nuclear weapons, but who see the problems of unilateral disarmament, have argued instead for mutual nuclear disarmament—the complete abolition of nuclear weapons on both sides. Some who make this argument are secretly unilateralists. They seek written agreements for sake of agreements, and ridicule those who question whether the enemy can be trusted to keep his word. However, many who argue for mutual disarmament are undoubtedly sincere. They call for genuine, gradual, and verifiable nuclear (and sometimes conventional) disarmament.

As I have already noted, the American Catholic bishops reached a strictly conditioned acceptance of deterrence. One of the conditions was progress in arms control negotiations. In particular, they stressed that "the numbers of existing weapons must be reduced" (1983, no. 204). They also quoted the words of Pope John XXIII, saying (1983, I.C.2):

> Negotiations must be pursued in every reasonable form possible; they should be governed by the "demand that the arms race should cease; that the stockpiles which exist should be reduced equally and simultaneously by the parties concerned; that nuclear weapons should be banned; and that a general agreement should eventually be reached about progressive disarmament and an effective method of control" (Pope John XXIII, *Peace on Earth*, no. 112).

Unfortunately, the attempt to escape the problems of nuclear weapons by getting rid of them creates several other moral problems.

One of the first problems is a practical problem, but it leads to a moral problem. That is the unity of science. Even if, in a historically unprecedented display of good will, all nuclear weapons were actually dismantled, the knowledge of how to build them would remain. So long as that knowledge remained, no one could be confident that nuclear weapons were not being constructed again. This knowledge cannot be eliminated because it is intimately linked with the rest of science. As Nye put it: ". . . it would be impossible to abolish nuclear knowledge without burning all books and all scientists" (1986, p. 121).

To eliminate the knowledge on which nuclear weapons are based would be to eliminate the knowledge that keeps modern civilization going. It is this knowledge that provides the means of survival for well over half the world's population. Without this knowledge, the world's population would be reduced to the maximum level that could be sustained by a preindustrial world.

In the case of North America, we know what that preindustrial population was. The continent supported about a million people as subsistence farmers and hunter-gatherers before the use of scientific knowledge allowed the land to sustain its current population. The rest of the quarter billion of us now living in North America owe our very existence to scientific knowledge.

Eliminating the knowledge of how to make nuclear weapons, and all the background knowledge on which nuclear science is based, would produce at least as many deaths as would a nuclear war.

We are faced, then, with the practical problem that knowledge of how to build nuclear weapons cannot be eliminated, and thus we can never be sure the weapons themselves have all been eliminated and not rebuilt. For moralists to continue to demand their elimination is to demand the impossible. At the very least, this is a waste of time. Worse yet, it can discredit entirely the idea of morality, since it appears to demand too much, and can cause people to conclude morality has nothing to do with politics or military matters. Indeed, these moralists ought to ask themselves, "Is it licit to demand the impossible, and to condemn leaders of our own government when they don't achieve it?"

In another sense, also, overemphasis on nuclear disarmament is a waste of time. Disarmament agreements negotiated between adversaries may simply lead each to seek new kinds of weapons not covered by the treaties. For instance, a clause in the Versailles treaty, which ended World War I, prohibited Germany from having military aircraft. Although this provision was promptly violated once Hitler gained power, it had already stimulated German planners to consider long-range rocket-powered missiles (Beard, 1976, p. 220). Similarly, if molecular biology makes the same degree of progress during the next fifty years that nuclear physics has in the past fifty, the moralists of the year 2040 may look back with fond nostalgia to a time when the worst weapons they had to worry about were nuclear ones. Too much emphasis on the impossible goal of eliminating nuclear weapons entirely may simply speed the day of "engineered plagues".

Beyond the perverse effects that overemphasis on nuclear disarmament can produce, there are some direct moral issues that are often ignored by those who demand nuclear disarmament.

The first of these is really a matter of moral confusion. The call for disarmament is based on the assumption that it is the *weapons themselves* that are the problem. The mutual disarmers assume that people threaten each other because weapons exist. In this regard it is worth noting the

Statement of the Holy See to 24th Session, International Atomic Energy Agency, Vienna, on October 1981:

> . . . the history, both ancient and more recent, of attempts at disarmament has proved to be a series of illusions and delusions. This demonstrates a truth that is fundamental: treaties are not effective unless they arise from and are sustained by a sincere and real desire for peace, because, in the final analysis, the danger and threat come not so much from the weapons as from the one who has them in his hand: man.

Thus in reality, weapons exist because some specific people threaten other specific people. When threats don't exist, neither do armaments. The U.S.-Canadian border is the longest unarmed border in the world, simply because both nations are confident the other isn't going to attack. The people in Canada and in Mexico may rightly be concerned about U.S. nuclear policy, but no one in either country seriously considers the possibility that the United States might attack them with nuclear weapons. Thus the people asserting that mutual disarmament is the way to peace are reversing cause and effect.

Some advocates of disarmament are at least willing to admit that people, not weapons, are the problem, but they still raise the spectre of overkill. These advocates argue that the United States and the USSR can each kill the other several times over; surely neither side would lose any security by reducing the level of overkill. This argument misses the critical point: what matters is not how many weapons each side has before the war starts, but how many deliverable weapons it has left after the enemy has made a first strike against its nuclear delivery systems. This is a point I will take up again in the next chapter, but it requires mention here. Determining whether nuclear overkill exists demands some thought about vulnerabilities of forces and the ways in which wars might be started and fought. It can't be determined simply by counting weapons, or even by counting the number of peacetime weapons per wartime target. Asserting that "morality demands a reduction", without taking practical considerations into account, and without recognizing that the problem is people not weapons, represents a high degree of moral confusion.

The second genuine moral problem faced by those who demand nuclear disarmament is the militarization of societies under threat. The primary reason for the Western alliance's emphasis on nuclear weapons has been that these are much less expensive than conventional weapons. Even before the Soviet Union obtained its own nuclear weapons, the NATO nations had begun to depend upon nuclear weapons to offset the conventional superiority of the Soviet Union and its Eastern European satellite nations.

James L. Payne has assembled data on "force ratios" (number of full-time active-duty military per 1000 people) for various nations. The results are quite striking. The eight Marxist countries in Europe have an average force ratio of 13.8; the seventeen non-Marxist countries have an average force ratio of 7.6. The Soviet Union has a force ratio of 16.3; the United States a force ratio of 9.1. East Germany has a force ratio of 14; West Germany a force ratio of 7.8. Even among the non-aligned countries, the contrast is striking: Marxist Yugoslavia has a force ratio of 10.9, while non-Marxist Austria has a force ratio of 5.3 (1986, pp. 270–89).

For the nations of NATO to achieve parity in conventional arms with the nations of Eastern Europe, they would have to become militarized to the same degree as those nations. Overall, this would mean roughly doubling the number of personnel in uniform, and increasing military budgets by the same ratio. This is not simply a matter of diverting resources from other uses such as health, education, and welfare, although such a diversion surely has moral implications. It is even more a matter of attitude. Whether the increase in military force were to be achieved by conscription or by attracting volunteers, matching the military buildup of the Soviet Union and the nations of Eastern Europe would require a permanent willingness on the part of the people of Western Europe to double the current peacetime military burden. Surely this, too, has moral implications that must be considered by those who are so eager to get rid of nuclear weapons.

The third moral problem arising directly from an emphasis on disarmament comes from the asymmetry that exists between the closed society of the Soviet Union and the more open societies threatened by the Soviets.

This asymmetry shows up first of all in attempts to negotiate arms-limitation agreements. Leaders of democratic countries are under domestic pressure to limit armaments. If they try to continue development or production of a weapon until the Soviet Union agrees to a mutual limitation, they find themselves attacked domestically. Three recent examples include the neutron warhead, the B-1 bomber, and the MX missile. All were targets of extensive domestic opposition. Then-president Jimmy Carter canceled the neutron warhead and the B-1 bomber unilaterally, achieving no comparable concessions from the Soviet Union. The Soviet leadership at the time asserted their researchers had already developed neutron warheads; they were completely silent on the question of whether they had deployed them. The Soviet BACKFIRE bomber was then already being deployed, and the Soviet Union currently has 270 of them, nearly three times the 100 B-1s the

United States will eventually deploy.[1] Congress placed a limit of 100 on the number of MX missiles to be deployed and has refused to fund even this many.

In the "Pastoral Constitution on the Church in the Modern World" (1965, no. 82), the assembled Catholic bishops of the whole world said:

> . . . everyone must labor to put an end at last to the arms race, and to make a true beginning of disarmament, not indeed a unilateral disarmament, but one proceeding at an equal pace according to agreement, and backed up by authentic and workable safeguards.

One-sided pressure on the United States resulted, in the cases of the B-1 and the neutron warhead, in unilateral reductions rather than the mutual and balanced reductions called for by the Vatican Council, several popes, and the American bishops.

Even when the executive branch is determined to maintain a strong negotiating posture, Congress often is not. In the United States, as soon as Congress senses that a weapon system is going to be used as a bargaining chip rather than be developed for actual deployment, it tries to reduce funds for it. The argument usually goes something like: "Why develop something that isn't going to be deployed anyway?" However, this makes it difficult if not impossible for the United States to put any pressure on the Soviet Union to negotiate.

The problems that can arise from failure to recognize this asymmetry are illustrated by Wohlstetter, who quotes responses of the leaders of the (German) Green Party to President Reagan's zero option for intermediate nuclear forces in Europe (1983, p. 33):

> Petra Kelly and Manon Maren-Griesbach, two of their principal leaders, explain that the zero option is "unrealistic" because the Russians would never agree to it. It is therefore "not even an honest step toward arms reduction".[2]

---

[1] There is some dispute over the extent to which the B-1 and the BACKFIRE are comparable. The U.S. Defense Department publicly credits the BACKFIRE with an unrefueled combat radius of 4000 km. versus 7500 km. for the B-1 (*Soviet Military Power 1986*, p. 33). However, the two aircraft are comparable in size, indicating that the disparity in range is smaller than the estimates allege, and the estimated top speed of the BACKFIRE is about 25 percent greater than that of the B-1. Even accepting the published United States estimates of range, the BACKFIRE is capable of striking the United States on a one-way mission from the Soviet Union. With in-air refueling, it is capable of making the round trip, or of recovering at bases in Cuba or Nicaragua.

[2] Ironically, as of this writing, the Soviets are asking for the zero option in Europe, now that they realize the Western European nations are serious about matching the Soviet SS-20 buildup. As usual, however, they have done so in a way that would permit them to filibuster once the negotiations started.

The attitude of the Greens is shared by many who advocate nuclear disarmament and put pressure on Western governments to achieve it. Such supporters take the view that it is up to us to make concessions that are acceptable to the Soviets. If we don't, we are not really attempting to achieve disarmament. Their attitude toward Soviet proposals is quite different. No matter how brazenly one-sided such proposals may be, they insist we must accept them as a starting point for negotiations.

A second example of this pervasive pressure on Western leaders is illustrated by the following extract from a story distributed by a national U.S. news service in the summer of 1986, announcing a proposal by President Reagan to Mr. Gorbachev regarding arms control:

> The new U.S. proposal offers no concessions to the Soviets on the *key stumbling block* to an arms agreement—the President's planned development of his strategic defense initiative or star wars (emphasis added).

This was not a signed opinion piece or an editorial. It was a news item. The assertion that strategic defense is "the key stumbling block" is presented as straight factual news. The implication is that if we abandoned strategic defense, Mr. Gorbachev would fall all over himself in his eagerness to sign a strategic arms agreement. In reality, of course, having achieved this concession from us without any matching concessions on his part, he would then negotiate vigorously over what our second concession would be in exchange for his first.[3] This unilateral pressure, so pervasive that news services begin to see Soviet propaganda claims made for negotiating purposes as objective facts, seriously hampers our attempts to negotiate with the Soviets.

Max Kampelman, head of the U.S. team at the Geneva negotiations on arms reduction, stated the issue clearly (August 10 and 17, 1986, passim):

> I've thought about this and I've concluded—reluctantly—that the antinuclear crusade of the so-called "peace movement", with which many religious leaders have identified, has made it *more* difficult to achieve a serious agreement with the Soviet Union (emphasis in original).

With regard to the effect of one-sided pressures, he stated:

> If there's a Soviet textbook called "How to Negotiate with the Americans", it says, "Be patient and take your time. The West and the Ameri-

---

[3] In the view of some, apparently, the mere fact that the Soviets agree to negotiate with us represents a concession on their part, and this concession justifies a "pre-emptive" concession on our part to get them to the bargaining table. People with this attitude apparently feel that arms negotiations are more important to us than they are to the Soviet Union. One can only wonder if this attitude is born out of a recognition that the Soviets are better armed than we are, and show less apprehension than we do about the prospect of using those armaments.

cans are impatient. If there's no agreement in a number of months, there will be criticism in the West that the Western negotiators aren't doing enough, or their governments aren't doing enough. And there'll be great pressure on them to make concessions. As the months go on there'll be more and more pressure, and they may make concessions to us without requiring that we make any concessions in return." I'm convinced that's a fundamental part of Soviet negotiating strategy.

He commented regarding the organized campaigns by religious groups to put pressure on Western negotiators:

> The organized religious community seems to have lost its basic moorings, to the extent it is promoting an approach to the problems of the world which ignores this understanding of values in a political community. . . . It also troubles me when so-called leaders stand behind the cloak of peace in order to be neutral in the real struggle for human dignity. . . . Their pressure is on the West because they have no influence on the Soviets. Don't they understand that their effort, if successful, can be damaging to human values because its result might well be unilateral disarmament?

Another person testifying to the potential harm from one-sided pressure for disarmament is Shin Kichi Eto, professor of International Relations at Tokyo University, and a survivor of the atomic bombing of Hiroshima. He stated on the op-ed page of the *Wall Street Journal*:

> When the bomb fell on the morning of August 6, I was indoors and was not burned. Although I was buried in the rubble and almost suffocated, I got away with a few scratches.
> As soon as the fires abated, we went into the blast area to clean away debris. We worked near ground zero for several days, and I was exposed to secondary radiation. . . .
> Every day, I worked in the intense heat, disposing of corpses. . . .
> My memories of those times are very painful still. I want to be second to none in my hatred for war and desire for peace. Yet I differ with some of the world's more outspoken pacifists. . . .
> The more powerful mass movements demanding the abolition of nuclear weapons become, the more influence they have on the U.S. government, but not on the Soviet Union. This could hamstring the United States while the Russians build up their nuclear arsenal with impunity (April 21, 1982, p. 28).

The massive amount of testimony about the folly of one-sided moral pressure on the West should encourage religious leaders to remember the advice of Dean Acheson: "We can never get a good arms control agreement unless we are prepared to live without one" (quoted by Adelman, 1984–1985, p. 241). These moralists should ask themselves, "Is it licit to apply moral pressure to one side only, when a possible result is unilateral disarmament and the triumph of those upon whom we can have no moral influence?"

The second place the asymmetry between our open society and the Soviet closed society shows up is in attaining adherence to disarmament agreements once they have been reached. It is very difficult to get the evidence needed to tell whether a closed society is violating a disarmament agreement. Worse yet, a democracy is reluctant to take seriously any evidence that the other side is cheating. There will always be those who want to put a good face on the matter, who will deny that the adversary's violations of the treaty are significant.

A good example of this situation is the current controversy over whether the Soviets are violating the Threshold Test Ban Treaty, which limits underground nuclear tests to 150 kilotons. Seismic signals from Soviet tests, as received in the United States, can be interpreted as indicating that the Soviets are setting off blasts far larger than 150 kilotons.[4] However, those who oppose U.S. testing and therefore wish to deny that the Soviets are violating the treaty, claim that our seismographs are improperly calibrated; or that the soil in the Soviet Union permits much more efficient coupling of the blast energy, so the shock waves are greater from a given size test; or some such thing. The supporters of the treaty once urged us to sign the treaty, saying that our measuring apparatus was good enough to tell whether the Soviets were violating the treaty and the treaty was therefore safe to sign. Now they deny this and assert our apparatus must be faulty because it makes it appear as though the Soviets are violating the treaty.

Another argument offered in defense of the Soviets by domestic opponents of testing and advocates of arms control is that even if the Soviets are exceeding the 150 kiloton limit, this has no military significance. It does not increase the threat to us. The resulting debate then focuses, not on whether the treaty is being violated, but on whether violations are important. This problem has its roots in the *arms control syndrome,* which works as follows.

The decision is made that some activity (such as nuclear testing) must be limited or controlled. A countable or measurable manifestation of

---

[4] The arguments on this issue can become quite involved. Prior to 1977, United States seismograph signals indicated that Soviet tests were significantly greater than 150 kilotons. However, the United States has twice raised the threshold for seismograph signals, until it is now above the level of all Soviet tests in 1976 and 1977. Assuming that until 1977 the Soviets were testing up to the 150-kiloton limit but not exceeding it, just as our tests approached the limit but stayed under it, then the average yield of their tests since 1977 is well over 150 kilotons. Conversely, if one assumes that their current tests are just barely within the limit of 150 kilotons, then their pre-1977 tests must have all been at 75 kilotons or less, which is entirely unrealistic. The situation cannot be resolved until the Soviets permit us to make accurate measurements of geological conditions at their test sites.

that activity is selected, with the emphasis usually being on its countability or measurability (ease of verification), rather than on its connection with the purpose for which control is desired. An arbitrary limit on the count or measure is then negotiated with the Soviets, usually after much haggling over whether it should be slightly higher or slightly lower. This inevitably leads to a debate on whether the other side is violating the limit or simply pushing as close to it as possible, with an occasional accidental violation. The arms control enthusiasts are usually quick to point out that a minor violation has no military significance anyway. This is of course true, since the limit is arbitrary anyway, and has only the most tenuous connection with the original purpose for wanting to undertake arms control.

The problem with this syndrome is that the debate completely loses sight of the original purpose for which control is desired. Instead the discussion degenerates to a debate over whether some arbitrary limit is being observed and what, if any, difference it makes if it isn't. This is one of the most serious problems with arms control as it is presently practiced. If we ignore enemy violations, we are releasing the enemy from the terms of the treaty while continuing to observe it ourselves. If we attempt to insist on the treaty, we end up in an endless round of haggling over whether the limit was actually exceeded. At the same time we find domestic supporters of the treaty arguing that we shouldn't worry about a minor violation that has no military significance, especially since insisting on the terms of the treaty may cause the other side to abrogate it completely.

The problem goes well beyond the issue of nuclear testing. Colin Gray quotes Senator Les Aspin (D-Wisc.) as saying (1986, p. 51):

> The violations [of SALT by the Soviet Union] are politically harmful because they undermine American support for arms control and because they cry out for an American response, but in military terms they don't amount to a hill of beans.

As Gray puts it (1986, p. 51):

> Arms control advocates like Les Aspin seem to think that the main problem with arms control violations is that silly Americans get all worked up about them.

However, the importance of arms control treaty violations goes far beyond the military significance of the violations themselves. Gray says further:

> Japanese, German, and Italian treaty violations before World War II were just about as militarily significant as Soviet violations in recent decades. For instance, . . . Japan violated the terms of the 1922 Washington Naval

Treaty by 70 to 100 percent on all 10 of its ships . . . while four ships exceeded the 35,000-ton displacement limit. Germany demonstrated its disregard for arms control . . . by constructing its two *Bismarck* class battleships with 42,000-ton displacements, considerably above the 35,000 tons permitted.

These violations were politically harmful not merely because they reduced public support in England for the arms control process, as Les Aspin would have it. They were politically harmful because they convinced Germany and Japan that the Allies were weak, that they could not enforce their treaties, that they were not even bold enough to insist on compliance, that there was constant handwringing and rationalization for hostile behavior. Thus arms control demonstrated weakness that could only have increased the confidence of Germany and Japan that increasing the military pressure would bring political capitulation from the Western democracies (1986, p. 51).

Here again, the asymmetry between open and closed societies means that pressure on democratic governments, not matched by pressure on their enemies, may increase rather than decrease the chances of war—especially if this pressure leads those governments to ignore violations of treaties. This is clearly a moral problem for advocates of disarmament.

There is yet another moral problem that can arise from efforts at arms control. Bernard Brodie states:

> [I]t was the Washington Naval Treaty of 1922 which made the Pacific phase of World War II possible, for it assured to Japan something much closer to naval parity with the United States than would have been anywhere near her reach in any real building competition ensuing from the absence of such a treaty. The Treaty did avoid for a time a "costly" naval building competition. But was not the war with Japan more costly? And would Japan have dared embark upon a war against an America boasting a naval power which was—as it easily could have been, without any untoward strain upon the American economy—two or three times her own? (1948, p. 27).[5]

[5] It was not just by signing treaties that granted military equality to economically inferior but hostile powers that the United States was brought into World War II. Former Chairman of the Joint Chiefs of Staff Admiral Thomas H. Moorer interviewed Japanese leaders for the Strategic Bombing Survey in Japan after World War II to determine why Japan attacked the United States when it did. He states:
> They all gave the same reasons: "Your Congress only passed the Selective Service Act by one vote, your defense budget had been at a low level for several years, your Congress refused to fortify Wake and other key islands, and the U.S. Army was training in Louisiana with wooden guns. So our *perception* of you was that the United States would not fight" (1987, pp. 65–68, emphasis in original).
One of the key lessons to come out of World War II was that failing to defend ourselves

The same problem appears in the world today. The United States has a gross national product roughly twice that of the Soviet Union. Moreover, a far smaller percentage of our GNP goes for basics. For instance, we need far fewer of our people on the farm to feed ourselves than they do. If we in the United States made up our minds to engage in an arms race, we could outdo the Soviets with no serious trouble, and without depriving the poor. The effect of mutual arms limitations, which always have to achieve something like parity to be acceptable, is to grant equality in weapons to a power that is hostile to us but economically inferior to us. Those who advocate mutual disarmament should ask themselves seriously, "Is it moral to cede, by treaty, to a hostile and aggressive power a level of equality it could not achieve otherwise?"

The moral problems arising from disarmament, then, fall in five categories. Demanding the impossible goal of total nuclear disarmament tends to discredit the idea that morality has any bearing on arms control. Failure to recognize that the problems are caused by people, not the weapons themselves, leads to moral confusion—that is, blaming the potential victims of aggression for the armaments of the aggressor. Failure to recognize that nuclear weapons cost much less than do conventional ones can lead to a much greater militarization of Western nations. Failure to recognize the asymmetry between closed and open societies can lead to one-sided agreements, and to a reluctance to enforce agreements, both of which make war more rather than less likely. Finally, granting an unnecessary equality to a hostile and aggressive power may increase the likelihood of war, as it did in the case of Japan prior to World War II.[6]

The issue is not, of course, to condemn those who for moral reasons press for mutual arms limitations. If they can achieve a mutual reduction in arms *without endangering security,* everyone benefits. The issue is that they must recognize that arms control presents moral problems that may be even more severe than those presented by armaments. They must not assume that just because a proposal is labeled "arms con-

---

only encourages the aggressor. An inordinate desire for disarmament can only have the same effect—this time in a world armed with nuclear weapons.

[6] The Washington Naval Treaty of 1922 restricted the ratio between the naval forces of Japan and the United States to three-fifths to one, rather than permitting full equality. However, even this ratio was much higher than the Japanese could have achieved in a real naval arms race. Also, by artificially restricting the level of our armaments relative to theirs, the treaty made Japanese violations far more significant. In an all-out arms race, the Japanese could never have come close to the United States. By cheating on an artificially low level of armaments, they came close to matching the United States' naval forces. The Pacific Ocean segment of World War II was a high price to pay for any "savings" made on naval armaments prior to 1939.

trol" or "mutual disarmament" it is automatically moral, and that anyone opposing it is automatically immoral. They should be particularly wary of disarmament proposals coming from nations that have a history of oppressing their own people and aggression against their neighbors; such proposals usually contain traps. They should refrain from attributing bad faith to those officials of their own government who don't enthusiastically support every proposal labeled *disarmament*. Finally, they shouldn't assume that once a treaty has been signed, all is well. Morality demands that treaties be kept, and that violations be publicized, and corrected or penalized, because failure to do so encourages aggressors.

Those who place a heavy moral emphasis on disarmament or arms control would do well to heed the words of Pope John Paul II, in his 1982 World Day of Peace Message:

> The production and the possession of armaments are a *consequence* of an ethical crisis that is disrupting society in all its political, social, and economic dimensions. Peace, as I have already said several times, is the *result* of respect for ethical principles. True disarmament, that which will actually guarantee peace among peoples, will come about only with the resolution of this ethical crisis. To the extent that the efforts at arms reduction and then at total disarmament are not matched by parallel ethical renewal, *they are doomed in advance to failure* (emphasis added).

The call for mutual disarmament is all too often simply another way of avoiding the hard moral questions. Its proponents seem to believe that if we abolished nuclear weapons, we wouldn't have to think about how to use them morally. But since we can't get rid of nuclear weapons without first ending distrust among nations, the pursuit of total mutual disarmament is at best a waste of time, and at worst an evasion of moral responsibility. Both the American bishops and John Paul II have emphasized that "peace is possible", but disarmament will come after peace, not before it.

REFERENCES

Adelman, Kenneth L. "Arms Control With and Without Agreements". *Foreign Affairs* (Winter 1984–1985), pp. 240–63.
Beard, Edmund. *Developing the ICBM*. New York: Columbia University Press, 1976.

Brodie, Bernard. "The Atom Bomb as Policy Maker". *Foreign Affairs* (October 1948), pp. 17–33.

Department of Defense. *Soviet Military Power 1986.* Washington, D.C.: U.S. Government Printing Office, 1986.

Eto, Shin Kichi. "A Hiroshima Survivor Reflects on Disarmament". *Wall Street Journal* (April 21, 1982), p. 28, col. 3.

Gray, Colin S. "Nuclear Delusions". *Policy Review* (Summer 1986), pp. 48–53.

Kampelman, Max. Interviewed in *National Catholic Register.* Part 1 (August 10, 1986). Part 2 (August 17, 1986).

Moorer, Thomas H. "Playing Politics With Our Defense". *Conservative Digest* (February 1987), pp. 65–68.

Nye, Joseph S., Jr. *Nuclear Ethics.* New York: The Free Press, 1986.

Payne, James L. "Marxism & Militarism". *Polity.* Vol. 19, no. 2 (Winter 1986).

Wohlstetter, Albert. "Bishops, Statesmen, and Other Strategists on the Bombing of Innocents". *Commentary* (June 1983), pp. 15–35.

CHAPTER NINE

EXISTENTIAL DETERRENCE

There is yet another attempt to escape the awful paradox of only being able to secure our safety by threatening something immoral; it goes by the name of *existential deterrence*, a term originated by McGeorge Bundy.
Bundy does not give a compact definition of the term. The meaning comes out only in an extended discussion.

> A [source of uncertainty] is intrinsic to the weapons systems themselves, which are now so powerful and varied on both sides that no one can hope to have any clear idea of what would in fact happen if "deterrence failed"—that is, if nuclear war began. . . . These terrible and unavoidable uncertainties . . . create what I will call *existential* deterrence . . . this fancy adjective is to distinguish this kind of deterrence from the kind that is based on strategic theories or declaratory policies. . . . As long as we assume that each side has large numbers of thermonuclear weapons which *could* be used . . . existential deterrence is strong. It rests on uncertainty about what *could* happen. . . . It deters quite impersonally; no provocative threats are needed. . . . It makes full and impartial use of one of the great realities of nuclear weapons: they are far more terrifying to adversaries than they are comforting to their possessors (1984, pp. 8–10) (emphasis in original).

Bundy also says of existential deterrence:

> . . . its deterrent power is unaffected by most changes in the arsenals on both sides . . . except those which might truly change the overall survivability of the forces on either side . . . [therefore] it makes no sense to base procurement decisions on refined calculations of the specific kinds of force that would be needed for a wide variety of limited nuclear responses (1984, p. 9).

Since the time Bundy coined the phrase, others have adopted it and given more compact definitions. Amstutz defines it as: ". . . a deterrence not based on any particular theory of war-fighting but on the capabilities of strategic nuclear arms in carrying out assured destruction" (1985, p. 34). Father J. Bryan Hehir characterizes it as: ". . . the objective deterrent which exists so long as both sides have weapons which *could* be used after any attack. This form of deterrence rests on 'uncertainty about what *could* happen' " (1984, p. 69) (emphasis in original).[1]

Others have recently expressed the same idea, without using the term itself. Ford states (1985, p. 111):

> The great irony in the convoluted debate over the optimum nuclear strategy is that it is hardly necessary to have a sophisticated nuclear weapons employment policy in order to hold the other side at bay. . . . Deterrence is not created by words. It is assured by thousands of weapons sitting silently in their silos and on board patrolling submarines.

For those who believe in it, existential deterrence avoids all the moral problems discussed in previous chapters. It isn't a bluff, therefore it doesn't amount to lying to our citizens and our allies. On the other hand, it doesn't involve the actual use of nuclear weapons, so it avoids the moral problems associated with such uses. Since it doesn't even involve planning to use nuclear weapons, it avoids the issues of whether it is moral to plan to use them.

Despite the new name, however, this is not a new idea. From the beginning of the nuclear age, many people took it for granted that deterrence was automatic and came from the mere existence of the weapons themselves.

Perhaps the earliest to give voice to this idea was Jacob Viner of the University of Chicago, who said in a talk to the American Philosophical Association in November of 1945:

> What difference will it then make whether it was Country A which had its cities destroyed at 9 A.M. and Country B which had its cities destroyed at 12 A.M., or the other way around (Kaplan, 1983, p. 27).

Political columnist Dorothy Thompson, trying to stress how nuclear weapons had changed the classical picture of warfare, wrote in 1946 that if Denmark had the atomic bomb and the Soviet Union did not, Denmark would be a more powerful country than the Soviet Union. Implicit in this statement was the idea that the bomb would be delivered with certainty, and in sufficient time to halt an otherwise overwhelming attack.

Likewise in 1946, speaking at a conference, Jacob Viner expanded upon his earlier views:

---

[1] Note that Hehir attributes objectivity to deterrence. This is a position often taken by people who believe deterrence is inherent in weapons. As I pointed out in Chapter 1, deterrence is inherently subjective, existing in the mind of the person whom we wish to deter.

The atomic bomb makes surprise an unimportant element of warfare. Retaliation in equal terms is unavoidable and in this sense the atomic bomb is a war deterrent, a peacemaking force (Kaplan, 1983, p. 27).

Richard Rovere, a political columnist, was quoted by Albert Wohlstetter as follows (1959, p. 213):

> If the Russians had ten thousand warheads and a missile for each, and we had ten hydrogen bombs and ten obsolete bombers . . . aggression would still be a folly that would appeal only to an insane adventurer.

Thus the early believers in existential deterrence took it for granted that retaliation would inevitably take place, and therefore deterrence was automatic. The first serious attempt to refute the idea that nuclear deterrence is inherent in the existence of the weapons was made by Albert Wohlstetter in his article, "The Delicate Balance of Terror" (1959, pp. 211–234). This article was an unclassified version of a "basing study" conducted at the RAND Corporation in the 1950s. The study participants had been asked by the Air Force to look at the most efficient arrangement of air bases from which to conduct a nuclear bombing campaign against the Soviet Union. The study participants came to what was, for the time, a radical conclusion: a rational enemy would strike first at our offensive forces, not at our cities, and therefore these forces should be defended.[2]

As Wohlstetter pointed out for the first time in the open literature: "To deter an attack means being able to strike back in spite of it. It means, in other words, a capability to strike second." He then pointed out that the Rovere statement implicitly assumed that the ten hydrogen bombs would inevitably be dropped on the aggressor, and they would be dropped despite the fact that: the aggressor would likely use several missiles against each bomber base, he would probably alert his air defense forces before launching his missiles, and he might even evacuate his cities or take other civil defense measures, since he knew the timing of the attack while the defender would be unprepared.

Wohlstetter listed a series of "obstacles to be hurdled" by any system that is to be able to strike second. These are paraphrased here:

1. The deterrent systems must be capable of stable operation for an indefinite period in peacetime at an acceptable cost, despite false alarms and despite both deliberate and accidental loss of individual units of the system.[3]

---

[2] This idea harks back to Churchill's views, described in Chapter 2, that the best way to protect yourself against the zeppelins is to bomb the zeppelin sheds.

[3] Bombers must be flown in peacetime to train their crews. This allows us to detect deterioration and wear, but exposes the bombers to accidental loss. Sample missiles must

2. The deterrent systems must be able to survive enemy attack.
3. The systems must be able to make and communicate the decision to retaliate.
4. The systems must have sufficient range to reach enemy territory and carry out the attack.
5. The systems must be able to penetrate enemy defenses (this is particularly important for bombers and cruise missiles).
6. The systems must be able to destroy the target in spite of "passive" civil defense in the form of dispersal or protective construction or evacuation of the target itself.[4]

Wohlstetter argued that the enemy would choose a time and method of attack that would make these objectives as difficult to achieve as possible and that he might even design his forces, or his mode of attack, to make one or more of them impossible. Any discussion of the inevitability of retaliation that failed to take these obstacles into account was simply ignoring reality.

Herman Kahn subsequently presented many arguments against the idea that deterrence was automatic, arguing that the deterrent forces must be protected. Kahn was more flamboyant than Wohlstetter, and he gained a great deal more notoriety for his work and words. In later years, however, he stated that he received a great deal of satisfaction from the fact that people began to take seriously the problems of preserving a retaliatory force against an enemy's first strike, and he felt his writings had contributed to that achievement.

While the earliest believers in existential deterrence assumed that deterrence worked because the attacker could count on being struck in retaliation, the newer believers assume that deterrence will work because the attacker cannot count on *not* being struck in retaliation. Bundy asserts that the weapons on both sides are "so powerful and varied" that the attacker could not be certain what would happen; he couldn't count on avoiding retaliation (1984).

But what about the hurdles Wohlstetter listed? What about the problems of striking second? Bundy simply slips by this issue. Consider his assertion that existential deterrence

> is unaffected by most changes in the arsenals on both sides . . . except those which might truly change the overall survivability of the forces on either side (1984).

---

be test-fired periodically in peacetime, to check for deterioration and wear, but this results in deliberate loss of the test-fired missile.

[4] Note that Wohlstetter implicitly assumes here that retaliation will be against cities, since those are the only targets left after the enemy has expended all his missiles against our forces and possibly our cities.

That is to say, existential deterrence is unaffected by any changes except those that affect it. This statement is true by definition and is therefore empty of any practical content. In reality, Bundy here is assuming away the very problem that is the crux of the issue: what does it take to be able to strike second?

Father Hehir likewise assumes away the problem when he says: "Existential deterrence . . . exists so long as both sides have weapons which *could* be used after any attack (1984, p. 69)." This, too, is true by definition, but it ignores the issue of how we can assure that we will still have weapons after the enemy has made a first strike.[5]

The emphasis on uncertainty and on weapons that *could* be used mean that existential deterrence boils down to saying "it wouldn't take much destruction to deter them, and they could never be sure they would escape it." This, too, is an old idea. Wohlstetter had addressed it already in 1959 (p. 216):

> . . . the enemy is free to use his offensive and defensive forces so as to exploit the weaknesses of each of our systems. . . . It would be quite wrong to assume that . . . the uncertainties . . . affect a totalitarian aggressor and the party attacked equally. . . . It is important not to confuse our uncertainty with his. Strangely enough, some military commentators have not made this distinction and have founded their certainty of deterrence on the fact simply that there are uncertainties.

In short, retaliation is not entirely certain. Moreover, the aggressor will take all the steps open to him to reduce both the probability of retaliation and the damage if retaliation occurs. It takes a great deal of effort to assure that the probability of effective retaliation is still high enough to deter a rational aggressor even after the aggressor has expended considerable effort to reduce that probability. The fact that *we* are uncertain does not mean *he* is deterred.

In addition to the fact that retaliation is not only uncertain but may be unlikely, there are some other things wrong with the idea that weapons deter by their mere existence.

First, weapons that are vulnerable may attract an attack instead of deterring it. The early Atlas ICBMs based in the United States, the Thor

---

[5] Existential deterrence is particularly important for Father Hehir, one of the chief architects of the American bishops Challenge of Peace pastoral. The bishops stated that *threatening* to retaliate was conditionally acceptable, but *executing* the threat would be immoral (1983, I.A.1, I.B). How, then, can we gain any deterrent effect if we publicly announce that the threat we are making is really empty because we have no intention of committing the immoral act of carrying it out? For Father Hehir and other believers in existential deterrence the problem disappears because the existence of the weapons themselves causes the enemy to be uncertain about whether we might retaliate, despite the fact that such retaliation would be immoral.

IRBMs based in England, and the Jupiter IRBMs based in Italy and Turkey were not protected by silos. They sat upright on a concrete pad, open not only to the weather but to attack. In a crisis, the existence of these Atlases, Thors, and Jupiters, far from providing stable deterrence, would have destabilized it.

The Thors and Jupiters were particularly bad in this regard. They had no protective construction to reduce the effectiveness of air attack. They had to be fueled with liquid oxygen before they could be launched, a process that took hours. However, they were within minutes' flying time of Soviet air bases. From the Soviet perspective, they had to look like first-strike weapons, because they obviously couldn't survive to deliver a second strike. Moreover, the Soviets could only believe that we would have seen that. Therefore, in their view, we had to be planning a first strike. In any crisis, the Soviets would have felt extreme pressure to knock out those missiles before they could be used—to preempt, in terms of their own doctrine.[6]

As early as 1959 Bernard Brodie had observed (p. 159):

> . . . a conspicuous inability or unreadiness to defend our retaliatory force must tend to provoke the opponent to destroy it; in other words, it tempts him to an aggression he might not otherwise contemplate.

Even Ford, who clearly subscribes to the existential-deterrence thesis, even if without the name, is concerned that in a crisis each side may be tempted to strike first to avoid losing its nuclear striking force to the enemy's first strike (1985):

> There is nothing, however, to guarantee that the mutual deterrence that prevails in peacetime can survive the stress of a major crisis, or that the conflicting interests and ideological differences of the two nations will not lead to severe clashes in the future. . . . It is in such an unstable situation that the existence of first-strike plans . . . could quickly and irreversibly lead to the rapid abandonment of all restraint and, in effect, propel the two nations into a nuclear war that neither wanted (p. 13).

The greater your suspicion of your opponent's offensive intent, of course, the greater the incentive to go on the offensive yourself. So much for mutual deterrence in a crisis. According to the script that each side has prepared for nuclear war, any previous hesitancy about attacking could

---

[6] From our perspective, however, the Thors and Jupiters were not first strike weapons. We fully intended to use them only in a second strike. However, that second strike made sense only in our "preferred scenario", in which the Soviets opened the war with a conventional attack in Central Europe, and we then punished them with a nuclear counterstrike. Our doctrinal and strategic thinking still hadn't caught up with the idea that the first objective of any sensible attacker is to destroy the most threatening weapons on the other side.

give way . . . before everything was destroyed by the other side. Ironically enough, the net effect of being prepared to strike first is to encourage the other side to make the preemptive attack itself (p. 14).

[T]he choice between using one's own first-strike weapons or waiting for the other side to use theirs is not, in military terms, one that calls for extended deliberations. Instead of both sides, as in peacetime, being deterred from attacking the other, they could both feel prompted to commence hostilities as soon as possible. The only question in such an unstable situation is who will fire first (p. 237).

By now it has become axiomatic that powerful but vulnerable nuclear forces make deterrence less rather than more stable because they provide the adversary with an incentive for a preemptive disarming attack. This alone is proof that the mere existence of nuclear weapons is not a sufficient condition for deterrence; a low degree of vulnerability is a necessary condition, and achieving that requires some thought about how the enemy might choose to initiate and prosecute a war. In short, deterrence requires that some thought be given to war-fighting, to intrawar deterrence, and to war termination; and it requires that some thought be given to determining which weapons to procure (all of which Bundy has specifically denied).

Second, even invulnerable weapons don't last forever. They wear out eventually in any case, and sometimes they deteriorate in unexpected ways. For instance, in the mid-60s, components of the warheads on our submarine-launched Polaris missiles were found to be damaged by warhead radiation. The missiles could have been fired, but the warheads would not have functioned. The Polaris boats continued their patrols while the warheads were redesigned and replaced. This situation was officially admitted only years later, and without much attention drawn to it. The continuing Polaris patrols were not a complete bluff, since the ICBMs and bombers still existed. However, this incident points up the dangers of depending on a single force or weapon, and particularly of assuming that the existence of that weapon alone is sufficient to provide deterrence.

Third, even the existence of multiple systems does not provide deterrence if they all share a common weakness that allows the enemy to disable them in the same way. The ability of complementary systems to offset each other's weaknesses is illustrated by the synergy that existed between bombers and ICBMs in the 1970s. At that time, Soviet Submarine-Launched Ballistic Missiles (SLBMs) were not accurate enough to attack missile silos. However, they were accurate enough to attack airfields. If launched near our coasts, they could reach inland

SAC air bases within a flight time of five to ten minutes, which meant they could catch most of the bomber force on the ground. However, an SLBM attack on airfields would give unambiguous warning that an attack was under way, and allow our ICBMs to be launched. Conversely, a launch of Soviet ICBMs at our ICBM silos, although a more ambiguous signal, would give a thirty-minute warning of the attack, allowing the bomber force to be launched, since the bombers could be recalled if the attack turned out to be a false alarm. Because the strengths of each system offset the weaknesses of the other, they provided stronger deterrence than either would have alone. However, to design systems that complement each other in this fashion requires that considerable thought be given to the various kinds of attacks the enemy might make. The synergy doesn't come automatically.

Some believers in existential deterrence, when pressed on these points, will admit that an aggressor may be able to convince himself that he can avoid retaliation, either by destroying our retaliatory force in a disarming first strike, or by tailoring his first strike to avoid as much civilian damage as possible. Then we would be faced with the problem that our surviving nuclear forces are too weak to do any serious damage to his remaining nuclear forces, while if we retaliate against his cities, he can make a third strike against our cities, doing more damage to us than we do to him. They respond that in case of a crisis, when an enemy first strike seems possible, we can go to a "Launch under attack (LUA)" or "Launch on warning (LOW)" posture for our nuclear forces. This, they argue, will strengthen deterrence because it will reduce the enemy's confidence in escaping retaliation (The Garwin article is typical [1979/ 80, pp. 117–39], but many others have advocated the same idea).

LUA means we execute a preprogrammed all-out retaliatory strike based on unambiguous evidence that an attack is under way, such as a nuclear explosion somewhere within the United States. LOW means we execute such a strike on the basis of early warning (radar, infrared, or other electromagnetic means) that the enemy has launched his missiles. The idea is that if we announce we have adopted either policy, the would-be aggressor will know he cannot get away with a disarming first strike, nor can he put us in a position where we must avoid attacking his cities with our surviving forces. Again, the mere existence of our forces provides deterrence, since a posture of LUA or LOW assures retaliation.

It is hard to believe anyone could argue for either LUA or LOW unless they were driven to it by sheer desperation. Consider LUA. It, at least, has the virtue of not calling for retaliation unless the attack is unambiguous—for example, warheads already exploding on targets in the United States. But then what? A nuclear force in an LUA posture doesn't wait to determine the nature of the attack: a limited strike at forces believed to be themselves preparing for a first strike; a strike tailored to reduce civilian casualties; an all-out strike against both weapons and cities; or even an accidental or unauthorized launch. Regardless of the nature of the attack, retaliation is done by reflex: "use the weapons before we lose them, and hit everything". Granted, the LUA posture might enhance deterrence. But once deterrence has failed, for whatever reason, LUA assures it will fail in the most catastrophic possible way. The attacker has no incentive to tailor his attack to reduce civilian casualties, or limit his attack to the forces he deems most immediately threatening. On the contrary, he has a perverse incentive to do as much damage as possible in his first strike, because of the damage he anticipates in our reflex retaliation.

LOW has every bad feature of LUA, plus one more: it is vulnerable to false alarms. If any of the electromagnetic devices that are supposed to warn of an enemy attack sound an alarm, nuclear forces in an LOW posture have only a few minutes to make the decision to launch. There may not be time to determine that the warning was false. After all, the LOW posture is likely to be adopted only in a time of crisis, and the presumption then is already tilted toward the likelihood of an enemy surprise attack. Thus an electronic glitch in the warning system might trigger a war. In addition, an accidental or unauthorized launch of an enemy missile, or even an unannounced test firing of an enemy missile, might trigger full-scale retaliation.

There have been numerous objections to "turning the decision to go to war over to a computer". These objections are well founded. And that is what LOW really amounts to, and to a lesser extent so does LUA. They can be advocated only as a means of preserving the idea of existential deterrence after there is some reason to believe the enemy is not deterred by the mere existence of our weapons.

In summary, existential deterrence is defective in its very definition. Some thought *must* be given to how nuclear wars might start, be fought, and be terminated, if deterrence is to be effective. Otherwise there is a serious risk that the wrong kind of weapons, by their very existence, will make deterrence less rather than more stable, especially if they have a weakness the enemy can exploit. The believers in existential deterrence should face up to the moral question, "Is it licit to build a retaliatory system without even thinking about whether it makes war more or less likely?" This attempt to avoid the hard moral questions about how to use nuclear weapons ends up like all the others. It presents us with even sharper moral questions.

REFERENCES

Amstutz, Mark R. "The Challenge of Peace: Did the Bishops Help?" *This World* (Spring/Summer 1985), pp. 22–35.

Brodie, Bernard. *Strategy in the Missile Age*. Princeton: Princeton University Press, 1959.

Bundy, McGeorge. "Existential Deterrence and Its Consequences". In *The Security Gamble*, edited by Douglas MacLean. Totowa, N.J.: Rowman & Allanheld, 1984.

Ford, Daniel. *The Button*. New York: Simon & Schuster, 1985.

Garwin, Richard. "Launch under Attack to Redress Minuteman Vulnerability". *International Security*. Vol. 4, no. 3 (Winter 1979/80), pp. 117–139.

Hehir, Rev. J. Bryan. "Moral Issues in Deterrence Policy". In *The Security Gamble*, edited by Douglas MacLean. Totowa, N.J.: Rowman & Allanheld, 1984.

Kahn, Herman. *On Thermonuclear War*. Princeton: Princeton University Press, 1960.

Kaplan, Fred. *The Wizards of Armageddon*. New York: Simon & Schuster, 1983.

Wohlstetter, Albert. "The Delicate Balance of Terror". *Foreign Affairs* (January 1959), pp. 211–234.

CHAPTER TEN

MAKING DISSUASION CREDIBLE

Since it is clear that nuclear weapons do not deter simply by existing, how do we make dissuasion credible? Fred Ikle has expressed the problem this way:

> [R]endering the use of arms so unattractive that a nation would rather tolerate existing conflicts or frustrations than start a war . . . requires that the antagonists hold certain views of how a possible war might end. Those with power to start a war must expect that the ending would be worse than what their nation would have to concede, or tolerate, to preserve the peace. This condition is well understood; indeed, it is what modern deterrence strategy is all about (1970, p. 108).

In short, dissuasion will be credible when the enemy believes war will leave him worse off than accepting the *status quo*. Even the proponents of MAD agree with this; they say nothing could be worse than having all of one's cities destroyed, therefore nations will accept anything rather than risk a counterpopulation nuclear exchange.

If dissuasion is to be credible, certain attitudes are required on the part of both the aggressor and the nation trying to dissuade aggression. Again Fred Ikle has stated the situation well:

> For deterrence to be effective against a *deliberately* planned attack—and only against this can it be effective—the would-be aggressor must give more thought than the defender as to how the war would end. Or more precisely, the would-be aggressor must be prudent enough to calculate how the victim's retaliation would deny him a desirable outcome in all circumstances. Yet to be deterred he must believe that the victim possesses precisely the opposite trait; that is, he must expect the victim to retaliate in a reflex fashion reckless of cost or consequences. History teaches us that these characteristics tend rather to be reversed between aggressor and defender, and that many an aggressor has counted on this being so (1970, p. 123).

This becomes a key point with regard to nuclear retaliation. Consider two alternative possibilities for first strikes by an aggressor. One is the all-out strike against our cities and our retaliatory forces. The other is a carefully tailored strike which attacks only nuclear forces distant from cities, so that cities suffer no blast damage, and there is adequate time for city-dwellers to evacuate or enter fallout shelters. What kind of retaliation is rational in each of these cases?

In the first case, our retaliatory forces are weakened, but some may survive to be launched against the undamaged enemy defense system. Since by assumption most if not all the enemy nuclear forces have already been expended, what is left to retaliate against? Only the enemy cities. Let us ignore the moral question for a moment, and ask simply, does it make sense to destroy the enemy's cities? What do we gain by it? Most of us may well be dead already. Is "vengeance from the grave" a rational response? The fact that we have nothing to gain from it, and the fact that it would be immoral, both argue that it really isn't a rational response.

In the second case, again our retaliatory forces are weakened, but let us assume we procured enough nuclear forces prior to the attack so that we still have the ability to destroy a significant fraction of the aggressor's population and economy. However, the assumed attack has left our cities undamaged. What would it be rational for us to do then? Should we use our nuclear forces against the aggressor's cities, knowing that his remaining nuclear forces are sufficient to do more damage to our cities than we will do to his? Should we use our nuclear forces against his remaining nuclear forces? Retaliating against the aggressor's cities certainly isn't rational at this point. Even retaliating against his remaining nuclear forces may be a less desirable move than opening negotiations to see what terms the aggressor will demand.

In short, once deterrence has failed, retaliation may not be a rational act at all. Since the aggressor knows this will be the case, deterrence may be weakened. The aggressor might even deliberately tailor an attack such that it would be obvious to us that retaliation would be irrational, in the sense that it would make us worse off than refraining from retaliation.

Numerous authors have argued for the value of finding ways to commit ourselves to carrying out an action that will be seen as irrational, if the occasion comes to carry it out. Gauthier presents an elaborate version of such an argument, dressed up with the mathematical apparatus of probability and expected utility (1984). Lewis attempts to escape the moral dilemmas by separating the intention to retaliate from the actual retaliation (1984). The basic point of all who make this argument, however, is that we can enhance deterrence by committing ourselves to do something that would be against our best interests to do if deterrence did fail.

As Ikle points out, this is difficult at best and may be impossible (1970, p. 123). For the aggressor to be deterred, he must be prudent and rational while we are irrational. Historically, it has been the victims of aggression who are prudent and rational. What this means is that the threat of an irrational action, while intended as a deterrent, leaves the threatener vulnerable to nuclear blackmail and to limited nuclear strikes. We will consider each of these in turn.

The French bishops discussed the problem of nuclear blackmail in their pastoral *Winning The Peace* (1983, no. 7):

> Some countries are very well-skilled at seizing the advantages of war without paying the price of its having been unleashed. Simply by fomenting the threat of war, they commit permanent blackmail. Hitler used this strategy with the Western democracies. They avoided any action rather than provoke him on the occasion of the rearmament of the Ruhr, the occupation of Austria, then of the Sudetenland, and finally of the whole of Czechoslovakia. It took the invasion of Poland to make them realize that they had postponed the inevitable. "The conqueror always loves peace. He would wish to penetrate our territory without meeting resistance", Clausewitz, a specialist in this matter, once wrote.

The German Catholic bishops, in their pastoral letter *Out of Justice, Peace* (no. 104), voiced similar sentiments:

> For this reason, the Church has always adhered to the necessity of protecting the innocent against brutality and oppression, combating injustice and defending justice and righteousness. As we know from the lessons of history, a universal renunciation of this protection and resistance may be understood as weakness and possibly as an invitation to perpetrate political blackmail. In fact, such a renunciation may foster the very things which it is designed to prevent, namely the oppression of the innocent and the infliction of suffering and brutality on them.

George Quester describes an instance of Hitler's successful use of blackmail:

> Aggressive German initiatives, until Munich, were often accompanied by subtle references to "total destruction" inevitably raining down from the air, if German demands should be militarily resisted; during the final takeover of Bohemia-Moravia, the threat (entirely a bluff) of a bombing of Prague was conveyed to Dr. Hacha, with significant influence on his decision not to resist (1966, p. 100).

Nor was Hitler the only dictator who pushed the democracies to see how far they would back down. In 1948 Stalin closed off all approaches to Berlin, ostensibly to repair the roads and railroads. James Forrestal, the Secretary of Defense, reported to Secretary of State George Marshall that "the Joint Chiefs of Staff do not recommend supply to Berlin by armed convoy in view of the risk of general war involved and the inadequacy of United States preparation for global conflict" (Johnson, 1983, p. 441).

And this was at a time when the United States had a monopoly on nuclear weapons (although in actual fact fewer than two dozen weapons were assembled and available for use). Later Nikita Krushchev admitted that Stalin was bluffing; he was "prodding the capitalist world with the tip of a bayonet" (Johnson, 1983, p. 441). Yet his bluff was successful in blackmailing the United States.

Albert Wohlstetter had the following comments on the effectiveness of deterrence through threats of irrational acts (June 1983, p. 30):

> Dogmas of "Minimum Deterrence" and "Deterrence Only" had their origins in the late 1950's in the writings of [French Air Force] General Pierre Gallois. Gallois believed that nuclear weapons spelled the end of alliance: no nuclear guarantee to a non-nuclear ally was credible since no nation would commit suicide for another. . . . However, the incoherence of the Deterrence Only view is thorough and applies to deterring an attack on oneself. If it is true that a nation will not commit suicide for another, neither can it commit suicide to assure its own survival. Suicidal threats are *in general* not a reliable means of dissuasion (emphasis in original).[1]

It is now popular to argue that the only use of nuclear weapons is to deter aggressors from using them; they have no military value, it is said. For instance, as McNamara and Bethe put it, ". . . nuclear warheads serve no military purposes whatsoever. They are not weapons. They are totally useless except to deter one's opponent from using his warheads" (1985, p. 45). Edward Doherty, who served as an adviser on political and military affairs to the U.S. Catholic Conference, during the writing of the bishops' Challenge of Peace pastoral, said in the same vein: "The pastoral letter does not make any sense unless you say there are virtually no uses of nuclear weapons."

However, this view presents too limited a perspective. In the hands of an aggressor, an important use of nuclear weapons is to intimidate the prudent and rational victims of aggression.[2] George Kennan noted that:

> Stalin said the nuclear weapon is something with which you frighten people with weak nerves. He could not have been more right (quoted by Dyson, 1984, p. 263).

[1] It might be objected that an enemy would believe we would use our remaining forces to retaliate if we were already destroyed, since we would then have nothing to lose. However, this would give the enemy an incentive to strike first only at our military forces, leaving us something to lose. It might even give the enemy an incentive to demand our surrender before he struck, if his offensive force was large enough that we could not seriously degrade it in a first strike, or if he threatened to destroy our cities in retaliation for our first strike even if we aimed only at his offensive forces. In short, in such circumstances we are more likely to cave in than a determined enemy is.

[2] A historical note is in order here. After Genghis Khan had finished consolidating his hold on the mountain tribes in Mongolia, and began attacking cities in the plains, he adopted a specific policy. If a city surrendered without fighting, he would spare the occupants. If it resisted, once he had conquered it, he would put every inhabitant to the sword.

The example of Bertrand Russell and the "better Red than dead" move-ment illustrates that the use of nuclear weapons for blackmail can be quite successful. The important point is that a threat of irrational re-sponse cannot protect us against nuclear blackmail.

Blackmail involves only a threat of nuclear strikes. However, an ag-gressor might be tempted to go beyond merely making threats, and launch a nuclear strike that is clearly limited in scope, one that would weaken us militarily but that would not result in major civilian casual-ties. Nor need we try to imagine a limited strike coming "out of the blue". Suppose we succeeded in defeating by conventional means a non-nuclear Soviet attack on NATO, and the Soviet Union then launched limited nuclear strikes against military targets in Europe. How would we respond then? With a massive nuclear attack on the So-viet Union? Is the irrational threat of massive retaliation likely to deter such a Soviet limited strike?

As far back as 1959, Bernard Brodie observed that one of the first things wrong with the doctrine of massive retaliation as a response to less than massive aggression is that "in many instances the enemy may find it hard to believe that we mean it" (p. 273).

More recently, Albert Wohlstetter has made the same argument (De-cember 1983, p. 16):

> If you believe that any nuclear exchange will almost surely destroy West-ern civil society and even bring on universal ruin, you may say you would respond to a limited nuclear attack, but if you are even moderately thoughtful, you will almost surely not really mean it. Even if you had so awesomely suicidal and homicidal a *conditional* intention, you would be unlikely, in the event of an adversary's limited use of nuclear weapons, *actually* to be willing to reply by ending the world. If your adversary un-derstands that you believe a nuclear reply would be suicidal, he may count on your being unwilling to reply, even if you say you will. But in more recent times, Western elites have ceased even to say it.

Former president John F. Kennedy gave a similar warning about the potential for the Soviets using the threat of nuclear destruction:

> [Soviet] missile power will be the shield from behind which they will slowly, but surely advance through Sputnik diplomacy, limited brush-

---

What was the point of killing those who were already his prisoners? His swords were really aimed at the minds of the residents of the next city he would attack; they were only incidentally aimed at the bodies of those he had just captured. He wanted to intimidate his next victims into surrendering without a fight. Ultimately all weapons, including atomic bombs, are aimed at men's minds and only incidentally at their bodies. Aggressors are well aware of this and are clever about using weapons for intimidation.

fire wars, indirect non-overt aggression, intimidation and subversion, internal revolution, increased prestige or influence, and the vicious blackmail of our allies. The periphery of the Free World will slowly be nibbled away. . . . . Each such Soviet move will weaken the West; but none will seem sufficiently significant by itself to justify our initiating a nuclear war which might destroy us (quoted in Enthoven, 1971, p. 165).

It simply will not do to assert that no aggressor would be so cunning as to think in this way. In this century alone we have the historical experience of Adolf Hitler. In 1940, Joseph Goebbels gave a secret briefing to a group of German journalists, in which we gave the following picture of how Hitler had succeeded despite the fact that his enemies were stronger than he was (quoted in Johnson, 1983, p. 341):

> Up to now we have succeeded in leaving the enemy in the dark concerning Germany's real goals, just as before 1932 our domestic foes never saw where we were going or that our oath of legality was just a trick. We wanted to come to power legally, but we did not want to use power legally. . . . They could have suppressed us. They could have arrested a couple of us in 1925 and that would have been that, the end. No, they let us through the danger zone. That's exactly how it was in foreign policy too. . . . In 1933 a French premier ought to have said, (and if I had been the French premier I would have said it): "The new Reich Chancellor is the man who wrote *Mein Kampf*, which says this and that. This man cannot be tolerated in our vicinity. Either he disappears or we march!" But they didn't do it. They left us alone and let us slip through the risky zone, and we were able to sail around all dangerous reefs. *And when we were done, and well armed, better than they, then they started the war!* (emphasis in original).

That is, from the beginning Hitler counted on gaining advantages over his opponents, both domestic and foreign, by presenting them with demands that always seemed less threatening than the prospect of taking action against him. In particular, his territorial demands never seemed worth a major war, for which he was apparently prepared but for which his opponents were neither militarily nor psychologically prepared.

Stalin and Hitler thus provide excellent reminders of how international blackmail works. They sized up their opponents, recognized these opponents would be prudent and rational in the face of "unreasonable" demands apparently backed by force, and made the demands. Thomas Schelling has referred to this as the rationality of irrationality (1960, pp. 15–19).[3]

---

[3] Schelling chose the term for its paradoxical-sounding nature. However, there is no need to invoke a paradox here. What is really meant is the rationality of *appearing* irrational.

What do we do when a Hitler or a Stalin "prods with the tip of a bayonet?" Do we go to war, or do we back down? Reliance on pure deterrence means that when blackmail comes, we face it with weapons that we really haven't thought about how to use, that weren't designed with any particular use in mind, and that our troops have not yet been trained to use in any particular strategy. The almost inevitable result is that we must back down, because we lack confidence in our ability to fight and win a war.

The point is simply this: if we have not thought about how to use our weapons, a clever and determined enemy can confront us with a situation in which it appears to us that the weapons we procured are useless, while his apparently are not. He can make it appear that our forces cannot seriously harm him, and that if we attempt to use them, especially against his population centers, the result will be our own devastation.

Under pressure, "pure deterrence" collapses into a choice between starting a war we haven't prepared for while the enemy apparently has, or admitting we've been running a bluff all along, and the bluff has finally been called. Going to war under those circumstances, as France and England finally did in 1939 when Hitler pushed them too far, will be all the more horrible because the weapons we have on hand will probably not have been designed to be discriminating or to allow proportionate attacks. The alternative, of an immediate surrender, brings all the injustices and disasters mentioned by the German and the French bishops, as well as those described in Chapter 7.

We can with certainty expect to face rulers such as Hitler and Stalin again, since history is full of them. Our plans for surviving in a world that knows how to build nuclear weapons must take into account rulers like these, who will attempt to intimidate us, confident in our lack of confidence in our own weapons.

The enemy may be wrong in his confidence. Hitler, after all, went to the well once too often. Poland finally proved his undoing. But the Western democracies paid a terrible price for their earlier failures to convince Hitler that the status quo was preferable to war, and that war was the real alternative.

Ultimately, this is the issue. As former Secretary of Defense Robert McNamara put it, "One cannot fashion a credible deterrent out of an incredible action" (quoted in Enthoven, 1971, p. 124). Dissuasion will be credible in the long run only if war *is* a real alternative—war that is in our interest in the sense that it will produce a better outcome for us than will surrender to tyranny. If we don't believe that war is a real alternative, in the long run the enemy won't believe it either, and dissuasion will fail. Its failure is even more likely if it amounts to pure deterrence, that is, the threat of an irrational act.

The American bishops recognized this link between dissuasion and war-fighting in their Challenge of Peace pastoral:

[An] issue of concern to us is the relationship of deterrence doctrine to war-fighting strategies. We are aware of the argument that war-fighting capabilities enhance the credibility of the deterrent, particularly the strategy of extended deterrence (1983, no. 184).

However, they went on to argue against development of a war-fighting capability:

But the development of such capabilities raises other strategic and moral questions . . . "counterforce targeting", while preferable from the perspective of protecting civilians, is often joined with a declaratory policy which conveys the notion that nuclear war is subject to precise rational and moral limits. We have already expressed our severe doubts about such a concept. . . . While we welcome any effort to protect civilian populations, we do not want to legitimize or encourage moves which extend deterrence beyond the specific objective of preventing the use of nuclear weapons or other actions which could lead directly to a nuclear exchange (1983, no. 184).

Thus the American bishops argued, on moral grounds, against the only thing that can make dissuasion credible in the long run. In our present circumstances, in which we are threatened by a nuclear-armed tyranny, we seem to be faced with a moral dilemma. We are told that anything we do to enhance the credibility of dissuasion is immoral, but surrender to tyranny is also immoral. This dilemma, however, is a false one, and arises from looking only at extreme alternatives. In the next several chapters, we will look at some alternatives other than the extremes of capitulation or catastrophe.

REFERENCES

Brodie, Bernard, Strategy in the Missile Age. Princeton: Princeton University Press, 1959.

Dyson, Freeman. Weapons and Hope. New York: Harper & Row, 1984.

Enthoven, Alain C., and Wayne K. Smith. How Much Is Enough? New York: Harper & Row, 1971.

Gauthier, David. "Deterrence, Maximization, and Rationality". In The Security Gamble, edited by Douglas MacLean. Totowa, N.J.: Rowman & Allanheld, 1984.

Ikle, Fred C. *Every War Must End*. New York: Columbia University Press, 1970.

Johnson, Paul. *Modern Times*. New York: Harper & Row, 1983.

Lewis, David. "Devil's Bargains and the Real World". In *The Security Gamble*, edited by Douglas MacLean. Totowa, N.J.: Rowman & Allanheld, 1984.

McNamara, Robert S. and Hans A. Bethe. "Reducing the Risk of Nuclear War". *Atlantic Monthly* (July, 1985), pp. 43–51.

Quester, George H. *Deterrence before Hiroshima*. New York: John Wiley & Sons, 1966.

Wohlstetter, Albert. "Bishops, Statesmen, and Other Strategists on the Bombing of Innocents", *Commentary* (June 1983), pp. 15–35.

Wohlstetter, Albert. Letter to editor. *Commentary* (December 1983), pp. 13–32.

CHAPTER ELEVEN

COUNTERFORCE/WAR-FIGHTING

[T]here are two schools of thought which have sought to influence declaratory [nuclear] policy—counterforce and assured destruction. The
latter approach assumes that nuclear arms are fundamentally indiscriminate and that no amount of refinement in targeting and weapons development can alter the character of such arms. Nuclear weapons are so
destructive that the preeminent objective is to ensure that they are never
used. The focus of assured destruction is on maintaining an assured retaliatory capability in order to avoid nuclear conflict. This approach does
not emphasize flexibility of options or discrimination among major targets. The counterforce approach, on the other hand, is concerned with
the maintenance of a wide variety of retaliatory options. It assumes the
credibility of threats depends on flexibility of the deterrent forces. This
approach, therefore, advocates a broad set of nuclear and nuclear-
conventional options both to deter as well as to respond to major aggression. The extreme view of this approach is articulated by those who
believe that nuclear weapons must be viewed as instruments of war-
fighting in which the goal is to prevail (Amstutz, 1985, p. 24).

Of the two schools of thought which Amstutz describes, so far we
have looked only at the one that says nuclear weapons are too destructive to be used: pure deterrence, which attempts to prevent their use
through a threat of vengeance; and various alternatives that say even
deterrence is immoral and that attempt to get rid of nuclear weapons—
all or only ours—one way or another. All of these approaches were seen
to present serious moral problems.

None of the options we have examined can be called war in the
Clausewitzian sense of military action in support of national policy.
Vengeance is not war, since it achieves no rational purpose. Indeed, by
the time it is carried out, there may be no nation left to have a purpose.
The other options are not "war" either, since in one way or another
they attempt to escape the actual use of nuclear weapons.

We look now at the possibility of genuine military action using nuclear weapons; of fighting a war in the Clausewitzian sense of rationally
coupling national policy with military strategy and tactics—of selecting
targets and battles to achieve some meaningful political goal. This
would mean employing nuclear weapons against military targets, in
pursuit of a rational strategy, just as other weapons are used. To begin

with, we will examine briefly the history of the idea of counterforce in American military doctrine.

We have already seen that the development of nuclear weapons seemed to lead directly to what Bernard Brodie called a dead end for strategy. The origin of the problem was the idea, widespread at the end of World War II, that nuclear weapons could be used effectively only against cities. This was coupled with the idea left over from World War II that cities were legitimate targets. Starting in 1950, however, military analysts began to question these ideas.

Wohlstetter (1983, p. 21) describes a series of studies carried out at the RAND Corporation which led to a different set of conclusions. The first of these was the basing study already mentioned in Chapter 9, which led to the recognition that the enemy's first strike would be at our bomber bases, not at our cities. The study concluded that "a strategic force, however powerful when left undisturbed to do its work, cannot deter an attack which it is unable itself to survive." The study found that not only the forces but also command-and-control (C & C) must be designed to survive an initial attack.

Later studies looked at targeting, not simply at protecting the nuclear forces without regard to the targets against which they might be used. Wohlstetter states that in

> these later studies of strategic aims, the authors become increasingly clear that to have only the alternative of indiscriminate attack would seriously compromise the credibility that there would be any response at all. . . . It had become apparent that to have a persuasive deterrent, we had not only to be able to protect command-and-control, but also to have some alternatives which a responsible political leader would be willing to command (1983, p. 21).

Wohlstetter (1983, p. 20) remarks on the results of these studies' conclusions:

> Inevitably, uneasiness about the sturdiness, as well as the morality of a balance based on threats of such massive destruction, however unintentional, led many sober critics to propose more limited applications of nuclear force, and especially the use of small nuclear weapons on the battlefield.

While the results of these studies were not immediately made public (in fact, the major conclusions of the basing study did not appear in the open literature until 1959, almost eight years after it was completed), they began to have an effect within the Department of Defense. Strategy and tactics began to seep back into military thinking about the use of nuclear weapons. This thinking affected ideas about both strategic and tactical uses of nuclear weapons.[1]

For instance, in 1958, I was project manager for an Air Force program to improve the guidance accuracy of ballistic missiles. A high-level defense civil servant remarked to me, "The simplest thing to do would be for us and the Russians to exchange serial numbers on our missiles." What he meant was, the primary targets for our missiles would be Soviet missiles, and vice versa. In a war, we and the Soviets would simply be exchanging missiles. The low accuracy then possible meant that large warheads were needed to dig out enemy missile silos. Those same warheads would be very effective at city-busting, but that wasn't our primary reason for wanting them. Thus, within the military, the notion was gaining ground that the first target should be the enemy's missile silos, not the enemy's cities.

The notion was also being accepted at higher levels in the government, as indicated by an article that John Foster Dulles published in 1957 (p. xxxvi):

> [T]he United States has not been content to rely upon a peace which could be preserved only by a capacity to destroy vast segments of the human race . . . [but now] it is possible to alter the character of nuclear weapons. It seems now that their use need not involve vast destruction and widespread harm to humanity. Recent tests point to the possibility of possessing nuclear weapons the destructiveness and radiation effects of which can be confined substantially to predetermined targets. . . . It may be possible to defend countries by nuclear weapons so mobile, or so placed, as to make military invasion with conventional forces a hazardous attempt.

This proposal was essentially to utilize small nuclear weapons against enemy armies in the field, instead of devastating the enemy's homeland.

The idea of war-fighting as opposed to devastation was reflected by the civilian leadership in the Kennedy administration. In 1962, in what became known as the "Ann Arbor Speech", then Secretary of Defense

---

[1] The distinction between strategic and tactical bombardment goes back to the pioneering airpower strategists of the 1920s and 1930s. For our purposes here, however, the following distinction will be adequate: *strategic* bombardment means missile or aircraft attacks against the enemy homeland, distant from any engaged armies, and especially attacks against enemy war industry or the enemy's strategic bombardment forces; *tactical* bombardment means missile or aircraft attacks against targets which are related to the engagement of armies, including military forces close to the line of engagement, as well as supply dumps and lines of communication of the enemy army.

Robert McNamara announced what was referred to as a *no cities* policy. He stated that if nuclear war grew out of an attack on NATO, our objective would be to destroy enemy forces, not enemy cities. We would, he said, retain sufficient power to destroy Soviet society if we were forced to do so. However, the objective was to give the Soviet government a strong incentive not to attack NATO or U.S. cities.[2] This no-cities policy represented the first official step away from the massive-retaliation policy of the Eisenhower administration.

As related in Chapter 3, Secretary McNamara later changed to an assured-destruction policy under which the size of U.S. nuclear forces was set at a level sufficient to destroy one-fourth of the Soviet population and half of Soviet industrial capacity, even after a Soviet first strike against our nuclear forces. However, as Enthoven and Smith note (1971, p. 195):

> The assured-destruction test did not, of course, indicate how these forces would actually be used in a nuclear war. United States strategic offensive forces have been designed with the additional system characteristics—accuracy, endurance, and good command and control—needed to perform missions other than assured destruction, such as limited and controlled retaliation.

This development of a capability to do more than just wipe out the Soviet Union in retaliation for a Soviet attack continued under the Nixon and Ford administrations. Donald Cotter, who was Assistant for Atomic Energy to Secretaries of Defense Schlesinger, Rumsfeld, and Brown, states:

> The United States, in the mid-70s, looked more soberly at policies for the employment of nuclear weapons in response to nuclear attacks and adopted a dual criterion for any possible use of this awesome force: to destroy Soviet military capabilities selectively and, at the same time, to minimize harm to innocent bystanders (1983, p. 11).

Harold Brown, Secretary of Defense under President Carter, noted that tension was beginning to develop between the requirements for assured destruction and those for war-fighting:

> [W]e cannot afford to make a complete distinction between deterrent forces and what are so awkwardly called war-fighting forces. Nor should we continue to plan the force structure on one basis and our employment policies on another—as we could when Soviet strategic forces

---

[2] This was a notion that Herman Kahn had earlier advocated under the name "intrawar deterrence". Even if deterrence of war itself failed, Kahn argued, to demonstrate during the war that you were refraining from destroying targets which it was in your power to destroy would give the enemy an incentive to restrain himself.

were more modest. Only if we have the capability to respond realistically and effectively to an attack at a variety of levels can we achieve essential equivalence and have the confidence necessary to a credible deterrent. Credibility cannot be maintained, especially in a crisis, with a combination of inflexible forces (however destructive) and a purely retaliatory counter-urban/industrial strategy that frightens us as much as the opponent (1979, p. 54).

In 1980 President Jimmy Carter issued Presidential Directive No. 59 (PD-59), which further stressed flexibility in targeting and the development of a war-fighting capability. This *countervailing strategy* emphasized counterforce targeting, flexibility, control of nuclear forces by duty constituted authority, and the ability of nuclear forces to survive repeated enemy attacks.

Under President Reagan, the policy of developing a war-fighting capability has been continued. Secretary of Defense Caspar Weinberger has asserted:

[S]ome believe that we must threaten explicitly, even solely, the mass destruction of civilians on the adversary side, thus inviting a corresponding destruction of civilian populations on our side, and that such a posture will achieve stability in deterrence. This is incorrect. Such a threat is neither moral nor prudent. The Reagan administration's policy is that under no circumstances may such weapons be used deliberately for the purpose of destroying populations.

For this reason, we disagree with those who hold that deterrence should be based on nuclear weapons designed to destroy cities rather than military targets. Deliberately designing weapons aimed at populations is neither necessary nor sufficient for deterrence. If we are forced to retaliate and can only respond by destroying population centers, we invite the destruction of our own population (1983).

Thus through five administrations, over more than twenty years, U.S. nuclear war strategy shifted from deliberate targeting of cities to two alternatives: deliberate targeting of military installations and defense industries instead of cities in the enemy homeland, and use of tactical nuclear weapons on and near the battlefield. The American Catholic bishops took specific note of this shift in strategy in their Challenge of Peace pastoral (1983, no. 179).

In parallel with this shift toward a counterforce rather than countervalue strategy came new technology that made missile guidance much more accurate than anyone could have imagined even in 1945. The atomic bomb dropped on Hiroshima actually exploded less than 100 meters, that is, less than the length of a football field, from its intended ground zero. But that was a bomb dropped in daylight, by a human bombardier who was tracking his target with a visual bombsight. That same order of accuracy is now possible at intercontinental ranges, day or night, with automatically-guided missiles.

An important consequence of this increase in accuracy has been a reduction in warhead yield. The warheads on the MX have a yield of about 335 kilotons, or roughly twenty-six times the yield of the Hiroshima bomb.[3] With the high accuracies available today, this is adequate for destroying a missile silo. No longer are multimegaton warheads needed to dig out a missile silo in spite of a sizeable miss. The reduction in warhead yield is reflected in a reduction in our total inventory. The U.S. nuclear inventory has one-third fewer warheads today than it did in the late 1960s, and the total megatonnage in the inventory has been reduced by 75 percent from what it was in 1960. Improved technology has actually allowed us to *reduce* the size of our inventory, while making it a more effective military force.

An important side effect of this increased accuracy coupled with reduced warhead yield is that it destroys the validity of the equation "one bomb equals one city". The individual warheads in the Polaris, Trident and MX missiles are unsuited for city-busting. At Hiroshima, earth-covered backyard shelters survived at 100 yards from ground zero. With the MX warhead, the same shelters could survive at just over 300 yards from ground zero (destructive radius increases as the cube root of warhead yield). To obliterate a large city with current U.S. warheads would require pattern bombing with several warheads per city, and there is still a good chance that people could survive in fairly modest shelters.[4]

These developments, which provided some alternatives to massive retaliation, welcome as they are, were driven by changes in technology, and by an unarticulated, almost inchoate horror at the thought of actually carrying out the threat of massive retaliation. It is important to recognize that they were *not* driven by any well-thought-out moral doctrines regarding the use of nuclear weapons.

This was not because there wasn't anyone calling for such moral doctrines in the hopes they would be used to select strategies and weapons. Over thirty years ago Thomas E. Murray, a member of the Atomic En-

---

[3] The Hiroshima bomb was for many years officially stated to have had a twenty-kiloton yield. More recent information has reduced the estimated yield to about 12.5 kilotons. If the higher value is used instead, the argument in the text is actually strengthened.

[4] None of this means that civilians would not suffer from a counterforce attack. Depending on the nature and location of the targets, and the availability of well-stocked shelters, noncombatant deaths from fallout could still number in the millions. What it does mean is that the common mental image of nuclear war as a spasm of city-busting with monstrous warheads is at least twenty years out of date. Most of those huge warheads have vanished from the U.S. inventory, and the remaining ones will be removed as the MX and Midgetman missiles replace Minuteman and Titan missiles.

ergy Commission under President Eisenhower, argued repeatedly that the United States must develop a strategy for the moral use of nuclear weapons in war, and design only weapons which could be used in pursuit of that strategy (1957, pp. 387–397). He called for us to determine the maximum size weapon that would be moral to use, to refrain from testing any which were larger than that, and to procure no more of that size than would be needed for the number of targets which required them. He called for us then to procure adequate numbers of low-yield weapons which could be used against military targets without excessive collateral damage. In short, he called for the development of a nuclear war-fighting capability, which would allow us to use nuclear weapons as moral means in pursuit of just national objectives.

Murray was not alone in calling for a counterforce/war-fighting capability. Kaplan mentions several people who promoted this objective (1983, passim): Bernard Brodie (although not consistently), Herman Kahn, and William Kaufman, among others. However, none of these advocates of counterforce/war-fighting were as consciously motivated by moral considerations as was Thomas Murray. The tragedy of the past forty years is that those who claimed to be concerned about morality spent their time either justifying or condemning deterrence achieved by a threat of massive retaliation—all the time overlooking the moral problems of both justification and condemnation—instead of responding to the crying need for a moral doctrine to govern the actual use of nuclear weapons. Conversely, those who concerned themselves with the problems of actually fighting a war with nuclear weapons lacked the moral doctrine that might have given them the means to connect nuclear strategy and tactics with just national objectives.

This isn't to say, of course, that counterforce/war-fighting provides an easy solution to either the practical or the moral problems presented by use of nuclear weapons. In the next chapter we will look at the most significant objections to nuclear war-fighting. In subsequent chapters, we will look at some approaches to moral analysis of the objections.

REFERENCES

Amstutz, Mark R. "The Challenge of Peace: Did the Bishops Help?". *This World* (Spring/Summer 1985).

Brown, Harold. *FY79 Annual Report of the Secretary of Defense*. Washington, D.C.: Government Printing Office, 1979, p. 54.

Cotter, Donald B. Letter to the editor: *Commentary* (December 1983), p. 11.

Dulles, John Foster. "Challenge and Response in United States Policy". *Foreign Affairs* (October 1957).

Enthoven, Alain C., and K. Wayne Smith. *How Much Is Enough?* New York: Harper & Row, 1971.

Kaplan, Fred. *Wizards of Armageddon*. New York: Simon & Schuster, 1983.

Murray, Thomas E. "Morality and Security: The Forgotten Equation". *The Catholic Mind* (March–April 1957), pp. 100–108.

Murray, Thomas E. "Rational Nuclear Armament". *The Catholic Mind* (September–October 1957), pp. 387–397.

Weinberger, Caspar W. "Report of the Secretary of Defense to the Congress". February 3, 1983.

Wohlstetter, Albert. "Bishops, Statesmen, and Other Strategists on the Bombing of Innocents". *Commentary* (June 1983), pp. 15–35.

PART TWO

JUST WAR AND NUCLEAR WEAPONS

CHAPTER TWELVE

OBJECTIONS TO NUCLEAR WAR-FIGHTING

Despite technological changes that have occurred since the 1950s, such as smaller warheads and more accurate weapons, and despite the strategic changes that reflect the new technology, the war-fighting option has essentially been ruled out by most opinion leaders and by the public at large. Arguments against a strategy of nuclear war-fighting can be grouped into two categories: the infeasibility of keeping nuclear war limited, and the immorality of fighting even a limited nuclear war. To some extent these categories overlap, since if it were infeasible to keep nuclear war limited, then it would also be objectionable on moral grounds. However, these categories are sufficiently distinct to be useful for analytical purposes. We will describe first the arguments against feasibility, then the arguments against morality. In most cases the same arguments are intended to apply to both strategic and tactical uses of nuclear weapons. However, when the arguments apply to only one of these categories, this will be pointed out specifically.

One reason often given for the technical infeasibility of nuclear war-fighting is that there is allegedly no possible defense against nuclear weapons. Before the invention of the ballistic missile, people acted as though they believed Stanley Baldwin's old dictum, "the bomber will always get through". After the invention of the ballistic missile, there seemed to be no serious doubt that the missile would always get through.

For instance, former defense secretary Robert McNamara and nuclear pioneer Hans Bethe wrote:

> "War" is only one of the concepts whose meanings were changed forever at Hiroshima. "Defense" is another. Before Hiroshima, defense relied on attrition—exhausting an enemy's human, material, and moral resources. The Royal Air Force won the Battle of Britain by attaining a 10 percent attrition rate against the Nazi air force, because repeated attacks could not be sustained against such odds. The converse, a 90-percent-effective defense, could not preserve us against even one modest nuclear attack (1985, p. 45).

The Catholic bishops, in their Challenge of Peace pastoral, sounded the same theme:

> The presumption of the nation-state system, that sovereignty implies an ability to protect a nation's territory and population, is precisely the pre-

sumption denied by the nuclear capacities of both superpowers (1983, no. 136).

The extent to which this view has penetrated the intellectual community can be seen in an announcement for a panel at the 1986 meeting of the World Future Society, titled "Beyond the Warfare System: Civilian-Based Peace Initiatives", chaired by W. Warren Wagar:

> States are armed in order to provide security for their citizens and to safeguard vital national interests. But nuclear arms have made warfare among states possessing them too destructive to serve any sane purpose. Warfare, armies, and the sovereign state itself have become obsolete. This panel will explore alternatives to the warfare system that rely on action by civilians and aim directly or indirectly at the dismantling of the warfare system to achieve a lasting peace on earth.

Thus the objection is that the inability of sovereign states to protect their citizens against nuclear weapons makes the actual fighting of a war with nuclear weapons infeasible.

A second reason given for the infeasibility of nuclear war-fighting is the allegation that control is impossible; that once nuclear weapons are used at all, the war is likely to escalate to the all-out level. Bundy, et. al. put it this way (1982, p. 757):

> . . . no one has ever succeeded in advancing any persuasive reason to believe that any use of nuclear weapons, even on the smallest scale, could reliably be expected to remain limited. . . . Any use of nuclear weapons in Europe, by the [NATO] Alliance or against it, carries with it a high and inescapable risk of escalation into the general nuclear war which would bring ruin to all and victory to none.

This argument was particularly intended to apply to tactical uses of nuclear weapons in defense of NATO.

Enthoven and Smith describe the conclusions about limited nuclear war reached during the time Mr. McNamara was Secretary of Defense (1971, p. 125):

> Another doubtful assumption underlying the limited nuclear war concept was the feasibility of adequate limitations on yields, targets, and numbers of weapons to keep collateral damage and civilian casualties down and thus to prevent the war from escalating to a general strategic level. Although theoretically the controlled use of small-yield nuclear weapons against strictly military targets could keep collateral damage low, the prospects for these limitations working out in an actual war appear to be very low because it would be extremely difficult for either side to determine whether restraints were being maintained—and the first side to violate them has an overwhelming, if not decisive, advantage.

Robert McNamara himself described U.S. strategy as follows:

> . . . the strategy calls for the [NATO] Alliance to initiate nuclear war with battlefield weapons if conventional defenses fail, and to escalate the type of nuclear weapons used (and therefore the targets of these weapons), as necessary, up to and including the use of strategic forces against targets in the USSR itself (1983, p. 67).

Kaplan argues that the inability to keep a nuclear war limited applies also to strategic uses of nuclear weapons:

> In the early 1960s, the U.S. needed to fire only a few hundred weapons to execute Option One of SIOP-63—destroying the Soviet strategic nuclear forces. Now, doing so would require firing a couple of thousand— at least one, often two, for each ICBM silo as well as one or two for each of the bomber bases, possible aircraft-dispersion bases and submarine ports. The critique of counterforce offered by Tom Schelling and, later, Jim Schlesinger—that such an attack would be so massive that the Soviets could not distinguish it from an all-out strike and, so, would respond with an all-out blow themselves—became particularly cogent (1983, p. 365). [SIOP stands for Single Integrated Operations Plan, which assigns targets to bombers, intercontinental ballistic missiles (ICBMs) and submarine-launched ballistic missiles (SLBMs) to avoid overlap and mutual interference.]

The American Catholic bishops reflected in the Challenge of Peace pastoral the view that limiting nuclear war was impossible:

> [T]he difficulties of limiting the use of nuclear weapons are immense. A number of expert witnesses advise us that commanders operating under conditions of battle probably would not be able to exercise strict control; the number of weapons used would rapidly increase, the targets would be expanded beyond the military, and the level of civilian casualties would rise enormously. No one can be certain that this escalation would not occur, even in the face of political efforts to keep such an exchange "limited". The chances of keeping use limited seem remote, and the consequences of escalation to mass destruction would be appalling (1983, no. 152).

The bishops listed several questions that must be answered before it will be possible to speak convincingly of limited nuclear war (1983, no. 157):

> While not trying to adjudicate the technical debate, we are aware of it and wish to raise a series of questions which challenge the actual meaning of "limited" in this discussion.
> —Would leaders have sufficient information to know what is happening in a nuclear exchange?

—Would they be able under the conditions of stress, time pressures, and
fragmentary information to make the extraordinarily precise decision
needed to keep the exchange limited if this were technically possible?

—Would military commanders be able, in the midst of the destruction
and confusion of a nuclear exchange, to maintain a policy of "discriminate targeting"? Can this be done in modern warfare, waged across
great distances by aircraft and missiles?

—Given the accidents we know about in peacetime conditions, what as-
surances are there that computer errors could be avoided in the midst
of a nuclear exchange?

—Would not the casualties, even in a war defined as limited by strategists, still run in the millions?

—How "limited" would be the long-term effects of radiation, famine,
social fragmentation, and economic dislocation?

Unless these questions can be answered satisfactorily, we will continue
to be highly skeptical about the real meaning of "limited".

The bishops gave further expression to their scepticism, specifically
stating that the moral attractiveness of counterforce was outweighed by
the risk of escalation:

Targeting civilian populations would violate the principle of
discrimination—one of the central moral principles of a Christian ethic of
war. But "counterforce targeting", while preferable from the perspective of protecting civilians, is often joined with a declaratory policy
which conveys the notion that nuclear war is subject to precise rational
and moral limits. We have already expressed our severe doubts about
such a concept (1983, no. 184).

The French bishops, in their pastoral, similarly expressed doubts
about keeping nuclear war limited: "The 'victor' (?) would find himself
ruined, and the advantage of ruling over a 'pulverized' adversary is not
all that evident" (Schall, 1984, no. 7).

A third objection to developing a war-fighting capability is that it increases the likelihood of nuclear war by making deterrence less stable.
The bishops stated the problem thus:

[An] issue of concern to us is the relationship of deterrence doctrine to
war-fighting strategies . . . a purely counterforce strategy may seem to
threaten the viability of other nations' retaliatory forces, making deterrence unstable in a crisis and war more likely (1983, no. 184).[1]

A fourth objection to developing a war-fighting capability is that a
nuclear war is unwinnable, in the sense that the "loser" can always de-

---

[1] Note that here the bishops completely ignore intrawar deterrence; for them, all deterrence ceases once war breaks out.

stroy the "winner" at the last moment. If Hitler had possessed deliverable nuclear weapons at the end of World War II, even though he could not have staved off defeat for Germany, he could have made victory hollow for the United States, Great Britain, and the Soviet Union by destroying them as viable societies. Moreover, if it appears to a desperate "loser" that he is on the verge of losing his nuclear striking capability, he will employ it before it is destroyed.

Jervis's entire book is nothing but a set of variations on this specific theme. For him, mutual vulnerability is an immutable fact, beyond the power of either side to alter: "mutual assured destruction exists as a fact, irrespective of policy" (1984, p. 146). He repeats, many times, that neither side's cities can survive without the cooperation of its enemy. This, for him, rules out any notion of nuclear war-fighting.

The fifth objection to the concept of limited nuclear war is that by apparently making nuclear war *thinkable,* we make it more likely. Father J. Bryan Hehir expressed this objection as follows (1978, p. 15):

. . . counterforce strategy is subject to the criticism that it makes nuclear war "thinkable", increasing the probability of wars being started with such weapons or of such weapons being employed because they are controllable, with one side or both tempted to escalate the conflict to an "all-out" nuclear exchange.

All of these objections express a basic doubt about the feasibility of keeping nuclear war limited enough to retain a meaningful distinction between victory and defeat. Father Hehir summed it up as follows (1984, p. 58):

The coming of the nuclear age has transformed the doctrine of Clausewitz that war is a rational extension of politics. The nuclear threat is such that to resort to these instruments of war places at risk the very values the use of force is supposed to protect.

Having listed the objections regarding feasibility, we next look at the issue of the morality of even a limited use of nuclear weapons. The U.S. Catholic bishops expressed doubts about the morality of such limited nuclear war.

[Proposals to avoid targeting population centers] do not address or resolve another very troublesome moral problem, namely, that an attack on military targets or militarily significant industrial targets could involve "indirect" (i.e., unintended) but massive civilian casualties . . . the number of deaths in a substantial exchange would be almost indistinguishable from what might occur if civilian centers had been deliberately and directly struck (1983, no. 180).

The bishops went on to say that the problem was not simply one of accuracy but of numbers:

> The problem is not simply one of producing highly accurate weapons that might minimize civilian casualties in any single explosion, but one of increasing the likelihood of escalation at a level where many, even "discriminating", weapons would cumulatively kill very large numbers of civilians (1983, no. 183).

The bishops also addressed the morality of first use of tactical nuclear weapons.[2]

> We do not perceive any situation in which the deliberate initiation of nuclear warfare, on however restricted a scale, can be morally justified. Non-nuclear attacks by another state must be resisted by other than nuclear means (1983, no. 150).

Since nuclear war-fighting is alleged to be both infeasible and immoral, the conclusion many have drawn is that nuclear weapons are unusable; the weapons' only purpose is to prevent their use. McNamara and Bethe put it,

> . . . nuclear warheads serve no military purposes whatsoever. They are not weapons. They are totally useless except to deter one's opponent from using his warheads (1985, p. 45).

Amstutz (1983, p. 23) quotes a similar view from George F. Kennan:

> A weapon is something that is supposed to serve some rational end—a hideous end, as a rule, but one related to some serious objective of governmental policy. . . . The nuclear device seems to me not to respond to that description.

---

[2] There is an important distinction between "first strike" and "first use". First strike means the initiation of hostilities with a nuclear attack. The United States has repeatedly declared that it will not employ strategic nuclear weapons against the Soviet Union unless the Soviets first make a nuclear attack against the U.S. homeland, that is, the United States will not make a first strike. The Soviet Union, by contrast, has repeatedly declared that in the event the United States prepares to attack them, the Soviets would make a preemptive nuclear attack against the United States; that is, it *will* make a first strike. First use, by contrast, means the introduction of nuclear weapons after hostilities have already been initiated with non-nuclear weapons. The United States and NATO have declared they will use nuclear weapons in response to a conventional Soviet attack. The Soviet Union has declared it will not be the first to use nuclear weapons in a European war and has called for a treaty banning first use. Thus a reliable ban on first strike would conform to current U.S. declaratory policy; a reliable ban on first use would conform to current Soviet declaratory policy.

The bishops specifically wanted to restrict use of nuclear weapons to a deterrent role:

> While we welcome any effort to protect civilian populations, we do not want to legitimize or encourage moves which extend deterrence beyond the specific objective of preventing the use of nuclear weapons or other actions which could lead directly to a nuclear exchange (1983, no. 185).

Edward Doherty, adviser on political and military affairs for the U.S. Catholic Conference, who helped write the bishops' Challenge of Peace pastoral, said "The pastoral letter does not make any sense unless you say there are virtually no uses of nuclear weapons."

Father Hehir made the following statement regarding the intent of the Challenge of Peace pastoral (1984, p. 58):

> The pastoral letter is designed to help build a political-moral barrier against the concept of nuclear war as a viable strategy of defense and to resist rhetoric which fails to convey the moral and political threat posed by the nuclear age.

Once one concludes that nuclear war-fighting is infeasible and immoral, one is led inevitably to assert an urgent need to maintain the "firebreak" between conventional and nuclear weapons. Bundy, et. al. put it (1982, p. 757):

> The one clearly definable firebreak against the worldwide disaster of general nuclear war is the one that stands between all other kinds of conflict and any use whatsoever of nuclear weapons.

The American bishops urged that the firebreak against use of nuclear weapons be maintained:

> We believe it is necessary, for the sake of prevention, to build a barrier against the concept of nuclear war as a viable strategy for defense. There should be a clear public resistance to the rhetoric of "winnable" nuclear wars, or unrealistic expectations of "surviving" nuclear exchanges, and strategies of "protracted nuclear war". We oppose such rhetoric (1983, no. 137).

As part of the firebreak, the bishops rejected first use of nuclear weapons, particularly the NATO strategy of using them to counter a conventional attack:

> We express repeatedly in this letter our extreme skepticism about the prospects for controlling a nuclear exchange, however limited the first use might be. Precisely because of this skepticism, we judge resort to nuclear weapons to counter a conventional attack to be morally unjustifiable.

Consequently we seek to reinforce the barrier against any use of nuclear weapons. Our support of a "no first use" policy must be seen in this light (1983, no. 153).

Before attempting to respond to these objections, we require an analytical tool that can be used to examine the morality of various possible uses of nuclear weapons. In the Catholic Church, as well as some of the major Protestant denominations (particularly Lutheran and Anglican), the Just War Doctrine has served that function. In the next chapter, we will take up that doctrine. In subsequent chapters, we will use it to analyze the issues of nuclear war-fighting.

REFERENCES

Amstutz, Mark R. "The Challenge of Peace: Did the Bishops Help?", *This World* (Spring/Summer 1983).

Bundy, McGeorge, George F. Kennan, Robert S. McNamara, and Gerard Smith. "Nuclear Weapons and the Atlantic Alliance", *Foreign Affairs* (Spring 1982), pp. 753–768.

Enthoven, Alain C., and K. Wayne Smith. *How Much Is Enough?* New York: Harper & Row, 1971.

Hehir, Rev. J. Bryan. "Moral Issues in Deterrence Policy". In *The Security Gamble,* edited by Douglas MacLean. Totowa, N.J.: Rowman & Allanheld, 1984.

Hehir, Rev. J. Bryan. "The Catholic Church and the Arms Race". *Worldview* (July–August 1978).

Jervis, Robert. *The Illogic of American Nuclear Strategy.* Ithaca: Cornell University Press, 1984.

Kaplan, Fred. *The Wizards of Armageddon.* New York: Simon & Schuster, 1983.

McNamara, Robert S. "The Military Role of Nuclear Weapons". *Foreign Affairs* (Fall, 1983).

McNamara, Robert S., and Hans A. Bethe. "Reducing the Risk of Nuclear War". *Atlantic Monthly* (July 1985).

Schall, James V., ed. *Out of Justice Peace and Winning the Peace* [Bishops' Pastoral Letters]. San Francisco: Ignatius Press, 1984.

Wohlstetter, Albert. "Bishops, Statesmen, and Other Strategists on the Bombing of Innocents". *Commentary* (June 1983), pp. 15–35.

CHAPTER THIRTEEN

JUST WAR DOCTRINE

William Tecumseh Sherman is quoted (somewhat imprecisely) as having said "War is hell". Philip Lawler has offered a correction to this: "War is not hell. Hell is hell". This is not just a witticism. Hell is the unrepentant sinner's final rejection of God, and God's eternal ratification of that rejection. The Christian who goes to war need not reject God. However, by waging war unjustly, he can do precisely that. War can become, then, not hell itself but the road to hell.

How can the Christian avoid rejecting God? How is he to know what is allowable in warfare and what is not? Saints Ambrose and Augustine began the development of what has come to be known as the Just War Doctrine. For over fifteen centuries the Catholic Church has developed and refined this doctrine as its official teaching on the subject of war. However, it is not a Catholic doctrine only. Protestant scholars from the time of the Reformation to the present have contributed significantly to it. Paul Ramsey, a Protestant theologian and one of today's leading authorities on Just War Doctrine, has written (1968, p. 261):

> . . . the just-war doctrine is not a Catholic doctrine; it is a common Christian teaching about the justice and limits upon the state's use of force, as Lutheran or Calvinistic as it is Roman Catholic.

However, even Ramsey's description is not broad enough. Just War Doctrine in no way depends upon Christian premises, but instead is based on Natural Law. As such, it is a product of human reason, and its results can equally well be reached by those who do not accept the Christian gospel as a source of morality. Thus in addition to the Christian Just War tradition, a purely secular version of the doctrine has been developed by diplomats and legal scholars since the seventeenth century. The Catholic, Protestant, and secular versions all draw upon each other and all reach similar conclusions—they are variations of a single doctrine, not three distinct doctrines.

Despite its roots in early Christianity and its widespread acceptance, Just War Doctrine has been subject to considerable criticism by religious leaders. Bishop Walter Sullivan, of Richmond, Virginia, stated that Just War doctrine is "an excuse to go to war, mental gymnastics, casuistry of the worst sort" (quoted in Spaeth, 1982, p. 12). This criticism is unfortunate, because it completely misrepresents Just War Doctrine. The doctrine begins with a presumption against war. It places the burden of proof upon those who would go to war, not upon those who would refrain from war. It then provides a set of criteria by which a proposed war may be judged. If the proposed war satisfies *all* the criteria, it may be waged, and the Christian can participate in it with a clear conscience.[1]

Just War Doctrine is conventionally divided into two parts: *jus ad bellum,* which governs recourse to war, and *jus in bello,* which governs conduct in war. The distinction between them is that between *waging an unjust war* and *waging war unjustly.* A war unjustly begun could still be waged justly (even though that would not justify the Christian's participation), and a war justly begun could be waged unjustly (which would not invalidate the original reasons for going to war).

There are numerous versions of the criteria for Just War, all essentially equivalent. For convenience, I will utilize the version employed by the American Catholic bishops in their Challenge of Peace pastoral (1983). For *jus ad bellum,* these are:

1. Just Cause. The side going to war must have sufficiently strong reason for doing so. The bishops list "to protect innocent life, to preserve conditions necessary for decent human existence, and to secure basic human rights" as causes sufficient to justify resort to war. However, war must be undertaken only in the face of "a real and certain danger" (no. 85).

2. Competent authority. "War must be declared by those with responsibility for public order, not by private groups or individuals" (no. 87). While in the past the declaration of war by a national government was taken to satisfy this requirement, the existence of nuclear weapons poses some unprecedented problems for this requirement.

3. Comparative justice. In this fallen world no party to the war can assume it has absolute justice on its side. However, the war may be justified if the party initiating it is comparatively more just than the enemy. Even so, because its justice is only relative, it must limit both its war aims and the means used in pursuit of those aims.

4. Right intention. Saint Augustine, in *De Verbis Domini,* stated this condition thus: "For the true followers of God even wars are

---

[1] O'Brien has suggested the term *permissible war* as being more properly descriptive. "Permissible war conveys the basic thought that recourse to war is an exceptional prerogative that has to be justified, not a right readily available to those who consider themselves just. It is also a general prerogative available exceptionally to all nations and other belligerent entities on grounds other than a subjective finding that they are just and their enemies are unjust" (1981, p. 14).

peaceful, not being made for greed or out of cruelty, but from desire of peace, to restrain the evil and assist the good." Thus the intention of those attempting to wage war justly must be to achieve only their legitimate objectives, not to go beyond them even in victory.

5. Last resort. "For resort to war to be justified, all peaceful alternatives must have been exhausted" (no. 96).

6. Probability of success. This does not mean certainty of victory, but it does mean one must not start a war when the prospects of victory are remote. It would be immoral to spill blood in vain.

7. Proportionality. ". . . proportionality means that the damage to be inflicted and the costs incurred by war must be proportionate to the good expected by taking up arms" (no. 99).

For *jus in bello*, there are only two criteria:

1. Discrimination. ". . . the lives of innocent persons may never be taken directly, regardless of the purpose alleged for doing so" (no. 104). Any military action must be aimed in a discriminating fashion against militarily relevant targets, not against innocent people.

2. Proportionality. In each individual military action, the damage to be done and the costs to be incurred must be justified by the military gain expected from the action. This is the proportionality criterion of *jus ad bellum* extended to the conduct of the war itself.

The Just War Doctrine encapsulates the accumulated wisdom of over fifteen centuries of Western thought on the moral issues of war. It provides a coherent framework in which these moral issues can be analyzed, and a nuanced vocabulary with which to discuss these issues. As such, it can provide an analytical tool we can use to deal with the moral issues raised by war.[2]

Many have argued that although Just War Doctrine was well suited to analyze the wars of the past, nuclear weapons have made it obsolete. In a neat turn of phrase, it has been said that nuclear weapons have "ex-

---

[2] Both Augustine and Aquinas, and most subsequent Just War scholars, took it for granted that nations had a right to self-defense. Therefore Just War Doctrine really didn't address that issue. Once the army of another nation had unjustly crossed one's borders, *jus ad bellum* was already satisfied. One's only concern from that point on was *jus in bello. Jus ad bellum* is intended to address the question of a nation making a preemptive attack before the enemy has crossed its borders, or a punitive attack in response to some extreme provocation or otherwise unresolvable *casus belli*. May the nation overcome the presumption against war and initiate a war against an enemy? Just War Doctrine says it may, provided it satisfies a set of quite stringent conditions. This implies, then, that a nuclear first strike, not merely first use in a war the enemy has initiated, might well be justified if the Just War conditions can be met. The argument of those who oppose the use of nuclear weapons, either first or second, is that the requirements of the doctrine cannot be met.

ploded" the Just War Doctrine. However, this kind of argument is erroneous. It is based on misunderstandings of both the Just War Doctrine and nuclear weapons.

Some who argue for the obsolescence of Just War Doctrine interpret it as Bishop Sullivan did: as casuistry; as a means of justifying a war one intended to wage anyway. To this group, if Just War Doctrine is capable of justifying an all-out nuclear war, then there must be something wrong with the doctrine. This group in effect says that since nuclear war cannot be justified, Just War Doctrine must be abandoned. Without Just War Doctrine, however, this group would be hard-pressed to condemn all-out nuclear war. Just War Doctrine, or something very much like it, is needed to condemn the obliteration of cities and the bombing of innocents.

Another group assumes that nuclear weapons can be used only against cities. This group argues that it may be necessary to use nuclear weapons, and because Just War Doctrine condemns indiscriminate destruction of cities, the doctrine must be abandoned. The problem with this argument is that it rules out all other uses of nuclear weapons by assumption. As Spaeth has put it (1982, p. 13):

> [I]t can be asserted with certitude that the just-war theory is not capable of justifying a war that launches nuclear bombs against enemy cities. But what does that say about the theory itself? Certainly not that it is deficient. . . . It would be a tragic mistake to conclude from the theory's incapacity to justify a counter-city nuclear war that no nuclear strategy, no nuclear deterrence, and no nuclear weapons can morally be considered at all.

While Just War Doctrine can be used to analyze the moral issues of nuclear war, unfortunately it can also be misused. Bishop Anthony Pilla, of Cleveland, issued a study paper on August 6, 1981, the thirty-sixth anniversary of the atomic bombing of Hiroshima. In this paper he attempted to apply Just War Doctrine to the issue of nuclear weapons. He stated the Just War criteria as follows (note that these rules are equivalent to those given above):

1. The decision for war must be made by a legitimate authority.
2. The war must be fought for a just cause.
3. War must be taken only as a last resort.
4. There must be a reasonable chance of "success".
5. The good to be achieved by the war must outweigh the evil that will result from it (proportionality).
6. The war must be waged with just means (in accordance with international and natural law).

Castelli quotes Bishop Pilla as saying:

If even one of these conditions were not met in a particular conflict, the conflict would be perceived by the church as contrary to the Fifth Commandment, morally reprehensible and a crime against God (1983, pp. 30–32).

Bishop Pilla's analysis of nuclear weapons is summarized by Castelli as follows:

Nuclear weapons make possible the total destruction of entire innocent civilian populations in a very short amount of time. Not only was such annihilation against rules 5 and 6 of the just war doctrine, it overstepped Rule 4 by giving the aggressor overwhelming odds for success. Also, the simplicity and power of one atomic warhead made Rule 1 . . . and Rule 2 . . . easily bypassable by anyone in control of a bomb. Finally, the presence of nuclear technology led to the "first-strike" philosophy and the arms race, thus negating Rule 3. So nuclear weapons break all of St. Augustine's standards for justice. Even more, they create the potential for mass destruction even if they are used in accordance with the just war doctrine (1983, pp. 30–32).

While we should be pleased that Bishop Pilla did attempt to apply Just War Doctrine to nuclear war, instead of taking one of the evasions described in previous chapters, his attempt was unsuccessful.

To begin with, consider the phrase "nuclear weapons break all of Saint Augustine's standards". It ought to be apparent that nuclear weapons themselves are incapable of either breaking or meeting the Just War criteria. Only people, by their objectives or their conduct, are capable of violating Just War criteria. In fact this problem pervades the whole analysis. It attempts to apply to *weapons* a set of criteria which are intended to be applied to *wars*.

Consider the assertion that Rules 1 and 2 are violated because some subordinate might launch a nuclear weapon without authorization. This is true of any weapon. For instance, a border guard might use his rifle without authorization to shoot at someone across the border, and thereby start a war. By this logic, even a rifle would violate Rule 1. The problem comes from focusing on the weapon that might be misused, rather than on the person who might use it legitimately or illegitimately. Even though a war *might* be started without legitimate authority, a war that *has* legitimate authority does not violate Rule 1.[3]

---

[3] It is often argued that the destructive potential of nuclear weapons creates a more serious problem than does, say, a border guard's rifle. This is true, but attempting to label the *weapon* as immoral is still inappropriate. The greater destructive potential of a nuclear weapon means greater controls must be placed on the *people* who might use it without authorization.

The same objection applies to the analysis of Rule 2. The fact that someone might use a nuclear weapon without just cause doesn't mean use of nuclear weapons in a just cause violates Rule 2.

Rule 4 is intended to prevent someone from starting a war which they cannot win, even though their cause is just. The suffering brought about by the war, even in a just cause, could not be justified if defeat is certain. However, the analysis appears to condemn nuclear weapons because they are *too effective*. This is not an appropriate use of Just War Doctrine. Moreover, the analysis has another, more subtle, flaw concerning this point. Nuclear weapons are presumed to give an advantage to the side which *uses them first*. The analysis appears to assume that first use, even by the victim of a non-nuclear attack, is equivalent to aggression. That is, the analysis appears to be implicitly condemning first use. However, the mere fact that first use conveys an advantage doesn't mean that the side that uses nuclear weapons first is by that very fact guilty of aggression. If first use is to be condemned, this must be done separately, not hidden in the analysis of Rule 4. In any case, the fact that first use may convey some advantage doesn't mean that the victim of aggression violates Rule 4 by employing nuclear weapons after the aggressor has done so.

The analysis of Rules 5 and 6 is similarly flawed. Just because nuclear weapons *can* be used in a disproportionate or unjust manner does not mean that all use of them is inherently disproportionate or unjust. That would have to be demonstrated separately.

Finally, the fact that nuclear weapons may convey an advantage to the first strike does not lead to the conclusion that their use by the victim of aggression violates Rule 3, or for that matter that use in a genuine last-resort situation violates Rule 3.

The problem with this analysis, again, is that it attempts to use Just War Doctrine to examine the morality of *weapons,* not of *wars.* Human beings can rise to being saints or sink to being sinners. A nuclear weapon has no volition. It is incapable of rising even to the dignity of sinning. It cannot be either evil or good, it can only *be.* Just War Doctrine must be used to analyze the morality of nuclear war, not the morality of nuclear weapons.

Unfortunately, the moral analysis of nuclear war is not easy. As Father Hehir has put it (1984, p. 58):

> The destructive capability of nuclear weapons forces the adherents of the just-war war ethic to declare themselves on the relationship of just-war moral criteria and the logic of nuclear war.

Despite the problems, however, if limited nuclear war is to be a moral possibility, it is the Just War Doctrine to which we must look for guidance.

In the next several chapters we will attempt to apply the Just War Doctrine to the problems of nuclear war, and do two things: either show where the application of the doctrine is clear or show where there are questions that need to be examined further to determine whether nuclear war can be conducted in accord with Just War Doctrine.

REFERENCES

Castelli, Jim. *The Bishops and the Bomb*. New York: Doubleday Image Books, 1983.

Hehir, Rev. J. Bryan. "Moral Issues in Deterrence Policy". In *The Security Gamble,* edited by Douglas MacLean. Totowa, N.J.: Rowman & Allanheld, 1984.

O'Brien, William V. *The Conduct of Just and Limited War*. New York: Praeger, 1981.

Ramsey, Paul. *The Just War*. New York: Charles Scribner's Sons, 1968.

Spaeth, Robert L. "Disarmament and the Catholic Bishops". *This World* (Summer 1982).

CHAPTER FOURTEEN

JUST CAUSE

Just cause is the foremost criterion that must be satisfied by a war. The cause is the ultimate end for which the war is fought. If the cause is not just, then it does not matter what weapons are used or how the war is conducted, it is still unjust. As O'Brien puts it, this cause must be a competing obligation of sufficient weight to overcome the obligation not to injure and kill others (1981, p. 20).

In the past, causes thought sufficient to justify offensive war included the protection of rights that had been threatened or injured, retribution for past wrongs, and vindication of righteousness against heretics or infidels.[1] That is, a state might justly break the peace and go to war for these causes.

The last of these legitimating causes is now archaic. As O'Brien notes: "Under the original concept of vindictive justice, an offensive war to free the Soviet people from communist rule would be just." Likewise, an offensive war to save a portion of the Soviet people from genocide would have been permitted under this older interpretation. He goes on to say, "A war of vindictive justice wherein the belligerent fights against error and evil as a matter of principle and not of necessity is no longer condoned by just-war doctrine" (1981, p. 22). The reason is simply that the cost is too high. Overthrowing a tyrannical government, or preventing genocide, important as these causes may be, cannot overcome the obligation not to injure and kill the many people likely to be injured and killed in modern war.

Likewise, at least for Catholics, the second of these causes is now ruled out. As the bishops put it in *The Challenge of Peace* (1983, no. 86):

> As both Pope Pius XII and Pope John XXIII made clear, if war of retribution was ever justifiable, the risks of modern war negate such a claim today.

That is, retribution for past wrongs is not a sufficient cause to justify the extent of injury and killing that accompany modern war.

---

[1] John Courtney Murray has listed the generally accepted just causes as *ad vindicandas offensiones, ad repetendas res,* and *ad repellendas injurias.* He goes on to add that Pope Pius XII appeared to have rejected the first two as just causes under modern conditions (1960, p. 76, note 4).

Under modern conditions, just cause is essentially limited to self-defense, and to "reasserting rights previously violated and to preventing recurrences of these and comparable injuries" (O'Brien, 1981, p. 22). Self-defense, as used here, includes collective defense and the defense of an ally. However, it must be *defense*, not retribution for past wrongs done to an ally. In essence, today just cause is limited to shielding against or preventing the violation of rights, and to reestablishing preexisting rights that have been violated. Just cause does not cover punishment for a prior violation of rights once that violation has ceased.

But now we come to the critical point. Reasons two and three are no longer just cause for a war as destructive as modern wars can be. Is reason one, the protection of rights, still an adequate justification? Can it be meaningful to talk of going to war to defend our rights, when the war itself may destroy both us and the aggressor?

We need to be clear about what is at stake. We are not talking about a war between two medieval kings, in which the main goal of the Church is to minimize the suffering of those who will gain nothing even if their king wins. We are talking about a war between the United States and the Soviet Union. The consequences of *not* resisting Soviet aggression, of *not* fighting a defensive war should the Soviets attack, would be horrendous.

To begin with, we are talking about an enormous cost in lives even from unresisted Soviet conquest. In Chapter 7, on unilateral disarmament, we have already looked at the Soviet death toll from the deportation of "untrustworthy" peoples, the labor camps, and Stalin's farm collectivization campaign. However, that is still not the total. During World War II the Germans killed an enormous number of Russians. Yet the careful counts of several Russian historians indicate that Stalin killed more Russians during World War II than did the Germans. Some estimates by dissident Russian historians put the total of untimely deaths due to Soviet tyranny, in the Soviet Union alone, as high as 100 million over a fifty-year period. This doesn't count Soviet-caused deaths in occupied countries, nor deaths due to other communist governments.

Rummel's careful and very conservative count of deaths caused by Communist governments leads him to state that:

It is a killing machine, responsible for the massacre, executions, starvation, and deaths from forced exposure, slave-labor, beatings, and torture of at least 95,153,600 people in this century, or 477 people per 10,000 of their populations. By contrast, the number of battle casualties from all wars in this century is 35,654, or 22 per 10,000 people of the populations involved. On a per capita basis, communism is at least 20 times deadlier than war. *Communism in this century has killed even more people, aside from Communist wars, than the 86 million that perished in all the wars and revolutions since 1740* (1986, p. 2) (emphasis in original).

If we extend this figure of 477 deaths per 10,000 population to the current world population of 4.85 billion, we conclude that a global victory for communism would result in 233 million untimely deaths from the causes Rummel has listed above. Could resisting the Soviet Union actually produce more deaths than this? The historical statistics for war deaths suggest resistance would actually produce fewer deaths than would conquest by communism.

But lives, important as they are, are not the only things at stake. We are all going to die eventually anyway. From a Christian perspective, we need to consider not just lives but the kind of society in which those lives are lived. We are talking about protecting the free portion of the world's population, the heirs to some 4000 years of Western and 2000 years of Christian culture, from a tyranny so monstrous it is hard to find a historical parallel. Therefore one thing that could very well be at stake is the denial of freedom, the imposition of slavery, on nearly five billion people.

Monsignor R. G. Peters, author of a weekly column on Catholic moral teaching, put the importance of freedom in a Christian perspective:

> God went to great lengths to show us how highly He prizes freedom. Knowing it could be abused and would lead to terrible loss, He nevertheless included liberty in Adam and Eve's Paradise. Knowing we would abuse it time and time again, He gave each of us a free will. He did it because He wanted to create us in His likeness, and one of the essentials of that likeness is free will or the power to choose either to act or not act. God, knowing all the tragedies that freedom would bring, nevertheless gives it to every human being. . . . Gold, oil, land, none of these things can justify even a war of defense. Liberty can (1983).

Even with the lives and freedom of billions of people at stake, we still have to recognize the need for limits. A nuclear war that destroyed everything could not possibly be a just cause. Nevertheless, a nuclear war which succeeded in preventing the establishment of a worldwide Soviet empire could be extremely horrible and still leave the world better off than it would be under that empire. It would be justified if it resulted in less death and suffering than not fighting it.

What Thomas E. Murray, a former member of the U.S. Atomic Energy Commission, wrote nearly thirty years ago is still valid, even though it has received little attention in the interim:

> Fear of War must not be allowed to confuse our counsels in the face of this threat. There are other ways in which civilization can perish than by the use of nuclear weapons. Civilization perishes when effective resistance is not opposed to injustice; when the sacred order of human rights is violated with impunity; when violent forces, that act without a conscience, are allowed to make successful defiance of the laws that conscience holds inviolable. Civilization has the right and duty to defend itself against these evils by all legitimate means; and in an extremity of need the use of armed force is a legitimate means of self-defense (1959, p. 154).

In the world today, there are human values that are sufficiently important to be just cause for a defensive and limited nuclear war. In subsequent chapters, we will look at whether the other requirements of Just War Doctrine can be met in defending those values.

REFERENCES

Murray, John Courtney. "Theology and Modern War". In *Morality and Modern Warfare,* edited by William J. Nagle. Baltimore: Helicon Press, 1960.

Murray, Thomas E. "Public Opinion and the Problem of War". *Catholic Mind* (March-April 1959), pp. 151–58.

O'Brien, William V. *The Conduct of Just and Limited Wars.* New York: Praeger Publishers, 1981.

Peters, Msgr. R. G. *Catholic Twin Circle* (July 17, 1983).

Rummel, Rudolph J. "Deadlier Than War: Non-Freedom". Paper, University of Hawaii Political Science Department, Honolulu, August 1986.

CHAPTER FIFTEEN

COMPARATIVE JUSTICE

Having observed that the United States does have a just cause worth defending, even to the extent of using nuclear weapons in a limited manner, we next need to look at the comparative justice of the United States and the Soviet Union. The problem is that in this fallen world no one can claim to have absolute justice on his side. Thus there are two important aspects to comparative justice.

The first aspect of comparative justice deals with the absence of absolute justice. There are some Christians who deny that the United States has the right to defend itself against the Soviet Union because the United States is itself imperfect. For instance, Bishop Raymond Hunthausen, speaking at the University of Notre Dame, was reported as saying:

> The "precise purpose" of the United States nuclear arsenal is "to protect our wealth". . . . Quoting Luke 6:24–26, the archbishop explained that Jesus said the rich would mourn and weep. "He [the archbishop] said, in essence, that if we go that way of outrageous wealth and power, we will get the very nuclear war with which we threaten others" (1982).[1]

Speaking at Gonzaga University, Bishop Hunthausen said:

> In considering a Christian response to nuclear arms, I think we have to begin by recognizing that our country's overwhelming array of nuclear arms has a very precise purpose: it is meant to protect our wealth. The United States is not illogical in amassing the most destructive weapons in history. We need them. We are the richest people in history (1982).

Bishop Hunthausen was also quoted as saying that Soviet conquest of America will be our "crucifixion", which we should accept willingly.

If we were to accept this view, then no nation could ever legitimately defend itself, by any means whatsoever, since no nation is ever perfect or can claim absolute justice for its cause. Instead, a nation should accept conquest as crucifixion for its sins, even when the conqueror is less just. The Just War Doctrine contradicts this alleged requirement for absolute justice. It says that comparative justice is sufficient to provide a basis for

---

[1] It is interesting that Bishop Hunthausen focused on protecting our *wealth*. Apparently in his view our liberties, and the humanly limited but nevertheless real achievements of justice in our society, are so trivial as to be unworthy of defense. Or possibly he values them himself, but believes the rest of us to be so mean-spirited we don't value them enough to defend them but would defend only our wealth.

defense. Those who demand absolute justice in a nation before conceding it the right to defend itself are being utopian, not Christian. The history of Christianity is littered with heresies teaching that the Kingdom of God can be realized in this world by human endeavors alone. Those who refuse to defend a comparatively just society because it isn't absolutely just, and who demand that it be replaced by an absolutely just order, are repeating these same heresies. Thus the first aspect of comparative justice is to say that perfection is not required; comparative justice is sufficient to warrant the use of force in defending a nation.

The second aspect of comparative justice is that it serves to limit the *means* by which a just war may be pursued. As the bishops put it (1983, no. 93):

> Every party to a conflict should acknowledge the limits of its "just cause" and the consequent requirement to use only limited means in pursuit of its objectives. Far from legitimizing a crusade mentality, comparative justice is designed to relativize absolute claims and to restrain the use of force even in a "justified" war.

Thus the extent of the means by which the United States may defend itself against the Soviet Union is limited by the comparative justice of the United States and the Soviet Union. If there is no essential difference between the justice of the United States and the Soviet Union, then the use of nuclear weapons in defense of the United States would be unjust. Indeed, the use even of highly destructive non-nuclear weapons would be unjust.

Many Christian writers who oppose the use of nuclear weapons have posited a *moral symmetry* (or perhaps *immoral symmetry* would be the better term) between the United States and the Soviet Union. Since we are no better than they, the argument goes, we have no right to use force to defend ourselves against them, and in particular we have no right to use nuclear weapons.

One version of this moral-symmetry argument involves referring to the United States and the Soviet Union as "the two superpowers", as in "the world is caught up in the struggle for dominance between the two superpowers". Both the United States and the Soviet Union are simply superpowers, doing things to and at the expense of the ordinary powers and the nonpowers. According to this view, whatever differences there may be between the United States and the Soviet Union are swallowed up by the similarities of their behavior as superpowers.

The American Catholic bishops reflected this view in their Challenge of Peace pastoral. For instance, they said (1983, no. 245):

> No relationship more dramatically demonstrates the fragile nature of order in international affairs today than that of the United States and the

Soviet Union. These two sovereign states have avoided open war, nuclear or conventional, but they are divided by philosophy, ideology and *competing ambitions*. Their *competition* is global in scope and involves everything from comparing nuclear arsenals to printed propaganda. Both have been criticized in international meetings because of their policies in the nuclear arms race (emphasis added).

And again (1983, no. 257):

Sensible and successful diplomacy, however, will demand that we avoid the trap of a form of anti-Sovietism which fails to grasp the central danger of a *superpower rivalry* in which both the U.S. and the U.S.S.R. are players, and fails to recognize the common interest both states have in never using nuclear weapons. Some of these dangers and common interests would exist in any world where *two great powers,* even relatively benign ones, *competed for power, affluence, and security* (emphasis added).

What is one to make of this inverse chauvinism that has replaced "My country, right or wrong", with "My country is always wrong"?

Perhaps the best place to start is to restate an oft-neglected truth: the world is *not* in the grip of a struggle between two superpowers. As Jeane Kirkpatrick put it:

[T]he United States has no unique rivalry whatsoever and . . . the United States has no unique interest in countering Soviet expansion. We and all of our friends and all of our adversaries ought to be clear that *in no sense is the United States involved in a contest with the Soviet Union for world domination.* Our disagreements with the Soviet Union are no different from those [the Soviet Union has] with any other country that seeks to maintain its own independence and hopes for a world of independent nations (1986, p. 13) (emphasis in original).

The point can be summarized thus: the Soviet Union wants to rule the world. We don't want *them* to rule the world, but we have no wish to rule it ourselves. They have repeatedly stated their belief in the inevitable triumph of Marxism-Leninism, and their duty to hasten that triumph. They have repeatedly acted in consonance with their stated belief. We have repeatedly demonstrated that we do not seek world rule. For instance, when we had a monopoly on the atomic bomb, we not only didn't use it to gain world domination, but proposed the Baruch Plan under which all atomic weapons and installations would be placed under international control. Can anyone believe the Soviet Union would have been equally generous had the situation been reversed? The simple historical fact is that we are not in a contest with them for world domination; we are only, like all the other not-yet-conquered nations, attempting to stay unconquered. Contrary to the bishops' assertion, we are not competing with the Soviet Union for power.

The bishops also asserted that the United States is competing with the Soviet Union for affluence. This statement is not only wrong but reveals a terrible misunderstanding of economics and of how wealth originates. It reveals a zero-sum mentality, which takes for granted that there is only so much wealth in the world, and some people can be affluent only if others are poor.[2] Affluence, in this view, comes from seizing more than one's fair share of the world's fixed amount of wealth. This is not the place to refute this view in detail. Suffice it to say that the affluence of the United States is based on the fact that wealth is not fixed but can be *produced*. It is based on the fact that one person's affluence is not gained at the expense of others, but on the contrary, that all can become more affluent simultaneously. And similarly, the affluence of one nation is not based on the impoverishment of others. We do not need to *compete* with the Soviet union for affluence; we and they can each *produce* it without denying it to the other.

The bishops further asserted that we are competing with the Soviet Union for security. This, strangely enough, reflects a Soviet view of the world, not an American view. We and the Soviets differ in our views on the nature of security. For them, security is a zero-sum situation. The more secure one party is, the less secure everyone else inevitably is. In their view, they can have absolute security only when everyone else has absolute insecurity.[3] For us, however, security is not a zero-sum situation. An increase in security for one party does not necessarily mean a decrease in security for everyone else. From our perspective, a world in which everyone is secure is conceivable, even if technically difficult to achieve. From the Soviets' perspective, such a world is a contradiction in terms. Our view is a reflection of our domestic situation. We view equality under the law as providing equal security to everyone. Their view is likewise a reflection of their domestic situation. The Soviet elite can have security only so long as their subjects have none.

---

[2] This zero-sum view may explain Bishop Hunthausen's focus on protecting our wealth, not our liberties. To an adherent of the zero-sum view, the mere existence of relative wealth is proof of criminal activity. We wouldn't have it if we hadn't stolen it. Therefore we need to defend ourselves against those who rightfully wish to recover it.

[3] This is particularly revealed by the Soviets' positions on arms-control negotiations. To them, equal security means they are as well armed as all the rest of the world put together. This is seen in their insistence that the French and British nuclear forces be counted along with U.S forces in balancing Soviet forces, and their insistence that the portions of their forces targeted at the People's Republic of China not be counted as part of the balance with Western forces.

This leads to a related point. Mr. Gorbachev has stated in an interview with the Western press that Soviet foreign policy is an extension of
Soviet domestic policy.[4] This is quite true. Soviet domestic policy includes the use of forced labor and the crushing of any dissidence.

Cronid Lubarsky, a Soviet astronomer now in the West and a former
inmate of the Soviet labor camps, stated:

> The punitive organs of governments, the Interior Ministry and the KGB,
> have their quotas to fill. It has long been evident that, whenever a major
> construction project is planned in a particular area, that district's newspa-
> pers launch a campaign against some particularly Soviet form of criminal-
> ity. A wave of arrests follows. The result: a rapid rise in the availability
> of cheap labor (quoted in *The New American*, 1986, p. 43).

Avraham Shifrin, another emigrant from the Soviet Union, has published a list and a map of 1100 labor camps in the Soviet Union, derived
from their post office addresses. Each camp contains a few hundred to a
few thousand inmates, including the camps *for children only*. Thus long
after the days of Stalin, the Soviet labor camps still contain several million inmates, and they must be refilled frequently because of high death
rates. There is also a new development since the 1960s. In addition to
the camp inmates themselves, there are some prisoners who are not actually interned, but are restricted to a certain area and forced to work at
specific jobs. A CIA study of 1982 claims the number of unconfined
forced laborers is at least equal to the number of people confined to labor camps.[5]

---

[4] This phrase of Mr. Gorbachev's was not one he casually tossed out on the spur of the
moment. It is fundamental to Marxist-Leninist dogma that the domestic policy of any
state reflects the interests of the ruling classes of that state, and the foreign policy of the
state likewise reflects those interests. Byely and his fellow authors spend most of a chapter
expounding this view in detail (1972, pp. 7ff.). Mr. Gorbachev was simply restating
Marxist-Leninist dogma when he made that statement. The ruling class of the Soviet Union is the *nomenklatura*, or what Milovan Djilas called "the new class". As authors such as
Simis and d'Encausse make clear, Soviet domestic policy is designed to assure the continued rule of this class. It is simply classical Marxism-Leninism, then, to state that the foreign policy of the USSR will be designed to protect and expand the rule of that class.
However, one need not accept Marxist-Leninist doctrine to agree that a ruling group that
oppresses its own people will not hesitate to oppress its neighbors.

[5] The Soviet use of prison labor is in no way to be compared with the trivial contribution that prison labor makes to the economy in the United States. Heller and Nekrich
state:

> The NKVD played an important part in the Soviet economy. With the most inex-
> pensive labor supply in the world, the prison and camp population, the NKVD
> functioned as a cornerstone of the economic system, as is shown by official Soviet
> documents. According to the "State Plan for the Economic Development of the
> USSR in 1941", the NKVD was responsible for 50 percent of the lumber produc-

In effect, the government of the Soviet Union is at war with its own people. And as Max Kampelman put it: "A country that declares war against its own people can't be trusted not to declare war against its neighbors (1986)."

Perhaps the most dramatic current illustration of how Soviet foreign policy is an extension of domestic policy is the war in Afghanistan. Several examples will illustrate the point. Here is an Associated Press despatch from New Delhi, June 26, 1984:

> . . . the southern Afghan city of Kandahar has turned into a cemetery and a virtual free-fire zone. . . . Once Afghanistan's second most populous city with nearly 250,000 inhabitants, Kandahar now looks like a vast graveyard. . . . Between 40 and 60 percent of the houses and shops have been destroyed. . . .

The Permanent Tribunal of Peoples, a European-based human rights organization, has conducted interviews with Afghan refugees and other witnesses. In January 1983 it issued a report giving the following findings about Soviet actions:

1. Soviet forces use dumdums and poisoned bullets, both prohibited by treaties to which the Soviet Union is signatory;
2. Soviet forces carry out summary execution of all captured guerillas;
3. Soviet forces make attacks on villages believed to shelter guerillas, without regard to the safety of noncombatants, including children, the elderly, and the sick;
4. Soviet forces burn out villages and destroy flocks and crops, to drive the inhabitants out of particular areas (Revel, 1985).

Dr. Claude Malhuret, executive director of the French medical relief organization *Medicins sans Frontieres* ("Doctors without Borders"), reports that his organization regularly sets up hospitals and provides medical care in war-torn areas throughout the world, without being molested by either side. In Afghanistan, however, his hospitals, clearly marked with red crosses on the roof, have been repeatedly bombed and destroyed by Soviet aircraft.

---

tion and export in the Far East and in the Karelian and Komi autonomous republics, more than one-third in Arkhangelsk and Murmansk provinces, and between one-fifth and one-fourth in Yaroslavl, Gorky, Molotovsk, and Sverdlovsk provinces and in the Krasnoyarsk territory (1986, pp. 319–20).

They also note that the 1941 plan called for the NKVD, using prison labor, to produce 40 percent of the total chrome ore mined in the Soviet Union, and that of all the money allocated for capital construction in 1941, the NKVD received 18 percent, more than any other single commissariat. Slave labor was thus an integral part of the Soviet planned economy.

According to Dr. Malhuret, as well as other witnesses, one of the common practices of the Soviet forces is to drop millions of antipersonnel mines throughout the countryside. These blow off feet and hands but don't kill people, leaving the crippled victims to be a drain on the able-bodied. One of the most vicious features of this campaign is the disguising of these mines as toys and other objects attractive to children. The result has been thousands of children whose hands or feet have been blown off, and who will be disabled for life (Revel, 1985).

The United Nations Human Rights Commission, in February 1985, issued a report prepared under the direction of Felix Ermacora of Austria. This report was based on refugee interviews, and accused the Soviets of "gross violations of human rights", including the use of toylike bombs targeted at children, the torturing of prisoners, and the massacring of whole villages. It concluded that

> . . . many lives have been lost, many people have been incarcerated in conditions far removed from respect for human rights and fundamental freedoms, many have been tortured and have disappeared, humanitarian norms have been flouted in the conflict taking place, and the resulting situation is fraught with danger for the population as a whole (quoted by Revel, 1985).

The UN report gave a figure of 12,000 persons killed between April 27, 1978 (date of the pro-Soviet coup) and January 1980 just in the Poli Charki concentration camp near Kabul. Most of these were doctors, lawyers, engineers, and religious leaders. As in the case of the Katyn massacre in Poland, the Soviet Union has decapitated Afghan society by murdering its educated leadership. Other observers, quoted by Revel, have presented a figure of 27,000 deaths in that camp for the same time period. This latter figure is claimed not to be an estimate, but simply a count of the names that the Afghan government posted in public places to avoid having relatives of the victims cluster around the camp gate.

Peter Samuel reports (1985, p. 1) that a Soviet draftee who served for two years in Afghanistan gave an interview in late 1984 to the Estonian journal *Isekiri*. The soldier described the attacks his unit made on Afghan villages. Here is his description of the orders he was given by his superior officers:

> Upon entering a village, all even slightly suspicious individuals were to be immediately shot. Generally all men who appeared capable of fighting were considered suspect. Similarly all those individuals whose appearance aroused suspicion were shot; for example, people clothed in a chador, which is generally worn by women, though men can go about in them. With a chador, the face is covered and thus it is easy to conceal

oneself. Those who began to run or tried to hide in any way were immediately shot. Those requirements were made clear to us before the beginning of operations.

This soldier also reported that in some operations in small villages his
orders were to kill every single person, including women and children.
The Soviets, aware of the damage the press did to the U.S. war effort
in Vietnam, are making sure that won't happen to them. They have a
very effective censorship policy—they shoot reporters. The Soviet ambassador to Pakistan warned two French journalists: "Stop trying to
penetrate Afghanistan with the so-called guerillas. From now on, the
bandits and so-called journalists accompanying them will be killed"
(quoted in letter to *National Review*, November 16, 1984, p. 4). This is
no idle threat. A Norwegian journalist was killed in 1982 and an Australian in 1983. In 1985, Charles Thornton of the (Arizona) *Phoenix Republic*
was killed, not as an accidental victim in a firefight, but in a deliberately planned ambush, the details of which were reported in TASS. In
addition to these deaths, three journalists and a doctor have been captured and tortured into "confessing".

Mao Tse-Tung, in his writings on guerrilla warfare, once compared
guerrillas to fish and the populace to the sea in which they swim. Several observers have summed up the Soviet strategy in Afghanistan as
one of attempting to dry up the sea. They have been trying, with
ghastly results, since 1979. From the standpoint of the Soviet leaders,
however, they are not doing anything to the Afghans that they haven't
done to their own people in one way or another. Armed resistance, such
as that in Ukraine after World War II, was crushed just as it is being
crushed in Afghanistan; any people showing themselves capable of
leading anti-Soviet activity are sent to a death camp.

The contrast between the Soviet war in Afghanistan and the U.S.
war in Vietnam is instructive. The most serious U.S. atrocity was the
Mylai massacre, in which some 200 Vietnamese were killed. Once the
U.S. government became aware of it, the army held an inquiry, and
the officer in charge at the scene of the atrocity was tried by court martial
and convicted. In Afghanistan, the atrocities are not an aberration but
official Soviet policy. There have not been, and will not be, any trials by
court martial for these atrocities.

It can be argued, of course, that Afghanistan is a temporary feature of
Soviet behavior. The war there will some day be over. We cannot, the
argument goes, take this temporary war as illustrating anything of a
permanent nature about Soviet society.

Nevertheless, a comparison of the world in 1939 with the world today is revealing. In 1939, there were nine European countries that

shared a border with the Soviet Union. Today three of those have disappeared from the map, five are occupied by Soviet troops, and only
one, Finland, remains even nominally independent. The term *Finlandi-
zation* has come into use to describe the type of independence which that
country still "enjoys". Moreover, the borders of even those countries
that still survive have all been adjusted in favor of the Soviet Union. For
instance, the Soviet Union now shares a border with Norway, because
the portion of Finland that in 1939 lay between the two countries has
been absorbed by the Soviet Union. Poland, which still exists even
though occupied, was forced to cede substantial territories to the Soviet
Union.

By contrast, in 1939 the United States shared a border with two nations. Those two nations are still independent (sometimes vociferously
so; they haven't been Finlandized), and the borders are the same as those
which existed in 1939. Moreover, since 1939 the United States has
granted independence to the Philippines, and offered independence to
Puerto Rico (the Puerto Ricans have voted resoundingly against independence).

In addition to the Soviet Union's political expansionism, it is worth
mentioning the issue of religious freedom. It is strange that Western
Christians who deny the United States has any moral superiority over
the Soviet Union completely ignore the condition of the Russian Orthodox Church. It is important to remember that the Russian Orthodox Church not only has never condemned Soviet nuclear plans and
weapons in the way Bishops Hunthausen and Gumbleton have condemned U.S. plans and weapons, it has never uttered even the slightest
criticism. If the Soviet Union should "win" through conquest of the
United States, or succeed in Finlandizing the United States through intimidation or moral paralysis, our churchmen would be no more free to
criticize their new masters than the Russian Orthodox Church is today
free to criticize those same masters. Indeed, many of our churchmen
would share the fate of thousands of Orthodox priests and millions of
believers, who died for their beliefs either through execution or the
slow death of the labor camps. They would then realize that there is a
moral difference, although it would be too late to say anything about it.

There is another point that deserves mention. It is often argued that
although the Soviet Union has a history of aggression extending to the
present, it will eventually mellow and become a status quo power instead of a revolutionary one. Therefore we needn't consider ourselves
morally superior to them, or consider them to be our enemy. We need
only be patient and wait for their "mellowing", perhaps hastening it
with some "education" and "cultural exchange".

This argument is historically unfounded. In all recorded history, there has never been a war between two nations with freely elected governments (for documentation see the articles by Rummel). All known wars have involved, on at least one side, a nation whose government was a tyranny. The United States, in particular, has never fought a war against a nation with a freely elected government. The evidence of all history is that if there were no tyrannical governments, there would be no wars. Thus the fact that the Soviet Union is a tyranny while the United States is not, is strong evidence of the latter's moral superiority. The United States, simply by having a freely elected government, is comparatively more just than the Soviet Union.

As a final illustration of the moral differences, consider the issue of *dezinformatsia*, a Russian word that has recently passed into English as *disinformation*. This term means the covert distribution of "information" which is either not attributed at all, or is falsely attributed. It contains intentionally false, incomplete, or misleading material, intended to deceive, misinform, or mislead the target. The target may be foreign elites, either in or out of government, or may be the public at large. The spread of disinformation may utilize rumors, forgeries, manipulative political actions, agents of influence, front organizations, and other means.

Numerous examples of Soviet disinformation campaigns are given by Shultz and Godson. Pincher gives an in-depth description of this practice up to the early 1980s. More recent examples include forged memoranda allegedly written by Secretary of Defense Weinberger, laying out a propaganda campaign to make the Chernobyl disaster look even worse than it was, and a massive, worldwide campaign to blame the AIDS epidemic on U.S. germ-warfare research. In this latter case, the Soviets always cite as their source a specific article appearing in an Indian newspaper, which is believed by U.S. officials to have been written on the basis of a forgery planted by the Soviets. This planting of a story, then citing the non-Soviet "source", is a common feature of Soviet dezinformatsia campaigns.

Dezinformatsia is not the ad-hoc actions of low-level agents. Forgeries are managed at the top level of Service A, of the KGB's First Chief Directorate. They are designed to fit into whatever is the Soviet Union's current propaganda campaign. This amounts to official lying on a massive scale. No other government in the world comes even close to this degree of blatant immorality.

We can conclude that despite the efforts of some Christians (as well as non-Christians) to argue that there is no difference in comparative justice between the United States and the Soviet Union, differences do exist and they are significant. Despite their erroneous ideas about super-power rivalry, the American Catholic bishops did recognize these differences (1983, no. 251):

> To pretend that as a nation we have lived up to all our own ideals would be patently dishonest. To pretend that all evils in the world have been or are now being perpetrated by dictatorial regimes would be both dishonest and absurd. But having said this, and admitting our own faults, it is imperative that we confront reality. The facts simply do not support the invidious comparisons made at times, even in our own society, between our way of life, in which most basic human rights are at least recognized even if they are not always adequately supported, and those totalitarian and tyrannical regimes in which such rights are either denied or systematically suppressed.

The differences between the United States and the Soviet Union, while not sufficient to justify a crusade, nevertheless are sufficient to justify the *limited* and *defensive* use of nuclear weapons to preserve those differences.

REFERENCES

Byely, B., et al. *Marxism-Lenimism on War and Army*. Moscow: Progress Publishers, 1972.

d'Encausse, Helene Carrère. *Confiscated Power: How Soviet Russia Really Works*. New York. Harper & Row, 1982 (translation of the 1980 French edition).

Heller, Mikhail, and Aleksandr M. Nekrich. *Utopia in Power*. New York: Summit Books, 1986 (translation of the 1982 Russian language edition).

Hunthausen, Bishop Raymond. "Why Challenge Nuclear Arms: Risking a Christian Response". Statement at University of Notre Dame, January 29, 1982. As reported in *Catholic Telegraph* (February 14, 1982).

Hunthausen, Bishop Raymond. Fifth annual Father Van F. Christoph, S.J., Memorial Lecture, Gonzaga University, Spokane, Wash. Reported in *Our Sunday Visitor* (February 28, 1982).

Kampelman, Max. Interviewed in *National Catholic Register*, Part 1 (August 10, 1986). Part 2 (August 17, 1986).

Kirkpatrick, Jeane J. *The United States and the World: Setting Limits.* Washington, D.C.: American Enterprise Institute, 1986.

Ingelbretson, Paul. "Our Contribution to the Slave Trade". *The New American* (July 14, 1986), p. 43.

Pincher, Chapman. *The Secret Offensive.* New York: St. Martin's Press, 1985.

Revel, Jean-François. "The Awful Logic of Genocide". *National Review* (October 4, 1985), pp. 22–29.

Rummel, Rudolph J., "Libertarianism and International Politics". *Journal of Conflict Resolution.* Vol. 27 (March 1983), pp. 27–71.

Rummel, Rudolph J. "Libertarian Propositions on Violence within and between Nations". *Journal of Conflict Resolution.* Vol. 29 (September 1985), pp. 419–55.

Samuel, Peter. "Policy: Shoot Civilians". In *Washington Inquirer* (January 25, 1985), p. 1.

Shifrin, Avraham. *The First Guidebook to Prisons and Concentration Camps of the Soviet Union.* Torrance, Calif.: Diane Books.

Shultz, Richard H., and Roy Godson. *Dezinformatsia.* McLean, Va.: Pergamon-Brassey's International Defense Publishers, 1984.

Simis, Konstantin. *USSR: The Corrupt Society.* New York: Simon & Schuster, 1982.

CHAPTER SIXTEEN

VICTORY

At least from the time of Pope Innocent IV (1243–1254), an important criterion for the justness of a war was the belligerent having a reasonable chance of victory—that there be "probable success" before initiating a war (Russell, 1975, p. 154). Clearly, a belligerent cannot be certain of victory. Often both sides go into a war confident of victory, and one of them turns out to have been mistaken. The American bishops stated, regarding the probability-of-success criterion (1983, no. 98):

> This is a difficult criterion to apply, but its purpose is to prevent irrational resort to force or hopeless resistance when the outcome of either will clearly be disproportionate or futile.

O'Brien has noted that there is a qualification to the requirement for a good chance of victory.

> A war of self-defense may be engaged in irrespective of the prospects for success, particularly if there is a great threat to continued existence and to fundamental values. . . . It seems to be conceded that a desperate, if not hopeless, defense is permitted if . . . moral values . . . are clearly threatened by the aggressor (1981, p. 31).

The bishops agreed with this assessment when they said (1983, no. 98): "The determination [of probability of success] includes a recognition that at times defense of key values, even against great odds, may be a 'proportionate' witness."

In earlier times, this criterion simply enjoined the potential combatant to determine (in the case of offensive war) whether the probability of success was sufficiently high to justify the destruction, injury, and death that going to war would bring; or (in the case of a defensive war) whether the values (survival and independence) to be protected were sufficiently important to justify a desperate defense. The problem in the nuclear age is different. The issue is no longer, "Can I achieve victory instead of my opponent achieving it?" but "Is there a victory to be had; can anyone speak, in any meaningful sense, of victory in nuclear war?"

The conventional wisdom is "No one can win a nuclear war". Politicians say it; churchmen say it; pundits say it. The apparently logical conclusion is then drawn: "Therefore we must never have one."

The problem with this conventional wisdom is that it fails to deal with the real world. It implies that when an aggressor threatens nuclear war, our only option is to surrender. *If victory is impossible, we are not morally permitted to resist.*

Aleksandr Solzhenitsyn warned of this problem, depicting the situation if the Soviet Union should be permitted to gain significant nuclear superiority over the West:

> At one time there was no comparison between the strength of the USSR and yours. Then it became equal. . . . Perhaps today it is just greater than equal, but soon it will be two to one. Then three to one. Finally it will be five to one. . . . With such nuclear superiority it will be possible to block the use of your weapons, and on some unlucky morning they will declare, "Attention. We're sending our troops into Europe, and if you make a move, we will annihilate you." And this ratio of three to one, or five to one, will have its effect: you will not make a move (1976, pp. 76–77).

Of course we won't make a move. In addition to the prudence (or even cowardice) that such overwhelming Soviet strategic superiority would naturally engender, the issue of concern here is that we have been told again and again that no one can win a nuclear war, and it is immoral to fight when there is no chance for victory.

The real problem, though, is that we haven't analyzed the meaning of the word *victory*. Before we can answer whether victory is still possible in the nuclear age, we have to know what the word means. Even if it is *no longer* possible, what is it that was *once* possible?

The French bishops had an implied meaning for the word *victory* when they pointed out the futility of ruling over a "pulverized enemy". Victory, it seems, means to rule over the vanquished. This was clearly the meaning of victory in World War II. The victors did rule over the former enemy. The Soviet Union still does rule over some of its World War II enemies. Even though the rule of the United States over Japan and portions of Germany was a benign one, eventually terminated, it was still a *rule*. Those who say we lost the war in Korea base that assertion on the fact that the North Korean state continued to govern itself after the war. There is no doubt that North Vietnam won the war; it now rules South Vietnam (not to mention Cambodia).

But before we accept this definition of victory uncritically, we need to look at the differences between a tyranny and a democracy.

For some rulers, conquest is a meaningful purpose for a war. A tyrant may meaningfully ask, "Will I be better off by keeping my country undamaged or by conquering the enemy, recognizing that the war will bring some damage to my country in the process?[1] Will the benefit to

---

[1] Note that for a tyrant the relevant question is "Will *I* be better off?" instead of "Will *the nation* be better off?" No elected official should be asking such a question.

me from ruling the enemy offset the loss from damage to my own country?''

A democracy can ask no such question. What is a democracy to do with the people it has conquered? Can it make them citizens and give them the vote? Only if they are few in number compared with the population of the democracy. The extent to which American politics were poisoned in the aftermath of the Civil War should give one pause. Here was a "conquered people" who shared most of the traditions and values of the "victors". It took nearly a century for the Civil War to be over, and even that required a Supreme Court decision that completely reversed more than half a century of constitutional history. To incorporate into a democracy a conquered people that has totally different traditions and values is nearly impossible. Consider the experience of France, which after 1945 tried to convince the Algerians that they were Frenchmen and that "France is one nation divided by the Mediterranean, just as Paris is one city divided by the Seine." French schoolbooks instructed Algerian children that "our ancestors were the Gauls." It didn't work, and the attempt to make it work destroyed the Fourth Republic.

If a conquered people can't be made citizens, can they be made subjects? An attempt to govern them without their consent, which is what it means to rule conquered subjects, will inevitably undermine the legitimacy of the democracy itself. Why should *government with the consent of the governed* apply only to the victors? That denies its generality as a principle, and paves the way toward denying it to the original citizens. The fate of the Roman Republic should be enough of a warning.

Thus for a democracy a war of conquest is an absurdity, regardless of the weapons used. Any attempt at it will doom the democracy. Therefore the issue of ruling over a "pulverized enemy", raised by the French bishops, simply does not exist for a democracy.

For a democracy, the only purpose of war is not to conquer, but to avoid being conquered and to restore Saint Augustine's "tranquility of order". This is true when the war is fought with conventional weapons. It remains true when the war is fought with nuclear weapons.

When we consider nuclear weapons in a political context, then, we can see that the political objectives of a tyranny differ from those of a democracy. A tyranny has the objective of intimidating its victim into surrender, or if that fails, of destroying the victim's defensive capability. A democracy, by contrast, has the objective of dissuading aggression, and of defeating aggression if dissuasion fails. A tyranny expects to gain by going to war. A democracy recognizes that war will be cost, not gain. If victory means to gain riches or power over others, a democracy can never "win" any war, nuclear or conventional.

Given that the best a democracy can hope for from a war is to "break even", the critical question is: what are the alternatives? For a democracy, victory has to mean the least bad outcome. Once this is recognized, the idea of winning a nuclear war is no longer an absurdity. Millions of casualties and enormous physical damage might still be better than the reasonably foreseeable consequences of surrender or defeat. To the survivors, the opportunity to live in political and economic freedom, to run their lives as they choose, to worship God as they wish, and to raise their children as they see best, may be well worth the suffering and deprivation of the war and its aftermath. To argue that loss of freedom is better than the loss of any wealth whatsoever is a purely materialistic outlook, and is unworthy of any Christian. Therefore, for a democracy, nuclear war may very well be winnable, not in the sense that it leaves the winner prosperous, but in the sense that it leaves the winner better off than the alternatives of surrender to intimidation or of defeat.

Thus, in short, victory, in the sense of acquiring wealth and subjects by conquering populated territory, *never was* possible for a democracy. Nuclear weapons have not changed that. Victory in the Clausewitzean sense of achieving the political objective of remaining free and independent is the only kind of victory that *ever was* possible for a democracy. Nuclear weapons haven't changed that, either.[2]

Even with regard to victory as we have defined it for a democracy, however, there is one more issue we must examine. As was pointed out in Chapter 12, a nation that is losing a nuclear war can always destroy the "winner" so long as it has sufficient deliverable nuclear weapons left. The "winner", although remaining unconquered, might be obliterated. How, then, can victory be obtained by either side? This simply means that *no nuclear-armed nation must ever be put in the position of seeing itself threatened with inevitable and total destruction*. It must always be left with an acceptable out. A defender must present the aggressor with the

---

[2] It might be asked, Suppose the United States resists nuclear aggression and loses, say, 95 percent of its population, but the remaining ten million people are indeed alive and free, and safe (at least for a time) from a recurrence of the aggression—is that victory? I suggest that the survivors would indeed count it as a victory. One achieved at frightful cost, to be sure, but nonetheless a victory. Note this says nothing about how many survive on the aggressor's side. It is not a case of "we won if there are two of us left but only one of them." Rather, it is a case of "we won if we achieved what we set out to achieve: freedom for the survivors." This issue will be discussed in more detail in Chapter 21, on proportion. However, the question itself is misleading. As we will see in later chapters, there is no reason to believe that the number of casualties would be that high. Postulating virtual annihilation of the defenders is simply one more instance of focusing solely on the case that is not only extreme but extremely unlikely, and ignoring more likely cases.

possibility of further destruction, but with the chance of avoiding that destruction if he ceases the aggression.[3]

Note that while this caveat is expressed in the context of nuclear war, it is not new. It really applies to conventional war as well. A common argument made in favor of the atomic bombing of Japan in 1945 is that it eliminated the need for an invasion that would have cost even more civilian lives than did the atomic bombing, not to mention the lives of troops on both sides. Thus, although by mid-1945 Japan was clearly on its way to defeat, it still had the power to inflict terrible costs on the inevitable winner. As Michael Walzer has observed, if U.S. war aims presented us with the choice of atomic bombing two cities, or carrying out an invasion that would inevitably cost the lives of an enormous number of innocent civilians, we should have reconsidered those aims (1977, p. 266). Were the defeat and occupation of Japan *really essential* to our purpose for being at war? Were they an essential part of defending ourselves and the other nations of the Pacific against Japanese aggression? If not, terms short of invasion and occupation, requiring less than unconditional surrender, should have been offered. Jeff McMahan makes the same point (1985, p. 146) and also quotes Anthony Kenny who argues that unconditional surrender is an immoral demand because it violates just cause. Once the enemy agrees to satisfy one's just cause for going to war, the war is no longer justified (1985, p. 146, n. 6).

Thus, once again we reach the conclusion that always applied to war with non-nuclear weapons, but that applies even more so to a war involving nuclear-armed nations: if a war fought with nuclear weapons is to be just, it must be *limited*. In this case, it must be limited in its objectives: the blocking and preventing of aggression. It must not aim at the complete destruction of the aggressor, not only because that was always immoral in itself, but also because such an aim against a nuclear-armed enemy *amounts to suicide*. It *precludes victory* and thus makes the war unjust for yet another reason.

Victory, then, is possible even in a nuclear war. Victory, however, merely means achieving the political objectives of remaining independent and free. It does not mean conquest. Moreover, if the aggressor is threatened with inevitable destruction, even this limited form of victory may become impossible.

---

[3] At this point we need not be specific about the nature of the destruction to be threatened. However, as was pointed out in Chapter 10, the threatened action must be a moral one to carry out, or it will amount to a bluff and may not have the desired intrawar deterrent effect. We will discuss some possibilities in subsequent chapters.

REFERENCES

McMahan, Jeff. "Deterrence and Deontology". In *Nuclear Deterrence: Ethics and Strategy*, edited by Russell Hardin, et al. Chicago: University of Chicago Press, 1985.

O'Brien, William V. *The Conduct of Just and Limited War*. New York: Praeger Publishers, 1981.

Russell, Frederick H. *The Just War in the Middle Ages*. London: Cambridge University Press, 1975.

Solzhenitsyn, Aleksandr. *Warning to the West*. New York: Farrar, Straus & Giroux, 1976.

Walzer, Michael. *Just and Unjust Wars*. New York: Basic Books 1977.

CHAPTER SEVENTEEN

RIGHT INTENTION

Just cause is required before one may fight a war. But just cause is not sufficient. As Saint Augustine put it in *De Verbis Domini*:

> For the true followers of God even wars are peaceful, not being made for greed or out of cruelty, but from desire for peace, to restrain the evil, and assist the good.

That is, right intention is also needed. Just cause may not be allowed to serve as the springboard for vengeance or for territorial conquest. Even in a just war, the combatant must enter the war with a desire to achieve a *just peace*.

The American Catholic bishops had this to say about the right intention criterion for a just war (1983, no. 95):

> Right intention is related to just cause—war can be legitimately intended only for the reasons set forth [in no. 86] as a just cause. During the conflict, right intention means pursuit of peace and reconciliation, including avoiding unnecessarily destructive acts or imposing unreasonable conditions (e.g., unconditional surrender).

In 1948 a commission of the Church of England carried out an analysis of nuclear war according to Just War Doctrine. The analysis was published in a report entitled *The Church and the Atom*. Among their conclusions was the following statement:

> To seek the entire subjugation of the enemy, or the abolition of his sovereignty, or unrestricted control over his life, labour and property, is not permissible; for such aims transcend the limits set by justifying causes (quoted in Batchelder, 1962, p. 255).

O'Brien lists three elements of right intention: limiting oneself to pursuit of the just cause; keeping in mind that the ultimate objective of the war is a just and lasting peace; maintaining charity and love toward the enemy (1981, p. 34).[1] Some general discussion of these elements is appropriate before we discuss their application to nuclear war.

---

[1] Joseph Kunkel has pointed out to me that the issue of right intention continues to matter even after the decision to go to war. During the war one must continue to have a right intention by being willing to stop fighting should the enemy satisfy one's just cause, by seeking only a just peace, and by maintaining love and charity toward the enemy.

Limiting oneself to pursuit of the just cause means that the belligerent may not add other objectives to his war goals, over and above those that justified initiating the war. For instance, a belligerent may go to war to repel an attack and to drive the invader out of his country. The defense and subsequent counterattack may be so successful that the original defender finds he can conquer a significant portion of the enemy country.

Just this situation occurred in Korea in 1951, with the North Korean armies not just halted and expelled from South Korea, but defeated utterly and put to rout. The objectives of the UN forces under General MacArthur were then expanded to include not just defense of South Korea but reunification of all of Korea. As it turned out this could not be accomplished without the defeat of the People's Republic of China, which had entered the war; and the effort necessary to do that was well beyond anything the United States and its allies were willing to undertake. The point, however, is not that expanding the goals widened the war (although that did happen), but that expanding the goals may have violated the criterion of right intention.

At the outset of the war, defending South Korea was definitely a just cause, but reunifying Korea did not seem part of the just cause because it would be too costly to free the North Koreans from their communist rulers. When suddenly the reunification of Korea appeared to be within the grasp of the UN forces, the goals were changed. As later events proved, the initial judgment was correct. Reunification was too costly to be justifiable.

Even had the expanded goal in Korea turned out to be realizable, however, the criterion of right intention might have been violated. In general, a belligerent should retain, throughout the war, the intention to pursue only the just cause for which the war was initiated. Broadening the war goals in response to events during the war may allow opportunism (if the war goes well) or desire for revenge (if the war goes badly) to lead the belligerent to turn an originally just war into an unjust one.

Pursuing a just and lasting peace means that the belligerent may not undertake actions that will unnecessarily increase the destruction of the war, or that will lead to lasting bitterness on the part of the enemy nationals, or that will appear so harsh as to prolong the war beyond what would be required to satisfy the just cause. The bishops specifically noted "unconditional surrender" as violating this element of right intention (1983, no. 95).

Even so, the distinction between waging a just war and waging a war justly is still valid. Lack of right intention violates the former, not the latter.

Unconditional surrender was the declaratory policy of the Allies in
World War II. We need not enter into a complete analysis of the reasons
for and against this policy. We can simply note that it prolonged the war
against Germany because it gave no hope of better terms from a conditional surrender that could be achieved sooner. The unconditional
surrender policy was not really applied to Italy, and it was ultimately
abandoned in the case of Japan, although it probably prolonged the war
before it was abandoned.

In 1944 a group of German officers attempted a coup, which was to
include the assassination of Hitler. The assassination attempt failed, and
the plotters were shot. Suppose, however, that the coup had succeeded
in killing Hitler. What terms might we have offered less drastic than
unconditional surrender? Had we from the beginning offered terms less
harsh than unconditional surrender, it is entirely possible that other attempts to overthrow the Nazi government would have been made and
might even have been successful.

What was the cost of prolonging the war against Germany? The cost
certainly included war casualties in the armies on both sides, as well as
civilian casualties from city busting air attacks, and civilian casualties in
the regions fought over. However, there was another important cost.

In 1945 the advancing American armies liberated several Nazi extermination camps. Thousands of Jews, Gypsies, Poles, and other
prisoners—walking skeletons, most of them—were saved from the
death that had already taken over ten million camp inmates, and would
have taken them within a few weeks. A conditional surrender at the
time of the attempted coup would have emptied the death camps a
whole year earlier, saving possibly a million or more innocent lives.

As it turned out, the policy of unconditional surrender did not actually keep us from obtaining a peace that has been just and that has lasted
for over forty years with the Federal Republic of Germany, with Italy,
and with Japan. However, this was a piece of good fortune, due primarily to the fact that we did not actually pursue the vengeance that was
implicit in the demand for unconditional surrender. We did not actually
carry out the Morgenthau Plan, for instance, which called for the total
deindustrialization of Germany.

Maintaining charity and love toward the enemy has implications for
modern war. During World War II Allied propaganda painted an evil
picture not just of the Axis leaders but of the German, Italian, and Japanese people. Allied government leaders considered this propaganda
necessary to keep their nations fighting vigorously. During the Vietnam conflict, the U.S. government made a deliberate policy decision
not to "crank up the propaganda machine" against the North Vietnam-

ese, out of fear that the resulting war spirit would make the American people demand unconditional surrender instead of accepting a negotiated peace.[2] The well-recognized power of propaganda means that using it to stir up hatred of the enemy would be a violation of this element of right intention.

It clearly will be difficult to maintain continuously a charitable attitude toward those who are conducting a war against us, possibly committing atrocities against our allies and our own people, and quite possibly not conforming to Just War Doctrine in the way they fight against us. However, important as interior attitude is from a Christian perspective, it is not the sole issue. Of at least equal importance is that *actions* toward the enemy be charitable. One must treat the enemy charitably even though one feels like killing every one of them slowly and painfully.

At this point it might be asked, how can it be charitable to wound and kill enemy soldiers? Saint Augustine answers that in his letter to Publicola, a professional soldier:

> Do not think that it is impossible for anyone to please God while engaged in active military service. . . . Think, then, of this first of all, when you are arming for the battle, that even your bodily strength is a gift of God; for, considering this, you will not employ the gift of God against God. . . . Peace should be the object of your desire; war should be waged only as a necessity, and waged only that God may by it deliver men from the necessity and preserve them in peace. . . . Therefore, even in waging war, cherish the spirit of a peace-maker, that, by conquering those whom you attack, *you may lead them back to the advantages of peace.* . . . Let necessity, therefore, and not your will, slay the enemy who fights against you (quoted in Fremantle, 1953, pp. 124–126, emphasis added).

The charity comes in leading the unjust enemy back to the ways of justice. Wounding or killing the enemy soldier is to be done only to the extent necessary to carry out this return to justice. It is not to be done out of vengeance or cruelty.

It is clear that maintaining right intention is psychologically difficult. To some it will sound utterly unrealistic. Nevertheless, the Just War Doctrine holds that a belligerent must maintain the intention to pursue

---

[2] This policy, while well intentioned, was carried too far. The failure of the government to inform the American people about what the issues were left the field clear for enemy propaganda and pacifist sentiments. The harsh rule imposed by the North Vietnamese on South Vietnam, followed by the exodus of hundreds of thousands of boat people, was the price ultimately paid for failure to convince the American people of the justice of the South Vietnamese cause. Fortunately for the American war protestors, the price was paid not by them but by the South Vietnamese people.

a *just peace* if the war he wages is to be a *just war*. It is worth remembering, in this regard, that during this century we have seen nations that were our allies become our enemies, and our enemies become our allies. In the case of China, the cycle has been complete: ally to enemy to de facto ally. A war waged without right intention is very unlikely to lead to reconciliation between enemies.

Having said this about right intention, what else must be said regarding a war between the United States and the Soviet Union, fought with nuclear weapons?

First, consider the Gulag Archipelago. Emptying the Gulag would be an act of humanitarianism to dwarf utterly the liberation of Nazi extermination camps. The Nazi camps resulted in the death of approximately twelve million people in total. The Gulag has in the past held that many people *at one time*.

Nevertheless, emptying the Gulag would not be a cause sufficient for a just war. Therefore, should the United States be forced to defend itself against the Soviet Union, its right intention must be limited to defense. Emptying the Gulag may not be part of the intention. If achieved at all, it must be considered a bonus from a just war justly waged. Moreover, if even as humanitarian an act as emptying the Gulag would exceed the bounds of right intention, actions such as securing the liberties of Soviet subjects would be even more outside the bounds of right intention.

Second, since just cause would be limited to defense, a policy of unconditional surrender would violate right intention. The intention of the United States must be to halt the aggression and achieve some assurance that the same aggression will not recur. The intention cannot include the overthrow of the Soviet government, much less the conquest of the Soviet Union. Therefore a policy of unconditional surrender would violate right intention. It would probably also preclude victory, as discussed in the preceding chapter, but that is simply one more count against it.

Third, right intention means we must intend only to thwart and blunt the Soviets' attack upon us. We may not seek revenge, *no matter what kind of attack they have carried out*. That is, we may not retaliate for a deliberate nuclear attack on our cities with a deliberate nuclear attack on their cities.[3]

Thus, once more we reach the conclusion that to remain just, a war fought with nuclear weapons must remain *limited*. In this case, the lim-

---

[3] More will be said in the chapters on discrimination and proportion regarding intention and attacks on targets within cities. The point here is that we may not *intend* to attack the civilians in the cities themselves, not even in revenge for intentional Soviet city-busting attacks.

its are placed on our *intentions*, and upon the *actions* we take in carrying out those intentions. Our intentions must be limited to the restoration of a just peace, and our actions must be consonant with those intentions. So long as we maintain those limits on our intentions, however, there is nothing about nuclear weapons which would make our use of them inevitably violate "right intention".

REFERENCES

Augustine. "To Publicola". In *A Treasury of Early Christianity*, edited by Anne Fremantle. New York: New American Library, 1953, pp. 124–126.

Batchelder, Robert C. *The Irreversible Decision*. Boston: Houghton Mifflin Co., 1962.

O'Brien, William V. *The Conduct of Just and Limited War*. New York: Praeger Publishers, 1981.

CHAPTER EIGHTEEN

LAST RESORT

The Just War Doctrine, starting from a presumption against war, teaches that even though a war may stem from a just cause and may be fought with right intention, it still should not be waged unless peaceful alternatives have first been exhausted. What does this mean, in the context of nuclear war?

With the establishment of the United Nations, many scholars argued that collective security, backed up by international enforcement, would satisfy the needs of nations for redress of injustices. A nation that took up arms without first attempting to settle a dispute by negotiation or arbitration would be by definition an aggressor. O'Brien notes that there are three problems with the idea of peaceful settlement using international peacekeeping machinery. First, nations are unwilling to put their vital interests at stake in such methods. Second, some differences are irreconcilable. Third, there is no recognized center to which to take international disputes. We need to examine each of these problems in order to determine how this Just War criterion applies to nuclear war.

Nations are unwilling to put their vital interests at stake because, in many cases, they recognize that calling something a court doesn't make it a court. Nations that have a tradition of impartial courts dispensing justice evenhandedly will refuse to entrust their vital interests to judges whose background involves settling cases according to theological or ideological criteria (for example, the Leninist doctrine that whatever advances the revolution is moral). By the same token, nations that are accustomed to judging questions by ideological or theological criteria will be unwilling to entrust their vital interests to judges who refuse to consider those criteria (for example, judges who would concede rights to class enemies or who would put unbelievers on the same moral plane as believers). In short, the problem with subjecting disputes to arbitration is that the very definition of justice differs from one nation to another. A nation will not submit its vital interests to a tribunal that is by definition biased against it.

The existence of irreconcilable differences is another barrier to peaceful resolution. There is no way, for instance, that the division of Korea or the status of Taiwan relative to mainland China can be resolved by peaceful negotiation between the two parties. In the two cases, neither party recognizes the other's right to exist. These same difficulties prevented peaceful settlement of the division of Vietnam and, as of this writing, continue to prevent peaceful settlement of the war in Nicaragua. At best, negotiation under such circumstances can lead only to some temporary resolution of the fundamental conflict. As O'Brien observes (1981, p. 32): "The Vietnam experience shows how utterly ephemeral such peaceful solutions may be if one side has the power and will to take it all." The fundamental problem in the case of irreconcilable differences is that there is no way to negotiate your own death, and when that is what the other side wants, there is nothing about which to negotiate. Hence to require that "all peaceful means" be exhausted before going to war in your own defense is futile.

The third problem amounts to the question of how do you know when you have exhausted all peaceful means? What is the sequence of international organizations to which you must submit your case before you reach the court of last resort? The fact is simply that there is none. The UN, in particular, has been a dismal failure as a means of finding peaceful solutions where vital interests are at stake. Nor is this a surprise. No one in his right mind would submit a vital interest to as irresponsible an institution as the UN. As O'Brien puts it (1981, p. 33):

> The United Nations . . . has always been a political organization to the extent that a state in the political minority could plausibly argue that it could not receive justice if it submitted to the jurisdiction of UN institutions.

What can we conclude about "peaceful resolution" with regard to use of nuclear weapons? We reach the discouraging conclusion that on the issues likely to be important enough to lead to use of nuclear weapons, *there are no peaceful means of resolution*.[1] If the aggressor intends to push the matter, on an issue where the differences are irreconcilable, there is nothing to negotiate. The defender is faced with a demand that amounts to "commit suicide or I'll kill you". Moreover, because of the risk that the defender might make a preemptive strike in the face of such a demand, the demand itself is unlikely to be made. Instead, the aggressor will *wage* war, not wait to *declare* it. Once the aggressor's tanks are rolling, and his warheads falling, there is no longer anything to negotiate. Negotiations can take place in such circumstances only if the aggression

---

[1] It may be objected that if I reject the UN, the World Court, and other similar institutions, I am obliged to suggest something better. But this objection misses the point. I am not obliged to offer to cook a better batch of soup before I am entitled to point out that the present batch is rotten. Unfortunate as it may be, there is no means available today for reaching a just settlement of unreconcilable differences. Until such a just means exists, limited nuclear war in defense against aggression remains legitimate.

can be contained or thwarted. Then the negotiations will be concerned only with cease-fire conditions, not with resolving the differences that brought on the war in the first place. The several wars involving Israel and the surrounding Arab states illustrate this case well. Even though they have not involved nuclear weapons, the survival of Israel has been the sole issue. So long as this is the sole issue, negotiations can involve only cease-fire lines and deployment of forces near them, and negotiations will begin only after the attack (by whichever side) has been halted.

In short, if the defender has satisfied the Just Cause criterion, which allows only defensive wars, the Last Resort criterion is not restrictive at all. In today's world it simply does not bind in the case of otherwise just wars involving nuclear weapons.

REFERENCES

O'Brien, William V. *The Conduct of Just and Limited War*. New York: Praeger Publishers, 1981.

CHAPTER NINETEEN

COMPETENT AUTHORITY

The idea behind this Just War criterion is that war should be declared only by those who have the right to do so. Saint Thomas Aquinas laid down the requirement thus:

> A private individual may not declare war; for he can have recourse to the judgment of a superior to safeguard his rights. Nor has he the right to mobilize the people, which is necessary in war. But since responsibility for public affairs is entrusted to the rulers, it is they who are charged with the defense of the city, realm, or province, subject to them.

Aquinas then quotes Augustine saying that:

> The natural order of men, to be peacefully disposed, requires that the power and decision to declare war should lie with the rulers (quoted in O'Brien, 1981, p. 17).

This rule was originally intended to prevent private wars. With the development of the nation-state, that intent has become obsolete. However, the criterion still has important consequences in the modern world.

Democratic states, in particular, often have constitutional provisions specifying how war may be declared. If these provisions are violated, then the war may be unjust in its lack of a declaration by competent authority.[1]

From the standpoint of justly fighting a nuclear war, the requirement for competent authority poses problems in three areas: the survival of competent authority long enough to declare war; the problems of communicating the decision to go to war; and the problems of controlling the use of nuclear weapons, that is, of preventing unauthorized use and of maintaining control by competent authority of actual use.

The problem of preventing unauthorized use of nuclear weapons was recognized from the beginning of the nuclear age; the other two prob-

---

[1] One interesting issue, which cannot be explored here, is whether tyrants have the competence to declare a just war. Does a ruler who has no accountability to his subjects, and who rules them without their consent, possess the authority to order them to go to war? Some writers on Just War Doctrine have argued that revolutionary war against a tyrant may be justified because the tyrant has lost the right to govern. An implication of this is that the tyrant lacks the authority to declare war. (Walzer specifically addresses this issue: 1977, pp. 82, 88–100).

lems were recognized only later, once it became apparent that the enemy's first target would be one's own nuclear striking forces and command structure, not one's cities.

The United States has addressed the problem of preventing unauthorized use of nuclear weapons by two approaches. Nuclear weapons utilized by the Air Force and the Army, and by carrier-based Navy aircraft, contain what is known as a *Permissive Action Link,* or PAL. This is a device into which the weapon operator must insert a coded number. If the number does not match the proper code built into the PAL, the weapon will not function. The codes are released to aircraft crews and to missile launch crews by higher authority as part of the process of authorizing use of nuclear weapons. The PAL means that a missile or aircraft crew cannot, on their own initiative, cause a nuclear explosion, even if they do launch a missile or drop a bomb.

Ballistic missiles launched from submarines do not have a PAL. This is because the process of launching a missile requires a large fraction of the submarine crew to participate. While the pilot of a one-man aircraft can drop a bomb on his own initiative, it would be impossible for one or a few submarine crew members to launch a missile by themselves. The fact that many people must be involved in launching a missile from a submarine is considered by U.S. government officials to provide sufficient safeguards against unauthorized launch.

Some critics of U.S. command-and-control (C & C) systems, such as Daniel Ford, have argued that submarine-launched missiles should also incorporate PALs, since at present a submarine crew acting on its own could launch the vessel's entire complement of missiles, carrying at least forty-eight warheads, without authorization from the President (1985, p. 119). That large a number of nuclear explosions on Soviet territory would almost certainly bring retaliation, in effect starting a war without competent authority.

Strangely enough, however, the critics who argue in favor of equipping submarine missiles with PALs also argue that a robust C & C system is not required for deterrence, since the submarine-launched missiles could achieve "revenge from the grave" no matter what the Soviets did to our government and its communications system (Ford, 1985, p. 46). These critics fail to explain how revenge from the grave is to be achieved if the submarine's missiles are equipped with PALs, and the Soviets destroy the communications system by which the weapons release codes must be transmitted. The very essence of the submarine missile force as the *invulnerable deterrent* requires that it be able to act even when the President is incapacitated. The submarine force is in effect *authorized in advance* to retaliate when competent authority is unable to act. Without that authority, the effectiveness of the deterrent threat is greatly reduced.[2] The ability to act in such circumstances, however, carries with it the risk (however slight) that nuclear weapons may be used without authorization.

This leads to the problem of survival of competent authority. This problem is now recognized as serious. There are two aspects to this problem.

The first of these aspects is that the Soviets may succeed in carrying out a "decapitating" strike against the United States. An attack on Washington, for instance, could eliminate the President, the Vice President, all the cabinet officers, and most congress members and senators. There are legal provisions for succession to the presidency, but in the wake of an attack, the official who would legally succeed to the office of President may well be several levels down the line of succession. He may not be certain that everyone ahead of him has been killed and he is now in charge. Those who should obey his orders may likewise be uncertain that he has actually reached the head of the line. Finally, even if he and everyone else is certain that he is the new President, he will not be on top of the situation to the same degree the late President was. He may be under pressure to "do something" while there is yet time to do anything. He may feel he has no choice but to authorize one of the retaliatory options prepared for the late President, or even to agree to whatever his (surviving) military advisers tell him must be done. All of which is to say that the person who has the *authority* may in an important sense not be *competent* to make a decision about going to war.

The second aspect of the problem of survival of competent authority is that even if the president himself survives, whatever decisions he makes may have to be made in a very short time. In the event of a Soviet nuclear attack on the United States, for instance, there simply would be no time to assemble the Congress and ask for a declaration of war. A state of war would have to be accepted, and the war waged, without satisfying Constitutional requirements. From the standpoint of other Just War criteria, this problem may not be particularly important, since a war of self-defense in response to an attack automatically satisfies the *jus ad bellum* requirements, including competent authority. Nevertheless, the lack of time to seek authority and/or approval for war activities does present a problem that should not be overlooked.

---

[2] This argument ignores the moral issues involved in the usual deterrent threat of retaliation on cities. However, those who support minimum deterrence while demanding PALs on submarine-launched missiles are in general also opponents of acquiring a nuclear war-fighting capability.

There is then the problem of communicating the decision to go to war, and linked to this, the problem of passing on orders about how the war is to be waged. Ford claims the problem of communicating the decision to go to war is a serious one for U.S. forces.

[A]ccording to several recent Pentagon studies, it may be very hard to find *any* working communications circuits once Soviet bombs have begun to fall on U.S. soil. This will be an especially severe problem if—as seems likely to the Pentagon—the key U.S. military command posts and message-relay stations are the highest priority targets of a major Soviet attack. In that case, the President will be put in the difficult position of having to make an extremely fast decision. . . . If he does not give the orders quickly, he may not be able to give them at all (1985, p. 22) (emphasis in original).

The number of warheads the Soviets would have to deliver to achieve this may be fairly small. Steinbruner provides a figure of at most one hundred, and possibly less than fifty (1981–82, pp. 16–28). Ford states that studies by Desmond Ball, an Australian defense specialist, and by the Pentagon, conclude that at most fifty Soviet warheads would be required to disable the entire U.S. command and control system (1985, p. 40).

The other part of this problem of communicating orders about *how* the war is to be fought is also a serious one. Ford points out that:

It is simply not possible to provide absolute central control over the multitude of actions that a complex military machine is programmed to carry out once it is put into action. The lesson of all this is that once a crisis turns into a strategic alert, once the safety catches that are on in peacetime begin to be taken off, a confrontation can become so volatile that its outcome may be out of the control of leaders on either side (1985, p. 51).

This can lead to difficulties not only in trying to keep the war under control, but in bringing it to a halt. Ford notes that:

Neither side may have the ability, while carrying on negotiations, to keep its own forces under control—for example, to prevent isolated submarine commanders from lashing out at the other side (1985, p. 166).

This problem of communication and control is of course not unique to nuclear war. Barbara Tuchman relates an incident that took place on August 1, 1914, in which a telephone order from the Kaiser to the Sixteenth Division, to hold up its advance into Luxembourg pending a reply from the British regarding their neutrality, was delayed in transmission, and arrived half an hour after the attack had started, thereby making British participation inevitable (1962, pp. 79–82).[3] However, the problem is particularly serious for nuclear war, because it directly threatens the requirement for competent authority to make the decision for war or peace, and to give the proper commands if the decision is for war.

The problem is not intrinsically unsolvable. Ford (1985) notes that the Soviet Union has paid much more attention to preserving the ability of competent authority to operate despite a nuclear attack than has the United States:

> The Soviets have a very different command system, one that has been extensively hardened to operate after a U.S. first strike. It is much less sophisticated in many ways, but has other features—such as a large network of underground facilities to protect Soviet leadership, and highly redundant communications systems—that make it far less vulnerable to disruption (p. 44).

By contrast, the U.S. C & C system has been neglected.

> The military's command-system machinery was installed in the 1950s and 1960s, and it has been left largely unchanged despite knowledge of its pronounced vulnerability to the kind of Soviet attack that would now be expected at the outset of a nuclear war (p. 16).

The vulnerability of the U.S. command-and-control system is to some extent deliberate. Bracken notes that when the Strategic Air Command underground headquarters was built in 1957, "it was only thirty feet underground. Even a small, inaccurate Soviet nuclear weapon could have destroyed it" (1983, p. 186). He suggests that the U.S. leadership failed to harden the headquarters because of the implicit recognition that once SAC had been launched, the SAC headquarters had no further function. It was left vulnerable because it was assumed that nuclear war would be a one-shot spasm.

Similarly, when plans were being made to harden the North American Air Defense Command (NORAD) underground command center, Bracken notes that SAC opposed the move (1983, p. 187). In SAC's view, once NORAD performed its function of giving SAC the warning needed to launch the bombers, NORAD had fulfilled its function

---

[3] The problem is not unique to the 1914 era. In the early 1960s, while stationed in Thailand, I worked on communications problems of U.S. forces located in that country. One day I was shown a message that had taken over twenty-four hours to travel from the Pentagon to its destination. By the time it had arrived, it had been bypassed by events. This delay occurred despite the fact that the message had been sent at a very high priority, only one level below that used for notifying U.S. forces of the outbreak of war.

and its survival was no longer important. In 1965 NORAD was eventually moved *inside* (rather than *under*) Cheyenne Mountain, in Colorado, but remained vulnerable to weapons such as the fifty-megaton warhead the Soviets tested in the 1960s. Moreover, the telephone lines that connected it to the rest of the world were even more vulnerable.

The vulnerability of C & C links to nuclear attack has led some to doubt the possibility of maintaining the control needed to wage a nuclear war. Richard Garwin, prominent critic of the U.S. Defense Department, has stated:

> After there have been many, many nuclear explosions in the United States, it is, in my opinion, fantasy—even a greater fantasy than before war starts—to imagine that you're going to have a capability for conduct of limited nuclear war, of flexible response, or sizing up what has happened and using your weapons efficiently. . . . How can we have a good old protracted nuclear war if we can't get the information as to what's happening and can't command the forces, and so on? (quoted in Ford, 1985, p. 104).

Garwin's opinion cannot of course be taken as definitive. It may represent nothing more than the fallacy of the argument from incompetence: "I don't see how to do it, therefore it can't be done." Nevertheless, it raises an important issue. The Just War criterion of competent authority cannot be satisfied if it is impossible to provide the necessary C & C arrangements for making the decision to go to war, and for directing the war once the decision is made.

Moreover, there is a problem in addition to the issue of hardening the command and control system. The thrust of Bracken's whole book is that our C & C system has been built largely from the bottom up rather than from the top down. It has an implicit strategy built into it, just as the inadequately hardened SAC and NORAD headquarters have built into them the implicit strategy of nuclear spasm. The implicit strategy built into our C & C system is one of reacting promptly to a Soviet attack, according to one of a fairly small number of pre-planned options.

The major difficulty with this implicit and built-in strategy is that it was not designed to support a national strategy developed by our responsible political leaders. Instead it was developed piecemeal, as the aggregated result of thousands of individual decisions by hundreds of individual "nuclear war planners" who, over the years, have worked on strategic targeting at SAC headquarters and the Pentagon. If we should be attacked, even if the President and the C & C system survive, the President may find that his options are severely limited because the system was designed only to transmit his selection from a limited menu of options, options that he had no part in developing and that may be completely unresponsive to whatever strategy he might wish to implement. Thus, even though a limited nuclear war can satisfy the Just War criteria considered in the preceding chapters, the competent authority criterion might pinch very sharply. Even if it were the case that with adequate C & C systems a nation *could* justly conduct a limited nuclear war, a nation *without* such systems might very well violate the Just War criterion of competent authority if it tried to wage a limited nuclear war.

In evaluating nuclear war according to Just War Doctrine, then, two issues need to be addressed. The first is whether it is intrinsically impossible to devise a C & C system that would function adequately during limited nuclear war. This is an empirical issue, not one which can be settled by theoretical discussion. If it should turn out there is no way to do it, however, then a just nuclear war would be ruled out by this criterion. The second issue is whether a particular country has sufficiently prepared itself to fight a just nuclear war by deploying an adequate C & C system. If a nation has not properly prepared itself it is incapable of conducting a just nuclear war.

REFERENCES

Bracken, Paul. *The Command and Control of Nuclear Forces*. New Haven: Yale University Press, 1983.

Ford, Daniel. *The Button*. New York: Simon & Schuster, 1985.

O'Brien, William V. *The Conduct of Just and Limited War*. New York: Praeger Publishers, 1981.

Steinbruner, John D. "Nuclear Decapitation". *Foreign Policy,* no. 45 (Winter 1981–82), pp. 16–28.

Tuchman, Barbara. *The Guns of August*. New York: Macmillan Publishing Co., Inc., 1962.

Walzer, Michael. *Just and Unjust Wars*. New York: Basic Books, 1977.

CHAPTER TWENTY

DISCRIMINATION

The Just War criteria we have considered in the preceding chapters have all dealt with *jus ad bellum*, the conditions which must be satisfied before going to war. *Discrimination* is a purely *jus in bello* criterion. It deals with conduct in a war. By failing this criterion, even a war that was justly entered can be waged unjustly.

The principle of discrimination means that one may not licitly make attacks in which noncombatants are *directly intended* to be killed. The words *directly* and *intended* have specific technical meanings in Just War Doctrine, which we will analyze in detail later in this chapter. Before taking that up, however, we will first take up the issue of who is a combatant, and therefore a legitimate target.

The primary moral consideration behind the principle of discrimination is expressed by the American Catholic bishops as (1983, no. 104):

> . . . the lives of innocent persons may never be taken directly, regardless of the purpose alleged for doing so. . . . Just response to aggression must be discriminate; it must be directed against unjust aggressors, not against innocent people caught up in a war not of their making.

The primary problem posed by the principle of discrimination in today's world is, "Who is innocent? Who among the enemy citizens is not a part of the war effort?"

Moralists usually begin their lists of the innocent with children, and then add the elderly, neither of whom, they allege, can be considered as contributing to the war effort. However, during World War II, I was merely one of many thousands of children who collected newspapers and scrap metal in formally-organized paper drives and scrap metal drives. Moreover, almost every American war has had its grandmothers who knitted socks or made bandages for the troops. These activities by both children and elderly were not simply continuations of peacetime activities. They would not have taken place except for the war, and they were intended as contributions to the war effort. Hence it cannot be argued that children and the elderly make *no* contribution to the war effort. Is their contribution sufficient to make them combatants?

The problem goes well beyond children and the elderly who aid the war effort within their limited capabilities. The claim is often made that in a modern economy, in which everyone is linked together, there is no one who does not in some sense participate in the war effort. The American Catholic bishops noted this problem in their pastoral (1983, no. 108):

> Mobilization of forces in modern war includes not only the military, but to a significant degree the political, economic, and social sectors. It is not always easy to determine who is directly involved in a "war effort" or to what degree.

What might be called the *bellicist* position (as opposed to *pacifist*) is simple: "They're all guilty." This, in effect, was the position adopted by the U.S. and British governments during World War II. The obliteration bombing of German and Japanese cities not only made no distinction between combatant and noncombatant, between innocent and guilty; it was not intended to make a distinction. The civilians supported the enemy war effort; they were therefore legitimate targets. In a condition of total war, everyone participated.[1]

Walzer quotes Marc Bloch, who wrote in *Strange Defeat* about the French collapse of 1940:

> Confronted by the nation's peril and by the duties that it lays on every citizen, all adults are equal and only a curiously warped mind would claim for any of them the privilege of immunity. What, after all, is a "civilian" in time of war? He is nothing more than a man whose weight of years, whose health, whose profession . . . prevent him from bearing arms effectively. . . . Why should [these factors] confer on him the right to escape the common danger? (1977, p. 144).[2]

Today it would be difficult to find many who accepted this view of universal guilt among the enemy. In discussions of possible war between the United States and the Soviet Union, the argument one hears today is that not only may one not licitly target Soviet cities as such, one may not even use nuclear weapons against genuine military targets in those cities *because the cities are full of innocents*. This is, for instance, the position of the American Catholic bishops, as shown by the quotations in Chapter 4. In essence, then, the bellicist position has been rejected.

---

[1] As was shown in Chapter 2, not all the bombing of German and Japanese cities was "obliteration" bombing. Most of the daylight bombing, and even some of the nighttime bombing, was genuinely precision bombing that was aimed at, and succeeded in hitting, specific targets. However, an enormously large fraction of the total tonnage of bombs was deliberately dropped with the intent of burning out the cities. This is what is referred to as "obliteration" bombing.

[2] Walzer quotes Bloch here only to refute him; he does not agree with Bloch's position.

But not completely rejected. Instead, a mirror image of it has been adopted with regard to our own people. Consider the argument made by Bishop Hunthausen, already quoted in Chapter 4:

> I was moved to speak out against Trident, because it is being based here. We must take special responsibility for what is in our own back yard. And when crimes are being prepared in our own name, we must speak plainly.

In Bishop Hunthausen's view, all Americans in the Seattle area are liable for what goes on in their name. Presumably this includes children and other nonvoters, not just those who took part in elections that resulted in appropriations for Trident submarines and missiles.

Markus (1961) has expressed the same view:

> Modern war is socially a complex phenomenon. Too many administrative decisions and too many phases of their execution are involved for it to be possible for any one involved in its machinery to claim that he is only doing "his bit", "let the other chaps look to what they are doing". Genuine ignorance of the total effect to which a man's individual action is a contribution may excuse obedience. But when I am knowingly taking part in organized evil-doing, I cannot plead that the blame is to be attached to the last link in the chain. In joining the gang, I have given it my support. . . (p. 79).

> In modern war, responsibility must be accepted for all that is not antecedently, clearly and publicly ruled out, by any one who in any way participates in its waging (p. 81).

> Even the farm-labourer behind whose willingness to carry on with his job is concealed a willingness "to do his bit in the war", is morally, compromised. He is a party to the crime being committed (p. 82).

Gollancz expressed the same view (1959, p. 21):

> Every Englishman is inescapably responsible for what his rulers of the moment may either do or fail to do in his name. . . .

Although the bellicists and the pacifists have different objectives, they use the same logic. The bellicist wants to implicate everyone on the other side to justify bombing them. The pacifist wants to implicate everyone on our side to justify laying guilt on all of us. Ironically, if we accept the conclusions of the pacifist about our own implication in whatever is done in our name, we must accept the conclusions of the bellicist about the complicity of everyone on the enemy side.

Markus recognized this problem, despite his efforts to implicate us all in the guilt:

> We have already encountered the difficulty of drawing a line between combatants and non-combatants when we were trying to discover the moral justification for the use of weapons capable of large-scale though not indiscriminate killing. . . . We are now faced with this same question in reverse: how can we draw the line between combatants and non-combatants in our own camp? . . . The answer to this question is not completely clear. The reason for this is the same as the reason for the difficulty of drawing a precise line between combatant and non-combatant earlier: it lies in the complex nature of a society geared to total war. . . . (1961, p. 81).

To accept the shared logic of the bellicists and the pacifists would make things easy. We would not need to concern ourselves with discriminating between the innocent and the guilty among the Soviet people; there would be no discrimination to make. However, this is a false escape from the problem. Just War Doctrine insists that there *is* a distinction, and we *must* make it, hard though it may be to do so. The American Catholic bishops were not able to draw the line between combatants and noncombatants precisely, but they had no doubt there was a line, and that some people were unquestionably on the noncombatant side of it (1983, no. 108):

> . . . not even by the broadest definition can one rationally consider combatants entire classes of human beings such as school-children, hospital patients, the elderly, the ill, the average industrial worker producing goods not directly related to military purposes, farmers, and many others. They may never be directly attacked.[3]

Father John Ford, in 1944, attempted to make an empirical distinction between combatants and noncombatants with regard to the morality of the British and American bombing campaigns against Germany. This was the first serious attempt to apply the criterion of discrimination to a bombing campaign. Unfortunately, it was apparently also the last. Everything since then has amounted to nothing but theoretical arguments.

Ford did not question the justice of the war against Nazi Germany. On the contrary, he accepted the justice of the war itself. His subject was solely the issue of attacks against cities, using high explosive and

---

[3] Note the contrast between the bishops' position and that of Markus, who definitely included farm workers among those implicated in the war effort.

incendiary bombs, which were intended not to destroy specific industrial or military targets, but to destroy the cities themselves and kill
their inhabitants. He expressed the issue as: "The principal moral problem raised by obliteration bombing, then, is that of the rights of noncombatants to their lives in war time" (1944, p. 269). Walzer, in arguing
against Bloch, made the same point. The issue is not that noncombatants in some mysterious way *gain* an immunity against attack which
their fellow-citizen combatants lack, but rather that they *retain* the immunity against attack that is "a feature of normal human relationships"
(1977, p. 145). It is the combatants who *lose* this normal immunity by
taking up arms and thereby posing a threat to other people.

Ford quotes numerous leading figures in the British and American
governments who had declared, in so many words, that the actual intention of the attacks was the destruction of civilian housing and the
deaths of civilians. With regard to this being a necessary feature of modern or total war, he goes on to say:

> If anyone were to declare that modern war is necessarily total, and neces-
> sarily involves direct attack on the life of innocent civilians, my reply
> would be: So much the worse for modern war. If it necessarily includes
> such means, it is necessarily immoral itself (1944, p. 268).

Arguing that one may legitimately target only those enemy subjects
who actually contribute to the war effort in the sense of posing a threat
or enabling others to pose a threat, Ford then takes an empirical approach to the question of who actually contributes. He identified some
150 occupations (for example, "foresters, lumberjacks, dressmakers,
milliners," etc.) that carry out essentially the same activities in both
peace and war, and argued that to include these among "a nation in
arms" was simply incorrect. He then took census figures on total number of people in a typical U.S. industrial town (Worcester, Mass.);
within that total he took census figures on the number employed in industry; of those, he found the number estimated by the War Production
Board to be engaged in essential war production; and finally he concluded that at least two-thirds of the civilian population of the area had
to be counted as innocent, even by the broadest definition of *war worker*.
Applying the same reasoning to Germany, he concluded that at least
half the people in the cities subject to obliteration bombing were likewise "innocent" in the Just War sense. Targeting them intentionally
was unquestionably immoral under Just War Doctrine. His conclusion
was that obliteration bombing was clearly immoral.

Several popes, the Second Vatican Council, and the American Catholic bishops have agreed with this position in regard to the use of nuclear weapons against cities. Deliberate attacks against civilians are immoral under the Just War criterion of discrimination.

Having concluded that even in "modern" war, half or more of the population of the enemy nation is *not* a legitimate target and may not be deliberately attacked, we come to what is really the crucial part of the discrimination criterion. Is it forbidden to carry out an attack in which some innocent enemy subjects will be killed? No, it is not forbidden. Under Just War doctrine, one *may* licitly carry out an attack against a legitimate target, even if that means some innocent people will die.

The problem falls naturally into two parts. One of these deals with the number of innocents who may be killed before an otherwise just action becomes unjust. This is covered by the Just War criterion of proportion, which will be taken up in the next chapter. The other deals with the matter of what actions the attacker takes to discriminate between combatants and noncombatants. The remainder of this chapter will deal with this issue.

The criterion of discrimination means more than just that there is a distinction between combatants and noncombatants. It means the attacker must recognize this distinction and try to maintain it in practice.

Father Ford's condemnation of obliteration bombing was essentially based on the recognition that Allied obliteration raids made no attempt to maintain this distinction. An entire city was taken as a target, not just factories engaged in war production, or war-essential installations within the city. Residential districts were included in the "target area" in an attempt to deprive factories of workers.

In particular, Ford analyzed obliteration bombing using the tool of moral analysis that is essential to the criterion of discrimination: the Principle of Double Effect. This principle is employed when an action intended to produce a morally licit effect also produces a second effect that would be immoral to procure directly. The principle states that if the second, immoral, effect is not directly intended, it is licit to carry out the action (we defer until the next chapter the issue of the proportion between the moral and immoral effects). There are two conditions here—"directly" and "intended"—that must be examined separately.

To say we do not procure the immoral effect directly means the moral effect, the one we desire, must not *flow from* or be a *consequence of* the immoral effect. The relationship between the two effects must be as two roads branching from the same point, not as two successive links in a chain. If the moral effect is produced as a consequence of the immoral effect, then the action is immoral. One cannot justify an immoral action on the grounds that it has a moral outcome.

This brings up a related distinction—that between physical evil and moral evil. Physical evils—such as death, disease, pain, suffering, and sorrow—are part of the fallen human condition. They are inescapable in this "vale of tears". Moral evils, such as the deliberate killing of an innocent person, are not inescapably part of the human condition. They are always the result of someone's deliberate choice. A principle upheld firmly by the Catholic Church and by most other Christian denominations is that one may never commit even the slightest moral evil, no matter how much physical evil one might prevent by so doing.

The killing of combatants is a physical evil. It is something dreadful, which we may have the right to do in self-defense, and may even have the duty to do in defense of the defenseless. The killing of noncombatants is a moral evil, something that we never have the right to do. In particular, we may never deliberately kill noncombatants as a means of alleviating some physical evil, such as our own suffering. If we kill noncombatants at all, it must be as an indirect accompaniment of something we have a right to do.

The bombing of munitions factories, *and of only those factories,* would clearly be a licit action. One does not even need to invoke the Principle of Double Effect. The question Ford addressed was whether this principle could be applied to bombing the workers' homes in order to achieve the morally licit outcome of halting munitions production. He concluded that it could not. The deliberate bombing of residential districts, killing workers who did not even work in war industries, and killing wives, children, and elderly parents of workers regardless of where they worked, in an attempt to deprive the factories of workers, meant that the moral effect *followed from* the immoral effect. The effects represented links in a chain, not a fork in the road. It was a case of doing evil that good might come of it, and this was itself evil. By the same token, destroying an entire city with a nuclear weapon, in order not only to destroy the factories but to deprive rebuilt factories of workers, would be immoral.

To say that the immoral effect is not *intended* means that the immoral effect must be genuinely unwanted. It must not be part of our objective. It must be merely *permitted* in the situation. The issue of whether the immoral effect is *intended* is distinct from that of whether it is procured *directly,* because even though the two effects following from the same action may be independent of one another, we may actually want both of them. To want the immoral effect that comes along with the moral effect would render the whole action immoral.

We can pass quickly over the case when both effects are actually wanted. This is really a fraudulent attempt to use the Principle of Double Effect. From the standpoint of the criterion of discrimination, the important issue is, when can we say we genuinely do not want the second, immoral effect that comes along with the wanted, moral effect? In the case of bombers dropping bombs at random on a city, or bombing under conditions when the target cannot be seen clearly,[4] or especially when bombing workers' residential areas, can one claim that one does not really want the deaths of the civilians, but only the destruction of the factories and the disruption of production? Can the bomber, in Father Ford's words, "let go his bombs but withhold his intention"? (1944, p. 289). Father Ford argued that in the case of obliteration bombing of cities in Germany and Japan, this was not possible. Even if we were to ignore the statements of Allied leaders that their intention was to burn out all major German cities, the Principle of Double Effect could not properly be applied to such a case. In fact, Father Ford argued that in reality the good effect of halting war production was an incidental and indirect accompaniment of the evil effect of destroying a city and the civilians in it, not vice versa.

The same argument would apply today. We could not claim that, in obliterating a whole city with a nuclear weapon, the deaths of the innocent people were merely incidental and unwanted effects of the destruction of whatever legitimate military objectives existed in the city.

What do we have to do, then, to claim legitimately the Principle of Double Effect? What is necessary to allow us to say honestly that we intended to destroy a legitimate military target, that the destruction of the target did not flow from the deaths of the innocent people who happened to be nearby, and that we did not intend to kill those innocent people?

The issue of *directly* killing the innocent people is generally not a relevant one, so long as we are actually targeting a military objective, not the people themselves. To destroy a factory means to destroy the machinery in it and to make it unusable. To destroy a missile site means to destroy the equipment there, either missile or launcher. In neither case does the destruction of the hardware flow from the deaths of any innocent bystanders who were also killed when the factory or the missile site was attacked. If the bystanders were somehow removed to safety, the

---

[4] During the World War II bombing campaigns against Germany, particularly during the winter, it was common to bomb through a cloud cover, when navigation instruments indicated the bomber was over the "target" city. Under these circumstances, it was ridiculous to claim that the bombs were "aimed" at a factory or other point target. Today, with radar, bombing through clouds is not significantly less accurate than bombing in clear weather. Miss distances of thirty to forty feet can be achieved readily; even smaller miss distances can be achieved with some effort.

factory or the missile site would be destroyed with equal effectiveness. To argue that we have somehow used those innocent bystanders in destroying the legitimate target is a failure to apply Double Effect correctly.

The real problem in applying the criterion of discrimination arises from intention. O'Brien says, regarding the use of Double Effect:

> If . . . the attacker knows that there are noncombatants intermingled with combatants to the point that any attack on the military target is highly likely to kill or injure noncombatants, then the death or injury to those noncombatants is certainly "intended" or "deliberately willed", in the common usage of those words (1981, p. 47).

This is true. The problem is that we are not concerned with the *common* usage of the words, but with a *technical* usage.

An example often used by Catholic moralists will illustrate the point. In some rare cases, a human ovum is fertilized and starts to grow, not in the uterus, but in some other location such as the Fallopian tubes. This is called an *ectopic pregnancy*. The natural outcome of an ectopic pregnancy is rupture of the tubes, peritonitis, and often death for the mother. The medical response to an ectopic pregnancy is to remove the fetus surgically. Technically this is an abortion. The innocent fetus is killed.

Despite its firm stand against abortion, the Catholic Church has never had any problem accepting the licitness of surgically terminating an ectopic pregnancy. The reasoning goes as follows. The fetus is growing in a place it doesn't belong. The direct intent is to remove the abnormality. The good effect, saving the mother's life, does not flow from the death of the fetus but instead flows from correcting the abnormality. It is a case of a fork in the road, not of two links of a chain.

The death of the fetus is *foreseen* and, in the common usage of the word, is *intended*. But in the technical usage, appropriate to the Principle of Double Effect, the death is not *intended*. It is merely *permitted*. It is an unfortunate outcome resulting from the fact that we lack the technology to save the fetus after the operation. If that technology existed, *failure to use it* would change the situation. Then the death of the fetus would be *intended* in both the common and the technical senses.

Applying this same reasoning to the bombing case, it is entirely correct to say that the deaths of innocent bystanders around a legitimate military target were *unintended* even though *foreseen*. Those Catholics who argue that in killing these bystanders we are "using" them should be fully aware of what they are doing. They are rejecting the Principle of Double Effect. They could not approve of aborting an ectopic pregnancy, either.

However, we must be careful not to distort this principle so that it can justify any kind of killing of innocents which doesn't also violate proportion.

Consider a military unit advancing along a road through a valley. A lone sniper in the woods on a hillside brings the unit to a halt. The unit then calls in an air strike that blankets the entire hillside with napalm. The sniper is killed, but so is a refugee who is hiding there to avoid the battle. Probably this would not violate proportion, but most people would conclude it violated discrimination. One just doesn't burn down a whole woods to get a single sniper. It would be excessive use of force even if one had no reason to suspect there were innocent people in there. It would clearly be excessive if one had any reason to think there *might* be innocent people there. If one *knew* there were innocent people there, it would be impossible to say their deaths were "unintended" in the technical Just War sense.

Walzer suggests a practical approach to judging whether an action satisfies the criterion of discrimination. This is that the attacker attempt to minimize the damage done, and accept some degree of risk to himself in so doing. That is, the attacker accepts a risk that could be avoided by making an indiscriminate or more destructive attack (1977, p. 155). An attacker who did this would be demonstrating that he was attempting to be discriminating. In the case of aerial bombardment, being discriminating usually means flying lower, or more slowly, or on a straight course for a longer time, to make the attack more accurate. All of these measures, however, increase the risk to the air crew of being shot down. U.S. Air Force pilots sometimes joke about "adding 1000 feet for the wife and 500 feet for each child" to the attack altitude specified for a particular air-to-ground weapon in the munitions manuals. This additional altitude reduces the risk to the pilot, but increases the chances of missing the target and hitting an innocent bystander.

The conflict between risk to one's own forces, and risk to innocents among the enemy, is illustrated by the following two quotations. Robert Tucker quotes General Thomas Power, then CINCSAC, at hearings on defense appropriations:

> . . . I have a deep moral sense as it applies to Americans, and I get a little indignant with people who become very lofty in their thinking and do not want to kill a few of the enemy but would gladly risk additional American lives. My crews are more important to me than the enemy (1960, p. 88).

Michael Walzer quotes former French premier Pierre Mendes-France, who flew bomber missions against factories in Occupied France during World War II:

It was . . . this persistent question of bombing France itself which led us
to specialize more and more in precision bombing—that is, flying at a
very low altitude. It was more risky, but it also permitted greater precision . . . (1977, p. 157).

The two situations are not completely analogous. General Power was
talking about the risks his crews would have faced attacking targets in
an enemy nation; Mr. Mendes-France was concerned about the risks to
both French pilots and the Frenchmen around their targets. Both positions represent legitimate goals. The point is, they illustrate how one
can show that he is attempting to satisfy the criterion of discrimination
by accepting a higher degree of risk in order to avoid killing innocents.
We will return below to the issue of how much risk one should accept.

Next, however, we will return to another part of Walzer's means for
demonstrating that one is being discriminating: minimizing excess destruction. This usually involves one's selection of weapons, or more
broadly, of one's selection of the method of attack. For instance, instead
of napalming the hillside to clean out a sniper, one might send in a rifle
squad.[5] This selection of weapons and attack method more closely
matches the degree of force used with the task to be accomplished.[6]

Turning again to aerial bombardment, discrimination then means
not only taking some risks to deliver a weapon accurately, but sizing the
weapon to the target. The power of the weapon should be great enough
to destroy the target if it is hit directly. The power of the weapon may
even legitimately be great enough to destroy the target with a near miss.
It should not be so great, however, that even with a direct hit it still
destroys a lot of other things in addition to the target. That is, to be
discriminating, the power of the bomb should be sized to the hardness
of the target and the likelihood that some innocents nearby will be killed
even if the target is hit directly.

Sizing the bomb to the target increases the likelihood that the target
will not be destroyed, since there is some chance the bomb will miss.
Failing to destroy the target imposes risks on subsequent attackers who
have to go back again to do the job. It also increases the risks from the
additional damage the target does to our own side until it is finally destroyed (additional production from a factory, additional launches
from a missile site, etc.). Sizing the weapon to the target therefore

[5] One can imagine cases where the urgency of the mission is so great that the delay
while a rifle squad kills or captures the sniper would be too great; it would jeopardize
some vitally important objective. However, we are not considering such a case here.

[6] Note that the match is between the force used and the task to be accomplished, not
between one's own force and the enemy force. Nothing in the principle of discrimination
says one may not outnumber the enemy. All it says is that one may not extend the destruction beyond the legitimate target in carrying out the task.

means accepting risks, just as does attempting to deliver the weapon more accurately, although the risks are different.

Having determined what it means to be discriminating in war, we next take up the question of whether nuclear weapons can be used in a discriminating manner. If they cannot be so used, then nuclear war founders on this criterion.

We can begin with the case of an attack on a warship at sea, or on a military force in a desert area. Here there are no civilians about. There is no question but that everyone in the target area is a combatant and has, in Walzer's terms, lost his normal immunity against attack. A nuclear weapon, sized so that fallout on distant locations would be insignificant,[7] clearly could be used in a discriminating way.

Stein has responded to this example as follows:

> Then there is that "fleet at sea" (it is remarkable how this fleet keeps turning up in this connexion): one has to admit, "a certain type of nuclear bomb" *could* be used against it—and used with impressive efficiency—whilst remaining discriminate in its effects; though this still leaves the question how many of these fleets, or armies concentrating in deserts, perhaps, are likely to be about (1961, p. 35) (emphasis in original).

While Stein has, with masterful British understatement, homed in on the one limitation of the example, he still concedes that nuclear weapons are not *inherently* undiscriminating. When used in such a way as to avoid killing innocent bystanders, they fully satisfy the discrimination criterion.

Nuclear weapons can be made which have an explosive yield comparable to the largest high explosive weapons currently available.[8] A weapon could be designed that has just sufficient power to destroy a factory if that factory were hit directly. Therefore just as with any other weapon, if a nuclear weapon is sized properly, and aimed with due care, it can be used in a discriminating manner. The attacker will have to accept some additional risks, but these very risks are what demonstrate that the attack is a discriminating one.

Before we try to answer the question of how much risk the attacker is required to assume in order to satisfy the criterion of discrimination, we need to look at one more issue. Father Ford quotes statements made by the Catholic bishops of France and of Belgium, protesting against British and American attacks against targets in those countries (1944, p.

---

[7] How small does the fallout have to be to qualify as insignificant? This must be dealt with under the criterion of proportion.

[8] The fact that nuclear weapons can be made this small is bothersome to some, because they fear it will lead to the use of nuclear weapons becoming *thinkable*. We will take up this objection in a subsequent chapter.

266). In attempting to prevent the occupying Germans from gaining any benefit from the industry and resources of these countries, the Allies bombed French and Belgian cities in the same way they bombed German cities. Ford quotes Cardinal Van Roey, Primate of Belgium, as stating:

> . . . except in a few rare cases where a small number of aircraft operating in daylight hit their objectives without causing great damage, explosives and even incendiary bombs have been dropped blindly, at random, and without distinction over densely populated agglomerations covering an area of several square kilometers.

The point here is that the targets were not in Germany, but in nations that were victims of German aggression. The people being bombed were presumably our allies; people we were trying to liberate from German occupation. If at least half the occupants of German cities were innocent, surely nearly all the occupants of Belgian and French cities were innocent. If Allied air forces were obliged to exercise due care in bombing legitimate targets in Germany (an obligation in which they often failed), they were even more obliged to exercise due care in bombing German targets in occupied cities. This was the whole point of the French pilots' accepting greater risks in order to bomb their homeland with greater precision and less loss of life among their countrymen.

What, then, would be the obligation of U.S. military forces making nuclear attacks against targets in the Soviet Union? The civilians who live near legitimate targets in the Soviet Union are, for the most part, not beneficiaries of the Soviet Government's tyranny but instead its victims. Conquest of the rest of the world by their government will not ease their lot; it most likely would make it even more difficult.[9]

From both a political and moral standpoint, these victims of the Soviet government are our natural allies, not our enemies. This factor

---

[9] The extent to which the existence of a free world outside the Soviet Union helps Soviet victims of their own government is illustrated nicely by David Goldfarb's letter of thanks to the scientific community for its help in his struggle to emigrate (1986, p. 801). Because of pressure from the outside, he was not fired from the editorship of a journal (loss of a job being the usual fate of applicants for emigration), and was rehired by the Institute from which he had already been discharged. An embargo on scientific samples sent to the Soviet Union, organized by the free world's scientific community, saved him from criminal prosecution when he attempted to bring his collection of scientific samples out with him. He states, of the support he received, "On several occasions during the past 7 years, I had a chance to witness how the authorities and the bureaucracies of the USSR Academy of Sciences softened their attitude to me as the result of this pressure." There would be no such opportunity for American and European scientists to bring pressure on the Soviet government, once they were subjects of a worldwide Soviet empire. On the contrary, they would suffer the same pressures as were brought to bear on Goldfarb. The Soviet people thus have a strong interest in restraining the expansion of Soviet rule.

should be taken into account in any moral analysis of attacks on installations in Soviet cities. As Raymond Aron once put it:

> [it] will be indispensable, but singularly difficult, to convince the masses in the Soviet Union that the West bears no ill will except toward their tyrants, if atom bombs unite in death Stalinists and their opponents: women, children, and the secret police (1954, p. 6).

That is, in making an attack on the Soviet Union we should place ourselves nearer the attitude of Mr. Mendes-France than that of General Power.

However, there is yet another consideration. Father Ford, in 1944, calculated that at least half the residents of German cities were innocent in the Just War sense. His calculations were reasonable, and could plausibly be applied to Soviet cities today. Since 1944, though, the civilized world has passed another judgment on the Germans of the World War II era. This has to do with guilt for the Jewish Holocaust. The consensus of moral judgment today is that the German people shared responsibility because they chose to allow that situation to develop. They are not permitted to plead they didn't know. It is generally taken for granted that they should have observed that people were suddenly missing. They should have spoken out, or taken some other action, to halt the killing. The fact that they didn't object means they bear some responsibility for what happened.

We are entitled to apply the same standard to civilians who live in a country committing aggression. Their responsibility may be to some degree attenuated, but the world has today come to agree that people have to be responsible for what their governments do, so far as they tolerate those governments. The civilians in an aggressor nation have moral obligations toward the victims of aggression. They have an obligation to protest, or even to remove themselves from the target areas. Therefore despite the fact that the Soviet people are really the first victims of their own government, it would be wrong to claim that the Communist government is a total imposition on them. They don't revolt against it.

This argument is different from the one that says the farmer who grows corn to feed the troops, and the grandmother who knits socks for the troops, are part of the war effort and are therefore legitimate targets. It says, instead, that although the Soviet people may be innocent of what their government does, their passive acceptance makes it easier for that government to carry out its aggression. By their presence they provide an "innocent shield" for that aggression.

Translating this to practical consequences, it means that we need accept no more risks, in demonstrating that we are discriminating between the Soviet people and their government, than they are willing to take in opposing that government. It is, after all, *their* government, not *ours*. We are trying to keep it from becoming ours. To increase the risk that we will become the next subjects of that tyranny, in order to protect the lives of those who refuse to revolt against it, is asking too much. For us to accept that additional risk might be an act of charity, but it cannot be demanded of us in justice.

There is yet one more aspect to the carrying out of discriminating attacks. Kaplan (1983, pp. 41–46) notes that U.S. strategic bombing forces in World War II failed to realize how fragile the German electric power system was and never targeted it. The post-war Strategic Bombing Survey discovered how fearful the Germans had been that the electric power system would be attacked, because they realized how vulnerable it was. As a result of this, post-war Air Staff planning called for attacks against the Soviet electric power industry. General LeMay, as CINCSAC, objected to this planning on the grounds that we didn't know where the electric power stations were. SAC would lose too many aircraft and crews, not to mention atomic bombs (which were then even scarcer than aircraft and crews), hunting for them. According to Kaplan, even Bernard Brodie, who was then a consultant to the Air Staff and a strong advocate of limited nuclear war rather than massive retaliation, agreed with this objection.

Thus we have to ask, if a government succeeds in closing off its society to the point where we cannot obtain the information we would need to conduct a discriminating attack, does that society thereby gain immunity against all attack? The answer has to be in the negative. While the guilt of a repressive government, which maintains a closed society, does not rub off on its subjects, the people in that society cannot in justice demand that other societies accept undue risks of defeat. The subjects of a tyrannical government are innocent; they may not be targeted directly. In defending ourselves against that government, we must try to discriminate between it and its people. But if the people refuse to take the risks needed to overthrow it, they must accept the risks of less-discriminating attacks from those who are defending themselves against it.

In summary, then, most enemy civilians are not combatants—they may not be targeted directly. One may not bomb a city as a city, with the intent of causing such horror that civilian morale collapses or on the grounds that "they're all guilty anyway". Civilians may be wounded or killed, however, if they are unavoidably close to legitimate targets. The attacks on those legitimate targets must be carried out in a way that attempts to discriminate between the target and the noncombatants. The attempt to discriminate can be exhibited in practice, even when using nuclear weapons, by selecting weapons that are sized to the target itself, not to the target plus the surrounding area, and by accepting some degree of risk in attempting to deliver that weapon accurately on the target.

How much risk must be taken? How much accuracy must be demanded? How much larger than the absolute minimum may the weapon be, to allow for a reasonable miss distance without being excessive in size and therefore undiscriminating? The answers to these questions will depend upon circumstances. They can never be answered with complete precision.

Even without complete precision in the answers, however, we can justly claim that nuclear weapons *can* be used in a way that allows us to discriminate between the aggressive Soviet government and the Soviet people. These weapons can be made sufficiently small and delivered with sufficient accuracy so that their use need not exceed the allowable limits set by the discrimination criterion. To stay within those limits, we must accept greater risks than we would have to accept with less discriminating weapons. However, in attempting to protect the innocents in the Soviet Union, we need not accept risks greater than those innocents themselves are willing to accept in protecting *us* against *their own* government.

REFERENCES

Aron, Raymond. *The Century of Total War*. New York: Doubleday, 1954.

Ford, John C., S.J., "The Morality of Obliteration Bombing". *Theological Studies*. Vol. 5, no. 3 (September 1944), pp. 261–309.

Goldfarb, David. Letter to *Science* (November 14, 1986), p. 801.

Gollancz, Victor. *The Devil's Repertoire*. New York: Doubleday & Co., 1959.

Kaplan, Fred. *The Wizards of Armageddon*. New York: Simon & Schuster, 1983.

Markus, R. A. "Conscience and Deterrence". In *Nuclear Weapons: A Catholic Response*, edited by Walter Stein. New York: Sheed and Ward, 1961.

O'Brien, William V. *The Conduct of Just and Limited War*. New York: Praeger Publishers, 1981.

Stein, Walter. "The Defence of the West". In *Nuclear Weapons: A Catholic Response*, edited by Walter Stein. New York: Sheed and Ward, 1961.

Tucker, Robert W. *The Just War*. Baltimore: Johns Hopkins University Press, 1960.

Walzer, Michael. *Just and Unjust Wars*. New York: Basic Books, 1977.

CHAPTER TWENTY-ONE

PROPORTION

The criterion of proportion applies to both going to war and waging war. That is, it is both a *jus ad bellum* and a *jus in bello* criterion, and is the only one which applies to both. We will consider these two aspects of proportion separately. However, proportion represents an important link between *jus ad bellum* and *jus in bello*. After considering the two aspects separately, we will examine this link.

With regard to *jus ad bellum,* much of the discussion of proportion is Just War Doctrine is obsolete. It belongs to a day when many more purposes for going to war were considered legitimate than are allowed today—reasons such as vindictive justice against unjust nations, or enforcing justice for someone else (for example, the Soviet people), or even such things as collecting defaulted debts and punishing unjust treatment of one's own nationals. One was supposed to ask, Does the good from punishing the unjust, from rescuing the innocent, and from deterring possible future injustices, exceed the damage to be done by the war? Today it is taken for granted that the good to be achieved could not possibly outweigh the damage done if war were initiated for these causes. Under today's conditions Just War Doctrine can permit only a defensive war, in which one is repelling aggression or enforcing justice for oneself. One should not even be in a war unless the independence and freedom of one's own nation, or of an ally, are under real and immediate threat. Even then, the only proper *jus ad bellum* question about proportion deals with the cost of defending against aggression versus the cost of submitting to it. If the cost of defending against aggression outweighs the cost of submitting to aggression, then one is obliged to submit to the aggressor.

In terms of human lives, the cost of defending against aggression is not small. R. J. Rummel has calculated the total war deaths in the twentieth century as 35.7 million (Rummel, July 7, 1986; March 15, 1986). This includes not only World Wars I and II, but Korea, Vietnam, and dozens of other wars, revolutions, and armed conflicts. This is equivalent to wiping out a nation such as Burma, Egypt, or the Republic of Korea.

However, the human cost of not defending against aggression is even larger. Rummel has calculated that systematic and unprovoked deaths by tyrannical governments have, since 1900, totaled over 120 million, equivalent to wiping out Brazil or Japan. Stalin's engineered famine in Ukraine caused more deaths than the total war-related deaths of all belligerents during World War I. The war in Vietnam cost 1.2 million lives on both sides. Since 1975, however, the victorious communists in Vietnam, Laos, and Cambodia have killed over two million people through oppression and deliberate elimination of *class enemies*.[1] According to Rummel's figures, during this century a person has had three times the likelihood of dying through government oppression as through war, and in a communist country, twenty times the likelihood.

If anything, though, Rummel's figures are an underestimate. He counts only 39.5 million people killed within Soviet borders by the Soviet government, and only 45 million killed within Chinese borders by China's government. Other authorities give much higher figures for both totals. Some authorities also put the total deaths from oppression in the three nations of Indochina, since 1975, at over four million.

Moreover, the totals for war deaths include both defender and aggressor. Thus while they include some innocent people on the aggressor side, in particular bombing deaths in World War II, they also include the deaths of those people who were legitimate targets on the aggressor side. The war death figures should be reduced by the number of *guilty* deaths on the aggressor side, whereas the tyranny death figures are essentially all innocent people. Thus the ratio of innocent deaths from tyranny to innocent deaths from war is larger than Rummel's figures would indicate. Even if one uses only Rummel's lower figures, however, one might conclude that going to war to prevent the expansion of tyranny actually saves lives.

While the comparison of deaths from war to deaths from tyranny is important, we must beware of a "cost-accounting" approach to the criterion of proportion, which would simply balance lives against lives. The concern of the Just War Doctrine is not merely with preserving lives, but with preserving *ways of living*. As Tucker observes, the criterion of proportion requires that "the *values* preserved through force must be proportionate to the *values* sacrificed through force" (Osgood and Tucker, 1967, p. 300) (emphasis added). Ramsey gives this same interpretation of the principle of proportion (1968, p. 404), as does O'Brien (1981, p. 28).

From the time of Augustine to the present day, Just War Doctrine has been concerned with establishing and maintaining *justice*. While Just War Doctrine begins with a presumption against war, it does not regard peace as simply the absence of armed conflict.

---

[1] It is ironic to recall that one of the slogans of those who opposed U.S. participation in the war in Vietnam was "Stop the killing".

The American Catholic bishops stressed, "peace is an enterprise of justice". The absence of justice implies the absence of peace. Pope John Paul II made this point even more emphatically in his homily in Singapore, November 20, 1986:

> Peace requires justice, an attitude which recognizes the dignity and equality of all men and women, and a firm commitment to strive and *protect* the basic human rights of all. Where there is no justice there can be no peace. Peace is possible only where there is a just order that *ensures* the rights of everyone. World peace is possible only where the international order is just (emphasis in original).

Therefore the empirical fact that since 1900 the reign of unimpeded injustice has killed more people than war itself should not be allowed to mislead us about the reasons for opposing injustice. Injustice deserves to be opposed simply because it is injustice. Even if the death toll from unimpeded injustice were less than the death toll from war, it might still be morally proportionate to oppose injustice by force of arms.

With regard to the calculation of proportion, Father John Courtney Murray points out that Pope Pius XII stressed the importance of making the comparison "between realities of the moral order, and not sheerly between two sets of material damage and loss". Murray went on to say:

> The question of proportion must be evaluated in a more tough-minded fashion, from the viewpoint of the hierarchy of strictly moral values. It is not enough simply to consider the "sorrows and evils that flow from war". There are greater evils than the physical death and destruction wrought in war. And there are human goods of so high an order that immense sacrifices may have to be borne in their defense (1960, p. 80).

That is, we must look not only at lives lost and property damaged, but even more importantly, at the values that are at stake.

Thus while the cost-accounting approach might say that we could permit the deaths, in discriminating attacks, of up to as many innocents on the enemy side as are threatened on our side by the targets we attack, the introduction of values changes the relationship. It says we may permit the deaths of *even more* innocents on the enemy side than the number of lives threatened on our side by the targets, provided that the values we are defending are sufficiently important.

Clearly the values being defended would have to be important human values; important not just to the defenders but also to the innocent victims of oppression in the enemy nation whose deaths are permitted. It is here that we run into a problem with the criterion of proportion. The cost-accounting approach seems to put a ceiling on the number of deaths we may permit in defense of our own lives. The "values" approach seems to put no ceiling over them.

It is one thing to say, with Pope Pius XII, that *we* must bear "immense sacrifices" in defense of important values. It is another thing entirely to say that innocent civilians on the *enemy's* side may have to be sacrificed in large numbers to defend important values on *our* side. If we are not careful, we may find ourselves justifying an enormous slaughter of innocents on the enemy's side, *so long as we do it in a discriminating fashion*. Tucker has made this particular criticism of the criterion of proportion, that it "lacks specificity and restraining force" (Osgood and Tucker, 1967). Because of this, he alleges, it provides no guidance to the statesman.

Tucker appears to be concerned that the lack of "restraining force" may make it too easy for the statesman to justify war. But it is equally possible that the lack of "specificity" may encourage cowardice on the part of a statesman, who would be willing to sacrifice values rather than defend them. Thus it is simply not the case that proportionality has a bias in favor of war.

Moreover, while it is true that the criterion of proportion does not provide a precise quantitative guide, this does not make the criterion worthless. To demand that the criterion of proportion provide specific limits on the damage that is acceptable in defense of values is to demand too much. The proportion criterion is not intended to provide the statesman with a way to automate the calculation. As Ramsey says, it is not to tell the statesman *what* to think about a particular war, but *how* to think about it. It tells him that he must take values into account. It does not tell him what the relative worth of these values is. While it is quite true that the statesman can deceive others, or even deceive himself, about the relative worth of the values at stake, this is not the fault of the criterion of proportion. It is simply the consequence of humanity's fallen state.

The most the criterion of proportion can do is serve as a reminder to the statesman of how he should think about the problem of going to war. For the Christian, the virtue of prudence is still a requirement for statesmen. It cannot be replaced by any routine calculations, especially not about the relative worth of the values to be preserved and sacrificed by a war.

Tucker has made another criticism of the criterion of proportion, particularly as it deals with values, that we must dispose of. He says the criterion merely makes it easy for the statesman to justify war against nations that don't share the values of his own nation (Osgood and Tucker, 1967).

Tucker here seems to be advocating a position of complete relativism, saying in effect "The enemy's values are as good as yours; don't try to use a criterion which merely allows you to exalt your own values." While being value-free is a popular intellectual position, it is not realizable in practice—"being value-free" is itself a value. The Christian, in particular, cannot accept this value-relativism. The Christian knows that some things *are* better than others, and that we *can* tell the difference. A nation which permits, for example, religious freedom, is better than a nation that denies it.

Even the secularist, however, rejects values-relativism in practice. Most secularists, for instance, support education on the grounds that literacy is better than illiteracy. Most secularists support legislatures, courts, and police on the grounds that some behavior *deserves* to be outlawed and punished.

In short, the person who argues that to be value-free is morally superior to being value-laden simply smuggles in his own values while denying the validity of other values. Tucker's apparent appeal to values-relativism must be rejected as an illegitimate attack on the criterion of proportion.

But if Tucker is really advocating values-relativism, then he ultimately undermines his own position. If values are only relative, there is nothing wrong with wiping out all the innocent bystanders who get in the way of military victory. The values of the one who objects to it are no better than the values of the one who does it.

What it comes down to is that the only person who is going to be concerned with the criterion of proportion is one who does believe that values matter—that some things are better than others. For such a person, the criterion of proportion serves as a worthwhile reminder that the war under consideration must be fought to preserve values. If it actually destroys those values, it is immoral regardless of how few lives it costs. Conversely, if the war preserves important values, the loss of many lives might well be justified. The statesman must still apply prudence in judging how important the values at stake are and what their defense is worth.

How does this apply to a war fought with nuclear weapons? To assert that any such war would inevitably violate the criterion of proportion is to say that there are no values of such importance as to outweigh the damage done by even the smallest imaginable nuclear weapon (which, as pointed out in the preceding chapter, may be comparable to the power of current high-explosive weapons). From the Just War perspective, this position is absurd on the face of it. To adopt it means to abandon the Just War Doctrine, adopting not just nuclear pacifism but complete pacifism. Thus going to war, even knowing that nuclear weapons will be used, need not be a violation of the *jus ad bellum* criterion of proportion.

Having said that, however, we must quickly add the caveat that has attended all our other conclusions about Just War criteria: the war must be *limited*. It must be limited in the means used, and ends sought. If the objective sought or the means used result in the destruction of the values the war was intended to preserve, or of other values of equal worth, the criterion of proportion would clearly be violated.

Thus before deciding whether or not to go to war, the statesman must take into account those values the war is intended to preserve, and those that will be sacrificed or at least put at risk. He must take into account not only damage to his own country, but harm to innocent bystanders in the enemy country, and harm to third parties who are not involved in the dispute (this latter group can be particularly relevant in nuclear war, with the possibility of radioactive fallout going beyond the borders of the belligerents).[2] If the damage to these parties exceeds the good to be achieved, the war is unjust. However, if the values to be preserved are worth more than the values sacrificed, the criterion of proportionality is satisfied, *even if the war includes the use of nuclear weapons*.

Having considered proportion with regard to *jus ad bellum*, we now turn to *jus in bello*. Here the issue of proportion deals not with a whole war but with a single military action in that war. The criterion requires that the good to be achieved by the action be proportionate to the damage done. Again, this means *values preserved* compared with *values sacrificed*, not a simple cost-accounting of lives and dollars.

From the standpoint of the moral use of nuclear weapons, the critical *jus in bello* issue raised by the criterion of proportionality is the death of innocent people in the vicinity of legitimate targets. The deliberate killing of innocent people who are *not* near legitimate targets would already violate discrimination, hence the issue of proportion would not even need to be raised.[3]

---

[2] Ordinarily even the slightest damage to third parties must be avoided if a war is to be judged just. Damage to third parties *should not* be part of the cost of defending oneself. However, when one is defending against an aggressor, the situation may change. One might justly argue that if we do not stop the aggressor now, those third parties will be the aggressor's next victims. Thus they might legitimately be asked to bear some loss, such as receiving radioactive fallout, provided that loss is smaller than what they would have to suffer should the aggressor be successful against us and then turn on them.

[3] A weapon that misses the target through mechanical or operator failure, or because of partially successful enemy defenses, may well kill innocent people remote from a legitimate target. However, this would not be *deliberate* killing of those people.

The criterion of proportion receives a great deal of attention in the Just War literature. Both O'Brien and Ramsey have more citations to it in the indexes of their books than to any other single term. Nevertheless, much of what is said in the Just War literature about proportionate use of nuclear weapons is unsatisfactory, largely because of the implicit assumptions that nuclear weapons are of necessity enormously destructive, and that cities are the only feasible targets for nuclear weapons. Since we are here dealing with the *jus in bello* application of the criterion of proportion, we must assume that all other Just War criteria have been met, including discrimination, as well as the *jus ad bellum* criterion of proportion. If they have not been met, then the *jus in bello* criterion of proportion is supererogatory; the war is already immoral. Thus in particular, we assume the war is fought in a just cause, that the values at stake are worth the values that might be sacrificed, and that the weapons used (whether conventional or nuclear) are aimed only at legitimate targets and are properly sized for those targets. We ask, then, if under those circumstances nuclear weapons still *inevitably* violate the criterion of proportion. If nuclear weapons do not *inevitably* violate proportion, then their use *can* be moral.

We begin the analysis by noting that to rule out all attacks on legitimate targets in populated areas is to give the enemy a sanctuary. For instance, during the fighting in Vietnam, U.S. air attacks against supply lines in North Vietnam were subject to severe restrictions, to reduce civilian casualties. Knowing this, the North Vietnamese deliberately located supply dumps in the middle of populated areas, in some cases simply stacking supplies in the main streets of villages, confident that under the ground rules imposed on our bombing missions, those sites would not be attacked.

Someone should have asked, how many casualties are those supply dumps going to cause our side? Are we obliged to protect enemy civilians to the extent of completely avoiding attacks on enemy weapons, particularly when many of those weapons will be deliberately used in indiscriminate attacks that will kill civilians on our side? (The enemy frequently bombarded villages, and even Saigon, with mortars and rockets, causing far more civilian casualties than did U.S. bombing of North Vietnam.) The failure to ask this question was itself a failure to apply the criterion of proportion. It was a failure to ask what values were at stake, and whether these were worth more or less than the values that would have been sacrificed by bombing the supply dumps.

What if the enemy installations are not simply supply dumps, but missile launching sites? Must the enemy civilians around them be protected, at the expense of our own civilians? If not, how many *unintended* deaths may be *permitted* in an attack intended to destroy the missile sites? The American Catholic bishops raised this same set of questions (1983, no. 109):

> Direct attacks on military targets involve similar complexities. Which targets are "military" ones and which are not? To what degree, for instance, does the use (by either revolutionaries or regular military forces) of a village or housing in a civilian population area invite attack? What of a munitions factory in the heart of a city? Who is directly responsible for the deaths of noncombatants should the attack be carried out? To revert to the question raised earlier, how many deaths of noncombatants are "tolerable" as a result of indirect attacks—attacks directed against combat forces and military targets, which nevertheless kill noncombatants at the same time?

The bishops attempted to answer their own questions (1983, no. 182):

> The location of industrial or militarily significant economic targets[4] within heavily populated areas . . . could well involve such massive civilian casualties that, in our judgment, such a strike would be deemed morally disproportionate, even though not intentionally indiscriminate.

The bishops went on to say (1983, no. 193):

> We are told that some weapons are designed for purely "counterforce" use against military forces and targets. The moral issue, however, is not resolved by the design of weapons or the planned intention for use; there are also consequences which must be assessed. It would be a perverted political policy or moral casuistry which tried to justify using a weapon which "indirectly" or "unintentionally" killed a million innocent people because they happened to live near a "militarily significant target".

While the bishops did raise the proper questions regarding *jus in bello* proportion, unfortunately, as indicated by these quotations, they failed to deal with the issue properly. The quotation from no. 182, for instance, not only makes no attempt to carry out a *jus in bello* analysis, it appears to deny the very possibility of one. The bishops seem to be saying that the casualties from an attack in a heavily populated area would exceed any possible justification. Any conclusion about the proportionality of a specific attack must involve a prudential judgment which must be made by a statesman, not by a moralist. Moreover, such a judgment can be made only at the time the attack is being considered. It cannot be made in advance, on some abstract basis.

In no. 193, however, the bishops appear to have failed completely in their attempt to deal with the question of proportion. To take their

---

[4] That is, countervalue targets that are not in themselves population centers. This would include dams, bridges, open-pit mines, and similar installations.

statement at face value, it would appear there is nothing whatsoever of such importance that it would justify the unintended deaths of a million people. Apparently, in their view a million lives goes beyond the "immense sacrifices" that Pope Pius XII said would be justified in the defense of important values.

In reality, it is very hard to imagine a legitimate military target that has a million people close enough to it that they could be killed by a discriminating attack. The target would almost have to be something like a strongly hardened missile silo buried in the middle of a high-rise apartment district. In this case, it would be a deliberate attempt by the enemy to use the civilians as an *innocent shield* for his missile site. In such a case, the blame for the innocent deaths falls not on the discriminating attacker, but on those who deliberately located a military target in a populated area.

However, let us go beyond the issue of what kind of legitimate target might result in that many innocent deaths when attacked in a discriminating manner. Even from a purely cost-accounting standpoint, one million innocent lives lost when an important military objective is attacked might not be too high a price to pay if *failing* to destroy that target would cost more than a million innocent lives.[5] Nor need the innocent lives saved be American only. When we consider how many of its own people the Soviet government has killed and is still killing through official terror, a discriminating attack that permits a million innocent deaths but weakens the Soviet government might save the lives of far more than a million innocent Soviet people, and therefore be morally justified without regard to the lives preserved on our side.

If important enough values are preserved, moreover, a million innocent lives might be a proportionate price to pay even if fewer than a million lives are saved on both our own and the Soviet sides. We already have ample evidence that the independence of the United States, and the pressure it can bring on the Soviet government, can to some extent ameliorate the conditions of the Soviet people. Thus preserving that value is worth some number of innocent Soviet lives.

In short, providing the enemy with a sanctuary violates the rights of those who will be innocent victims of whatever the enemy places in the sanctuary. At the very least, we must weigh the values lost on our own side by permitting the sanctuary with the values destroyed on the enemy side by denying the sanctuary. Beyond this, however, we must include the values threatened or destroyed *on the enemy side* by the installation they have placed in the sanctuary. The continued reign of in-

---

[5] Note that by prior assumption, the weapon used was aimed accurately and sized to the target. In short, the criterion of discrimination was satisfied.

justice on the enemy side destroys values among the victims of that injustice. Shortening or weakening that reign may well preserve more values than the attack destroys. Finally, as pointed out in the preceding chapter, those who are already victims of tyranny still have some obligation to those who are fighting to remain free. At the very least, they have an obligation not to permit themselves to be used as innocent shields. If the loss they would suffer from their own government is less than the loss from attack, they have an obligation to resist their tyrannical government. If the loss they would suffer from their own government is greater than the loss from attack, they have an obligation to accept the smaller loss simply as part of their own government's injustices.

We can summarize the sanctuary issue by saying that the enemy need not be allowed to protect his weapons and other legitimate military targets with innocent shields. It may very well be proportionate to attack an important target that the enemy has located in a densely populated area. The people who will be innocent victims of the power the enemy derives from that target have a right not to be attacked, and to defend themselves by destroying the target. Moreover, one cannot put an arbitrary limit on the number of deaths that may be *permitted* in an attack on a legitimate target. If the values at stake are important enough, the loss of millions of lives may be a proportionate cost.[6]

How many lives represent a proportionate cost? As already discussed for the *jus ad bellum* case, the criterion of proportion does not give us precise guidance here. Nevertheless, it seems clear that there are cases in which a million unintentional deaths would be proportionate to the values preserved. Unfortunately, the bishops have not only not acknowledged this, they have attempted to foreclose all analysis by referring to

---

[6] It is worth noting that the largest cost of Hitler's Holocaust was not the six million Jews and the six million non-Jews who died in the death camps. Ultimately the largest cost was the destruction of the value of the inviolability of innocent life. Hitler's breach of this value did not start with the Holocaust, but with his mass murder of Ernst Roehm and other leaders of the SA (Brownshirts) in 1934. As Paul Johnson observes (1983, p. 299),

It was the sheer audacity of the Roehm purge, and the way Hitler got away with it, with German and world opinion and with his own colleagues and followers, which encouraged Stalin to consolidate his personal dictatorship by similar means.

Nor was the encouragement all one-way. Hitler's death camps were in turn patterned after the death camps established by Stalin (Johnson, 1983, p. 304). Thus failure to preserve the value that innocent life is inviolable cost millions of innocent lives, not only under Hitler and Stalin, but under such successors as Idi Amin and Pol Pot, admirers respectively of Hitler and Stalin. In 1934, millions of lives would have been an entirely proportionate price to pay to preserve that value. Because that value was not preserved, the loss of innocent life since then has been staggering. The loss of innocent lives will likely be even higher before that value is restored to the level of adherence it enjoyed in the 1920s.

it as "perverted" and "casuistry". This issue deserves analysis, not rhetoric.

We will return later to the issue of how many deaths may be *permitted* without an attack becoming disproportionate. First, however, we need to look at another issue.

The American Catholic bishops wrote (1983, no. 180):

> . . . an attack on military targets or militarily significant industrial targets could involve "indirect" (that is, unintended) but massive casualties. We are advised, for example, that the United States strategic nuclear targeting plan (SIOP—Single Integrated Operational Plan) has identified 60 "military" targets within the city of Moscow alone, and that 40,000 "military" targets for nuclear weapons have been identified in the whole of the Soviet Union. . . . The number of civilians who would be killed by such strikes is horrendous.[7]

The bishops seem to be saying, by their emphasis on the fact that sixty targets are located within Moscow, that a series of attacks, each of which is proportionate, can add up to something disproportionate. This is an idea we need to analyze.

Consider the case of sixty legitimate targets, each located in a separate city. Assume one nuclear weapon is used, in a discriminating manner, against each target, and the permitted innocent deaths are proportionate to the values preserved by destroying each target. Under these assumptions, clearly these attacks are justifiable.

Now suppose those same sixty targets are concentrated in one city, and each is attacked in the same discriminating and proportionate way. Does the fact that the deaths are concentrated in one city make the total disproportionate? If this is what the bishops are claiming, they offer no moral argumentation to support the claim. They have simply reacted to the horror of the total number of deaths.

From the perspective of Just War Doctrine, concentrating an otherwise acceptable number of casualties in a small geographic area does not alter the acceptability. If the values preserved are proportionate to the values sacrificed, then the geographic distribution of the casualties within the enemy nation is irrelevant. Hence we have to reject the view that several discriminating and proportionate attacks on targets within a single city can add up to a disproportionate number of deaths.

---

[7] Note, however, that it is not necessarily the case that one nuclear weapon would be used per target, nor that all sixty targets in Moscow would be attacked. Note also that the United States simply does not possess the 40,000 nuclear warheads needed to attack every single one of those targets. In fact, most of the U.S. nuclear arsenal consists of tactical warheads, which cannot even be delivered on targets deep in the Soviet Union.

Indeed, what the bishops appear to be saying is not only wrong but dangerous. The bishops could be interpreted as saying that it makes no difference how the deaths occur, it is only their number that matters; that is, if reaching a certain outcome one way is immoral, then all other ways of reaching the same outcome are also immoral. This borders on a consequentialist view of morality that is entirely alien to Catholic moral thinking.

Consider a defender who kills an aggressor soldier in battle. A consequentialist argument would assert that morally the defender is no different from a mugger who kills that soldier for his purse, when he is home on leave. After all, the soldier is dead either way. Yet Catholic moral thinking has never confused the two. The former was always permitted, the latter always prohibited. There is as much difference between the intention to blow up the city and the intention to target only military objectives in a discriminating and proportionate manner, as there is between the intention of the mugger and that of the defender. If each strike on a single target is legitimate, then so is the cumulative result. The bishops' apparent lapse into consequentialism is simply wrong.

This apparent consequentialism is also dangerous because it might lead someone to conclude that if there is no moral difference between using sixty small weapons against sixty individual targets and using one big weapon against the whole city, then we should use the one big weapon because it is cheaper and involves less risk to our own forces. This apparent lapse into consequentialism implicitly rejects the Just War Doctrine's emphasis on right intention, discrimination, and proportion.

In summary, then, we have to reject the view that simply concentrating the deaths in one location makes the total disproportionate when the same total would be proportionate if it were distributed widely. The *jus in bello* criterion of proportion deals only with the total of the deaths and its relation to the values preserved by permitting those deaths. Concentrating or dispersing the deaths is irrelevant.

However, we are not finished with the issue of accumulated casualties from individually proportionate attacks. Can a series of proportionate attacks add up to a disproportionate war? The answer is "no", but it requires some analysis. In fact, it requires us to examine the connection between the *jus ad bellum* and *jus in bello* criteria of proportion.

Suppose it were argued that we have enormous values at stake on our side. Freedom and justice are clearly at stake, not to mention the lives of large numbers of people who would be eliminated as class enemies if the Soviets were to win. It might be argued, then, that if the Soviets successfully use the tanks produced in a particular factory, they could destroy all those values that we are defending. Thus the number of innocent deaths that could be permitted in destroying the tank factory would be proportionate to the values we are defending.

But here we run into a problem. We can't throw all the values on our side into the balance against this tank factory, and then against that helicopter factory, and once more against the missile site over there. If we allow the values sacrificed *in each attack* to be proportionate to the total values at stake on our side, the total values sacrificed would come to far more than the values preserved. We could subdivide the targets on the enemy side as finely as we wished, attack each in a proportionate manner, and justify wiping out everyone on the enemy side. Clearly this leads to a contradiction. If the values sacrificed in each attack are proportionate to the total values preserved on our side, the entire war is disproportionate; it fails the *jus ad bellum* criterion of proportion.

What it comes down to is that the total values to be preserved by going to war, the values forming the basis for the *jus ad bellum* proportion, amount to a *budget* of values. Some portion of that budget can be allocated to each action against the enemy, but the total budget may not be exceeded without the war becoming disproportionate. Thus to ask if a series of proportionate attacks can add up to a disproportionate war is to get things backwards. It is the individual attack that is disproportionate if it uses up too much of the budget of values that justifies the war; if the values sacrificed in the attack exceed the share of total value that is preserved by the attack.

Of course, use of terms like "budgets" and "allocations" implies a degree of precision that is simply not possible. The values to be preserved and those sacrificed cannot be totaled on an adding machine, like the dollars and cents of a financial budget. Nevertheless, even though precision "to the penny" is not possible, we are obliged to use as much precision in our judgments of the values preserved and the values sacrificed as we can possibly manage. The criterion of proportion demands that we make an honest attempt, to the best of our ability, to balance values sacrificed against values preserved. In every action we take against the enemy, we must attempt to assure that the values we sacrifice do not exceed the values threatened by the particular enemy action or installation we are trying to counter.

Among other things, this means we may not attack anything and everything of some military value in the enemy nation, simply "because it's there". It must present a sufficient threat to the values we are fighting to preserve in order to justify the destruction of values that will result from the attack.

This idea is not as strange as it may seem. It is merely unfamiliar. Ordinary military strategy prescribes that we shouldn't attack a target simply "because it's there". When we attack a target, the risks we ask our troops to take, and the combat power we use up, should be warranted by the importance of the target. But how is that importance to be judged? In the military sense, it is judged in terms of the loss we would suffer if the target were not attacked. Militarily, it makes no sense to attack something if the losses we suffer in neutralizing it exceed the losses we would suffer from allowing it to continue to exist and operate against us.

The U.S. Army makes this point in its doctrine on "The Objective", one of the nine "Principles of War" recognized by the Army. The Army's Doctrine manual states:

> Strategic, operational, and tactical objectives cannot be clearly identified and developed . . . until the political purpose has been determined and defined by the President and Congress . . . these objectives must . . . reflect not only the ultimate political purpose but also any political constraints imposed on the application of military force. . . . Operational efforts must also be directed toward clearly defined, decisive, and attainable objectives that will achieve the strategic aims . . . operational and tactical objectives must quickly and economically contribute, directly or indirectly to the purpose of the ultimate operational or tactical objective. The selection of objectives is based on the overall mission of the command. . . . Every commander must understand the overall mission of the higher command, his own mission, and the tasks he must perform. He must communicate clearly the intent of the operation to his subordinate commanders (1986, p. 173).

Just as in a narrowly military context we judge the need to attack a target by comparing the military cost of attacking it with the cost of not attacking it, in the broader moral context we must judge the need to attack it by comparing the values it will destroy if not attacked with the values *we* destroy by attacking it. Neither judgment admits of a great deal of precision. But just as we would condemn a military commander who cost us unnecessary casualties by attacking a militarily unimportant target, so should we condemn the commander or statesman who destroys more value by attacking a target than he preserves from the threat posed by that target.

It is the link between *jus ad bellum* proportion and *jus in bello* proportion which gives us the opportunity to evaluate (albeit only in a rough manner) the extent of the damage we may legitimately do in a single action against the enemy. If we are at war because the enemy has in some way threatened important values, then from the military perspective we should be acting against only those enemy forces and installations that have the capability to destroy some of the values we are defending. To do otherwise is to dissipate our combat power for no purpose. But if we are acting against an enemy force or installation because it is a threat to what we are defending, then the extent to which it is a threat is the measure of the damage to innocent bystanders that we may *permit*. To kill a dozen innocent bystanders while destroying a relatively harmless installation in the middle of a village might be totally disproportionate, while to kill a million innocent bystanders while destroying a critical installation in the middle of a large city might be entirely proportionate. If every attack on an enemy force or installation would be disproportionate in this sense, it can only be because the war itself is disproportionate. We shouldn't even be in it.

In summary, then, the *jus ad bellum* criterion of proportion says one mustn't go to war unless the values to be preserved by the war exceed the values to be sacrificed. Within the war, the *jus in bello* criterion of proportion says that when one takes action against enemy military units or installations, the values sacrificed in the attack must not exceed the values that would be threatened by the continued existence of the target. This judgment cannot be made with a high degree of precision, but it is not significantly different from the kinds of judgments we already expect military commanders and statesmen to make in determining whether the military cost of neutralizing a target is more or less than the military cost of leaving the target untouched. Therefore it is reasonable to expect that people could make these judgments about individual targets and entire wars. Finally, these considerations apply with equal force to nuclear and non-nuclear weapons. The idea that nuclear weapons are inherently and intrinsically disproportionate is simply wrong. However, because of their greater power, nuclear weapons are more easily used in a disproportionate manner than are non-nuclear weapons. Satisfying the criterion of proportion depends upon the user, not the weapon. It is incumbent upon those who use nuclear weapons in combat to select the weapons and the targets in such a way that the values they sacrifice do not exceed the values they are preserving. To the extent that they do this, the use of nuclear weapons satisfies the Just War criterion of proportion.

REFERENCES

Department of the Army. Field Manual FM 100-5. *Operations*. May, 1986.
Johnson, Paul. *Modern Times*. New York: Harper & Row, 1983.

Murray, John Courtney. "Theology and Modern War". In *Morality and Modern Warfare*, edited by William J. Nagle. Baltimore: Helicon Press, 1960.

Murray, Thomas E. "Public Opinion and the Problem of War". *Catholic Mind* (March–April 1959), pp. 151–8.

O'Brien, William V. *The Conduct of Just and Limited War*. New York: Praeger Publishers, 1981.

Osgood, Robert E., and Robert W. Tucker. *Force, Order and Justice*. Baltimore: Johns Hopkins University Press, 1967.

Pope John Paul II. Homily in Singapore, November 20, 1986. Reprinted in *The Wanderer* (December 11, 1986).

Ramsey, Paul. *The Just War*. New York: Charles Scribner's Sons, 1968.

Rummel, Rudolph J. "War Isn't This Century's Biggest Killer". *The Wall Street Journal* (Monday, July 7, 1986).

Rummel, Rudolph J. "Deadlier Than War: Non-Freedom". Manuscript, University of Hawaii, March 15, 1986.

CHAPTER TWENTY-TWO

AGAIN COUNTERFORCE/WAR-FIGHTING

In Chapters 1 through 11 we examined the alternatives to the preparation for and, if necessary, actual use of nuclear weapons as military weapons—war-fighting. We found that all attempts to escape actually using nuclear weapons to defend against aggression presented serious moral problems. In Chapter 12 we listed the common objections to nuclear war-fighting and saw they were of two types. The first type posited that such a war would inherently be immoral. The second type held that such a war would be infeasible to conduct—that nuclear weapons are not really weapons in the sense of being usable in pursuit of political objectives the way guns and high-explosive bombs are.

In Chapters 13 through 21, we examined the moral issues, using the analytical tool of Just War Doctrine. We concluded that the actual use of nuclear weapons *can* be moral, provided that their use can be kept *limited*. That is, the objectives of the war must be limited to the pursuit of the just cause for which it was begun, the actual fighting must be confined to military objectives, and any damage to noncombatants that is *permitted* as a concomitant of an attack on a military objective must be proportionate to the values being preserved by attacking that military objective.

We still face the practical question: Can nuclear war be kept limited in that fashion? Can the level of destruction be kept low enough so that it doesn't outweigh the values the war is fought to preserve and the political objectives it is fought to achieve? That will be the topic of this chapter. We will take up the *infeasibility* objections presented in Chapter 12 and see to what extent they are valid. If one or more of the objections are valid, then nuclear war fails the Just War proportionality requirement, and possibly other requirements as well.

The first objection we consider is the one saying that nuclear weapons cannot be used for war-fighting because there is no defense against them. The meaning of the objection itself is not clear. Does it mean that we cannot prevent a nuclear weapon from being delivered to the target, or does it mean instead that when a nuclear weapon is delivered to a target, the target is inevitably destroyed?

Neither one of these possible meanings is necessarily true. However, we will defer the discussion of active defense (keeping the weapon from getting through) to Chapter 25, and passive or civil defense (preventing a delivered weapon from fully destroying the target) to Chapter 28.[1]

At this point, we can simply note that the assertion is actually a non sequitur. Even if "the bomber will always get through", and even if every warhead completely destroys its target, this has nothing to do with the issue of whether the use of nuclear weapons can be kept limited to levels that would satisfy both Just War criteria and political requirements.

Mr. McNamara's attempt to justify this non sequitur by an argument based on attrition is simply obfuscation. It is simply not the case that war necessarily relies on attrition to defeat the enemy, nor that the victorious belligerent is the one who outlasts the other. Mr. McNamara and his successors conducted an attrition war in Vietnam, in which the objective was to wear down the enemy. They (and we, and especially the ordinary Vietnamese people) lost. The Vietnamese communists did not conduct an attrition war. Instead, as Colonel Harry Summers has shown, they focused on the critical objectives, and won the war *despite the fact they never once defeated the American Army in battle* (1982, pp. 20–29).

Luttwak has called the attrition approach to war-fighting the *dumb-rich* style of war (1986, p. 242). It substitutes overwhelming material resources for strategy, for tactics, and even for thought itself. Moreover, it ignores intangibles, such as morale, that can enable an army to overcome the enemy's material resources, as the morale of the Vietnamese Communists (at least the leaders) succeeded in overcoming our material resources. (It was our army, not theirs, that had drug problems, murdering ["fragging"] of officers, and a worrisome desertion rate.) The "materialist bias" (as Luttwak calls it) inherent in the "attrition" approach, fails to recognize that in most wars in history, the outcome was decided by the intangible factors rather than the material factors.[2]

In short, the argument that "there is no defense" does not lead to the conclusion that wars fought with nuclear weapons will inevitably be-

---

[1] It is worth noting that those who make the strongest claim that there is no defense against nuclear weapons are also those who most vigorously oppose any attempt to build defenses. For instance, Mr. Robert McNamara, during his term as Secretary of Defense, opposed both civil defense measures and attempts to develop a defense against strategic missiles and deliberately dismantled U.S. defenses against air attack. He is currently one of the most vigorous opponents of developing a missile defense. It appears he wishes the statement "there is no defense" to continue to be a self-fulfilling prophecy.

[2] Luttwak gives some examples (1985, p. 145ff.). Summers gives several citations from Clausewitz that make the same point (1982, p. 82). Sun Tzu (1963) bases his entire teaching on the notion that the intangible factors outweigh the material factors; and the

come unlimited. If anything, it leads to the conclusion that a dumb-rich war fought with nuclear weapons would be even more frightful than one fought with non-nuclear weapons, and reinforces the conclusion that we ought not plan to fight dumb-rich wars regardless of the weapons used.

The majority of the arguments quoted in Chapter 12 to the effect that nuclear weapons cannot be used in a limited manner boil down to the assertion: "The Soviets will escalate, and therefore we'll have to escalate too." This statement really contains two separate assertions, each of which must be considered on its own merits. Thus we need to consider two distinct issues: (1) Can we limit our own actions to those that are morally acceptable? (2) What do we do if the enemy doesn't limit his actions to those that are morally acceptable?

This second issue has a particular importance. It would be moral *for us* to fight a war with nuclear weapons even if the enemy exceeded the bounds of morality. After all, the atrocities of the Nazis didn't make *our* participation in World War II immoral. On the contrary, they justified our participation. However, if the enemy could win by escalating while we exercised restraint, victory would be impossible from the outset, and the war would fail one of the important Just War criteria.

We will defer for the moment consideration of what the Soviets might do. Let us consider first the problems we would face in trying to keep our own use of nuclear weapons within Just War limits. To do this, we need to make clear just what is involved in limiting the war. The American Catholic bishops, for instance, expressed doubt that "precise rational and moral limits" could be maintained. Others have described the problem as one of "fine-tuning the war" and have expressed doubts as to whether this would be possible.

Those who argue this way are demanding too much. No war has ever been fine-tuned. However, Just War Doctrine doesn't demand that war be fine-tuned. It doesn't demand micrometric precision. It allows room for accidents, for mistakes in judgment, even for *safety margins*— doing more than might be absolutely necessary, for example, because at the outset you don't know exactly how much will be necessary. As we have already seen in the preceding chapters, Just War Doctrine demands only that you be fighting for something worth the damage the war will cause, that you exercise due care that the damage isn't any worse than it has to be, and in particular that avoidable damage to innocent parties actually be avoided. Thus we need to see if there is some intrinsic prop-

---

essence of B. Liddell Hart's arguments (1974) is that the proper strategy is to use "indirect" methods rather than grinding down the enemy.

erty of nuclear weapons that would prevent us from maintaining an adequate, even if not micrometric, degree of control over our own use.

The American Catholic bishops quoted several anonymous "experts" as advising them that in the confusion of battle, commanders would not be able to exercise control over use of nuclear weapons. There are several possible interpretations of this statement:

1. Commanders won't know where the targets are.
2. Commanders will start using nuclear weapons in an indiscriminate way.
3. Commanders will use nuclear weapons in ways which violate proportionality in the damage they cause to bystanders.

It is almost certain that in the confusion of battle the commanders will not know where all the targets are. However, under these conditions the commanders should not be authorizing the use of even conventional weapons, let alone nuclear weapons. Rhodes presents the views of two Air Force colonels regarding use of non-nuclear ordnance in the vicinity of friendly troops (1986, p. 50). One colonel is quoted as saying, "In close air support, there are specific rules of engagement, and certain criteria have to be met before the release of any weapons. . . . The targets become a function of where the friendly troops are on the ground." Another is quoted as saying, "[C]lose air support is extremely complicated because of the coordination required. . . . There are also certain restrictions you have to put up with when delivering lethal ordnance next to your own troops." That is, the problems of locating targets accurately, and of avoiding accidental attacks on our own troops, are already recognized and are being dealt with in connection with use of conventional munitions. Do the bishops' "experts" believe that commanders would be *less* careful with targeting and delivery of nuclear weapons?

The task of avoiding damage to civilian bystanders may have to be emphasized to commanders by our political leaders, but it would fit within the framework of what commanders are already used to thinking about with regard to non-nuclear weapons. Thus the fact that commanders might not know where the targets are doesn't mean the war *has to* become unlimited.

As for commanders using weapons indiscriminately or losing sight of proportionality, this becomes a matter for the nation's political leaders. We simply cannot delegate to military commanders the task of determining how much damage to innocent bystanders is *proportionate*, or how much care they must take in being *discriminating*. The political leaders, who were responsible for the initial decision that the values the war would preserve were proportionate to the damage it would do, must ensure that commanders attack only military targets and do not exceed the limits of proportionality on individual targets. This means, among other things, that the political leaders must be able to transmit their decisions to the field commanders and in turn know what the commanders are doing.[3]

Once we recognize that the issue really amounts to maintaining discrimination and proportionality, we see that the confusion of battle is only an excuse, not a reason, for losing control of the level of destruction caused by nuclear weapons. Commanders make individual decisions about where to detonate nuclear weapons and about what size weapons to use. They must be told by proper authority what constraints they will operate under and be held accountable for staying within those constraints.[4]

But this, of course, deals with only one side. War involves two sides. Is there some inner logic in the interaction between two sides that makes escalation to an all-out level inevitable?

Bundy, et. al have written that they see no "persuasive reason" to believe that the use of nuclear weapons can be kept limited (1982, p. 757). However, they have asked the wrong question. Can they offer any "persuasive reason" to believe that war will inevitably escalate to the all-out level once the first nuclear weapon has been exploded in anger? Can they offer any "persuasive reason" to believe that even if the initial use of nuclear weapons is restricted to military objectives, with civilian casualties kept as low as possible, this is only the first step to an inevitable catastrophe?

---

[3] This statement may sound frightening to military leaders, who have nightmares of another Lyndon Johnson nightly reviewing the next day's target lists. However, that is not the proper way for political leaders to exercise control. Abraham Lincoln did it properly. Instead of micromanaging the decisions of his generals, he fired one general after another until he found one who would fight the Civil War the way he wanted it fought. He achieved the proper division of labor, as he himself decided the political objectives and overall strategy, and his generals pursued those objectives with their full professional talents. In reality, this issue is the same one mentioned in Chapter 21, in the citation from Army Field Manuel FM 100-5, regarding the Principle of the Objective. Just as the political leadership is responsible for telling the military commanders the political objectives of the war, and therefore the political constraints under which it must be fought, the political leadership is responsible for telling the military commanders the moral constraints under which the war must be fought. In either case, the political leadership is responsible for either assuring that the military commanders adhere to those constraints or replacing them with commanders who will do so.

[4] There is yet another objection sometimes raised: that nuclear weapons will be used *in spite of* the orders of commanders. However, as described in Chapter 19, the Permissive Action Link is intended specifically to prevent this from happening. Launch crews cannot, on their own initiative, decide to fire a nuclear weapon. Even less can the weapons accidentally launch themselves.

Clearly they cannot offer any such reason, because the war does not have a mind of its own. Decisions to use or not use a particular size weapon on a particular target are made by individuals. There is nothing inevitable about the decision to escalate.

It is unfortunate that the term *escalation* has come into such widespread use. It implies complete automaticity, something along the lines of a department store escalator. One simply gets on it and rides up, with no further volition required. However, when Herman Kahn introduced the concept of an "escalation ladder"[5], he specifically described it in terms of successive "rungs", with passage from one rung to the next one up coming as a deliberate decision, not as the automatic result of a process over which one no longer has control (Kahn, 1962, p. 185). He later described escalation as a "competition in risk-taking" (Kahn, 1965, p. 3), with each side demonstrating its resolve by taking another step up the "ladder". However, the implication was that each side could stop at any point, conceding that the enemy had raised the ante too high to make the further risks of taking the next step worthwhile. Kahn thus clearly recognized that, in war as in peace, decisions are made by people. They are not the automatic outcome of some inevitable logic of war.

Thus, although no one can guarantee that nuclear war will inevitably remain limited, there is certainly no reason to believe that it will inevitably escalate to an all-out level. In particular, we can refrain from escalating it ourselves, if we choose to do so.

This brings us to the objection by Enthoven and Smith that even though we wish to keep the war limited, and even if the enemy has agreed to limits, it will be difficult to tell whether the limits are being observed in practice (1971, p. 125).

This objection arises from the same arms-control syndrome discussed in Chapter 8. It assumes that the limits will be agreed to by both sides, formally or tacitly, and they will be arbitrary numerical limits on things such as warhead yield (like the 150-kiloton yield of the Threshold Test Ban Treaty) or on the allowable range of weapons with nuclear warheads (like the limits on the range of cruise missiles in SALT II). Given such types of limits, the problem seen by Enthoven and Smith could readily arise, just as it has already arisen with regard to nuclear testing and SALT II.

In wartime, of course, the problems of verifying warhead yield or missile range would be even more difficult than they are in peacetime monitoring of arms control agreements. Any enemy nuclear burst that

---

[5] In retrospect, this is a mixed metaphor if there ever was one.

appeared to be close to the limit would lead to a debate, with our "hawks" urging, "They've broken the limit; let's saddle up and go get 'em!" and our "doves" urging, "It may have been an accident. Let's reduce the yield of the next bomb we use, to signal that we're continuing to observe the limits."[6]

Consider a war in defense of NATO. Suppose the Soviet Union explodes a nuclear weapon over, say, Antwerp, in an attempt to prevent reinforcements from arriving. We don't want to have a debate (either between our hawks and our doves, or between ourselves and the Soviets) over whether the warhead was 149 or 151 kilotons. Thus we must reject at the outset any limits based on the kinds of arbitrary numerical quantities that have provided the arms control community with employment the past three decades. Instead we must say that (for instance) targeting Antwerp *as such*, rather than targeting militarily important installations in a discriminating and proportionate manner, is unacceptable regardless of the size of the warhead.

The objective of the limitations, whether formal or tacit, (at least on our part) is to keep the war within moral bounds. As we have already seen, the morality of using a nuclear weapon does not depend upon its yield as such, but rather on whether it is aimed at a legitimate target and properly sized for that target. Hence we must break away from the arms control tradition and establish limits that are directly related to the moral bounds we want to preserve. The limits must be set in terms of whether a particular enemy attack was indiscriminate or disproportionate in the Just War senses. Whether we establish the limits through formal agreement or only tacitly is not particularly relevant. We must be able to determine unequivocally when they are violated, and we must have means for penalizing the violation.

It is at this point that those who deny the feasibility of limited war raise their ultimate objection. "Granted the enemy isn't forced by some inner logic of nuclear weapons or nuclear war to escalate; *suppose he does anyway*? Then we have to escalate to avoid losing." Hence we now examine this issue.

Suppose the enemy does make an attack that is indiscriminate or simply disproportionate (for example, the use of a large warhead against Antwerp, as mentioned above). What is our response? Do we go to the use of bigger warheads against enemy forces on our own soil or on the

---

[6] In reality it may be the doves who argue for abrogating the agreement. In numerous war games conducted by the Pentagon, it has frequently been found that the more dovish a participant is initially, the more upset he becomes, and the more likely he (and especially she) is to "go nuclear" or to escalate when he finds the enemy doesn't reciprocate his dovishness.

soil of our allies? This hardly seems the way to restore a lost balance. It amounts to retaliating for the enemy's killing our people by killing more of them ourselves. Do we then use bigger warheads against targets in the enemy's homeland (thus violating proportion), or even without increasing warhead size, do we start attacking the enemy's cities (thus violating discrimination)? In the case of the Soviet Union, this amounts to killing the slaves to punish the slaveholders. Soviet leaders have already demonstrated they are willing to kill their slaves by the millions. It is doubtful we can influence their behavior by competing with them to see who can kill their slaves first.

If we are to control their behavior, and induce them to keep their attacks on us discriminating and proportionate, we must pose a credible threat to targets that they value and that would be moral for us to attack if we needed to carry out the threat. There is a broad class of targets that are of great economic value to the Soviet leadership but that are remote from any battle area and thus would be of little direct relevance to a war. Therefore we would not ordinarily bother attacking such targets. This class includes things such as rail and highway bridges, dams, power plants, canal and river locks, oil and natural gas fields, open pit mines, quarries, aqueducts, and airfields. All can be destroyed by nuclear weapons, and most are (for good reasons) located away from population centers. Because of the minor contribution each makes to the war, but because of their importance to the continued functioning of the Soviet economy, they are ideal targets to be held hostage for the good behavior of the Soviet leaders. Moreover, it would be moral for us to attack them in retaliation for indiscriminate or disproportionate attacks by the Soviets.[7]

There is another class of targets even more important to the Soviet leadership than these economic targets: namely, the things that keep them in power, their apparatus of repression. These would include their means of internal communication and their means of enforcing their orders, such as Party organizations and prison camps. We can do far more to influence their behavior by posing a credible threat to deny them these things than we can by threatening Soviet civilians.

---

[7] Even though these targets are located away from population centers, and therefore attacks on them would not result in blast-damage to cities, fallout from the attacks could well cause casualties in cities downwind. This means that the yield and burst-height of the attack should be selected to reduce fallout as much as possible. In addition, the possible fallout casualties must be taken into account in calculations of proportion. It should be noted that with the weapon-delivery accuracy available today, most of these targets can be destroyed with a warhead smaller than the one used at Hiroshima. Thus the problem of minimizing remote casualties would be difficult but not unsolvable.

The threat of a successful revolt by the Soviet people is perhaps the most important thing which we can hold over the heads of the Soviet leadership as a *stick* to induce them to exercise restraint in the attacks they make upon us.[8] A credible threat to destroy their means of repressing the Soviet people, and of suppressing rebellion, especially in the conquered provinces of Asia, might well be sufficient to induce them to bring the war to a halt.[9]

Finding and attacking the proper targets to threaten the rule of the Soviet leadership would not involve us in an attrition or dumb-rich war. Instead, it would allow us to concentrate on the objectives that really mattered, just as the communists did during the war in Vietnam. Finding means of attacking these targets successfully would be difficult, but the payoff would be worth the effort.

The objection of Enthoven and Smith dealt primarily with verifying the observance of limits on tactical use of nuclear weapons, that is, use in conjunction with combat between two armies (or even two fleets). Kaplan's objection, that the enemy might not be able to tell the difference between a large-scale attack on legitimate targets, conducted with discrimination and with due attention to proportion, and an all-out attack, was concerned primarily with strategic use of nuclear weapons. Hence we must yet consider that issue.

Kaplan's objection can be interpreted in either of two ways: one, even a counterforce attack would be so destructive to cities and people that the Soviets couldn't distinguish the difference between it and a counter-population attack; or two, that the number of warheads seen on the way, and the number of explosions, would look like an all-out attack even if they were all aimed at purely counterforce targets. Regardless of

---

[8] It may be objected that we would be betraying the Soviet people by refraining from attacking their rulers' apparatus of repression; that we would in effect be striking a deal with the slaveholders not to free the slaves as long as the slaveholders desist from attacking us. However, as Aleksandr Solzhenitsyn and others have argued, getting rid of the Soviet leadership is a problem for the people of the Soviet Union, not for anyone else. We must not let the historically unique events of World War II, with our overthrow of Hitler, of Mussolini, and of the military government of Japan, and our liberation of Western Europe, Indochina and the islands of the Pacific, become our sole guide regarding how we deal with tyrannical governments.

[9] Aleksandr Solzhenitsyn describes several revolts in the Soviet prison camp system, some of which not only took over the camps but also marched on nearby towns. Some succeeded in resisting for over a month, but all were eventually suppressed by troops brought in for the purpose. Strikes with low-yield nuclear weapons that knocked out road and rail bridges and that destroyed troop garrisons might well lead to revolts by millions of Gulag prisoners, since the Soviet government would then be in no position to suppress them.

what Kaplan may have meant, we need to examine both interpretations.

It may be useful to look at the issue from our own side. Cole describes the targeting the Soviets would need to do if they attempted to execute a disarming first strike against the United States.

> First-strike targets in the U.S., those that must be destroyed in the critical first few minutes of any attack, include 1,000 Minuteman silos, 16 test silos at Vandenberg Air Force Base, the last few Titan II silos, 105 launch-control bunkers, 17 Strategic Air Command bomber bases, 17 Strategic Air Command tanker bases, 16 Navy bases with nuclear-armed ships, 9 nuclear-weapon storage facilities, the White House, the Pentagon, NORAD Command at Cheyenne Mountain, Strategic Air Command headquarters, the Alternative National Headquarters at Fort Ritchie, two SAC alternate command posts, 5 early warning radars, 10 Navy communications stations, 9 SAC communications facilities, and 9 satellite communications bases. Allowing two bombs per target, with extra bombs around the air bases to knock down any escaping aircraft, this would require about 2,840 weapons (1986, p. 41).[10]

Note that most of the targets listed are remote from cities and heavily populated areas. In such an attack, only a few cities would be obliterated. Most of the nation's cities would suffer no blast damage whatsoever. Immediate American casualties would be fewer than the Soviets suffered at the hands of the Nazis in World War II, when their population was about the same size as ours is now. The radioactive fallout from such an attack would be heavy, but it would take hours to arrive at the undamaged cities. If properly-stocked fallout shelters were available, total casualties could probably be limited to those killed directly in the attacks on installations near cities. Hence from the *damage* standpoint, we can reject the interpretation that says there would be no significant difference between a massive counterforce attack and a counterpopulation attack. The casualties from a counterforce attack would probably be a tenth or less of those from a counterpopulation attack.[11]

What about the *appearance* of the attack? While this hypothetical at-

---

[10] Cole notes that the Soviets have, under SALT II, deployed 308 SS-18 missiles, the largest missiles ever built. These may carry up to thirty warheads, although they are limited by SALT II to ten. This force makes up only 22 percent of the number of missiles the Soviet Union is allowed. These 308 SS-18s (allowing for those with fewer than ten warheads and discounting reports that some have more) have about 2900 warheads. That is, the SS-18 force alone would be sufficient to carry out the "first strike" described above.

[11] Note that casualties from a counterforce attack arise primarily from locating military targets near population centers. This is an argument for locating strategic-missile and bomber bases in remote and lightly populated areas and for basing nuclear missile submarines away from large cities. We could go a long way toward preparing ourselves to fight

tack is still on its way, our early warning radar would show about 300 incoming *hostile tracks*. We would have no idea of the targets, since the individual warheads would not yet be deployed from their *buses*. If we had battle-management radars (we don't because they are prohibited by the ABM treaty), once the buses deployed their individual warheads, there would be about 3000 hostile tracks, and we could begin to identify specific targets for each warhead. As it is, we would be able to discern the nature of the attack only as the warheads began to explode on their targets.

How would we respond to this massive attack when we saw it coming? The United States has never disavowed a policy of Launch Under Attack (LUA). However, we concluded in Chapter 9 that such a policy is very imprudent. It denies us the opportunity to discern the nature of the attack before responding, and it removes any incentive on the part of the attacker to avoid doing unnecessary damage, since an announced policy of LUA expressly denies any willingness on our part to reciprocate the attacker's restraint. Despite the imprudence of such a policy, however, we might launch our land-based missiles before they were destroyed, employing a "use them or lose them" philosophy.

What about the Soviets? Would they, as Kaplan suggests, be unable to tell the difference between a counterforce strike and a countercity strike *before the warheads had landed*? They probably couldn't tell the difference any better than we could and might respond by launching their missiles before they were destroyed.[12] However, this really isn't relevant. A massive strike of the type described by Cole is intended as a disarming strike—to so disable the enemy's strategic forces that a significant second strike is impossible (or, as the Soviets would argue, to "preempt" the first strike the enemy was planning to make, and abort it).

Every American president since Eisenhower, and several of their secretaries of defense, have stated, as declaratory policy, that the United States will not strike first. *Preemption* has never been part of our publicly announced policy. Since the demise of the doctrine of "massive retaliation" for non-nuclear attacks, our announced policy has been that of "second strike" only. Even "first use" would occur only in the context of a massive conventional attack on one of our allies.

---

a nuclear war by defeating Congress members from densely populated areas who get a military base located in their district, and electing those who will keep them out.

[12] In reality, the Soviets could probably tell much better than we can the nature of a massive missile attack. In violation of the ABM Treaty, they have embarked on the construction of several battle-management radars, which could identify the targets of individual warheads after the buses have crossed the Soviet border and deployed those warheads.

Given this policy, there would never be a need on our part to execute a massive strike such as that described above, not even at counterforce targets.[13] Hence the problem should not arise. This doesn't completely dispense with Kaplan's objection, of course. It simply means that our actions in a nuclear war must be such that we would never put the Soviets in a position of uncertainty about the true nature of an attack—countercity or counterforce. Since our objective must be to stay within the limits of the Just War, this does not impose any additional constraints on us.

In nuclear war involving strikes against both U.S. and Soviet homelands, just as in tactical nuclear war, the objective on our part will be to keep our own use of nuclear weapons within Just War limits and to penalize the enemy for exceeding these limits. Again, we would be looking for targets that are of great value to the Soviet leaders (though not necessarily to the Soviet people) but whose destruction is not of great *direct* value to us, in terms of prosecuting the war, and whose destruction would not violate Just War limits. The justification for destroying these targets, under Just War Doctrine, would be to discourage further violations of Just War limits by the enemy. Their *indirect* value to us is thus worth the cost of destroying them. Many of the same types of targets listed above for the tactical case would be suitable for the strategic case as well.

In short, we can keep our own use of nuclear weapons limited, regardless of what the Soviets do, if we choose to do so. In addition, we can penalize the enemy for exceeding Just War limits, if necessary, without exceeding those limits ourselves.

Would our restraint, and our ability to impose a penalty on the Soviets if they don't observe restraints, be certain to keep them from escalating? Nothing depending on human choice is certain. Nevertheless, it is worth noting that the United States and the Soviet Union have each been successful at interwar dissuasion for over thirty years, ever since the Soviets acquired their own nuclear weapons. Even once nuclear war has broken out, both sides should be able to see the merits of intrawar dissuasion and have an incentive not to escalate to all-out levels. The ability to threaten either high-value targets, or the Soviet command structure itself, gives us *bargaining power* within the war. Thus intrawar dissuasion has a good chance of working to keep the war limited, and it *doesn't* depend upon the threat of killing innocents.

---

[13] An exception to this might be an attempt to overwhelm Soviet antimissile defenses. However, if the Soviets have as much confidence in their defenses as we would be showing by making such a massive attack, they should be able to ride out the attack and see what targets are hit, rather than launching their own missiles before ours arrive.

Will the Soviets accept this view? There has been a great deal of arrogance among U.S. arms controllers for the past three decades. They have assumed from the outset that the Soviets knew nothing about war, particularly nuclear war, and it was our task to educate them. For instance, our arms controllers decided we had to educate the Soviets to the idea that defense was bad and vulnerability was good. As an example of this attitude, consider the following statement by Paul Warnke, made in 1977 when he was head of the Arms Control and Disarmament Agency, regarding the Soviet view that victory in nuclear war was meaningful and achievable:

> Instead of talking in those terms, which would indulge what I regard as the primitive aspects of Soviet nuclear doctrine, we ought to be trying to educate them into the real world of strategic nuclear weapons, which is that nobody could possibly win (quoted by Glynn, 1984, p. 33).

Thus the matter of the *fightability* of a nuclear war would not be another instance of the same kind of arrogance on our part. We don't need to teach them that yes, indeed, you can fight a nuclear war if you keep it limited. On the contrary, they believe it already. Our arms controllers have spent a great deal of effort, so far without success, trying to "educate" the Soviets out of this notion.

To see how the Soviets view nuclear war, it is worth looking at some of the documents they publish for their own internal use, rather than for propaganda purposes.

Cohen (1985) presents several quotes from *Military Thought*, the official journal of the Soviet General Staff. They are repeated here to illustrate official Soviet thinking regarding the feasibility of nuclear war-fighting, and the Soviet attitudes toward nuclear weapons.

> Theses of Soviet military strategy primarily reflect the political strategy of the Communist Party of the Soviet Union. It is in the interests of political strategy that military strategy makes use of the achievements of scientific-technical progress which materializes in weapons of varying power . . . [certain weapons can] lead to defeat of the enemy's armed forces without doing essential injury to the economy or populace of states whose aggressive rulers unleashed the war. Only political leadership can determine the scale and consistency of bringing to bear the most powerful means of destruction.
>
> The objective is not to turn the large economic and industrial regions into a heap of ruins . . . but to deliver strikes which will destroy strategic combat means, paralyze enemy military production, making it incapable of satisfying the priority needs of the front and rear areas and sharply reduce the enemy capability to conduct strikes.
>
> Initial attention is given to the selection of those enemy targets against which nuclear means could be used. Depending on the features of the

strike targets, a selection is made of the nuclear weapons carriers . . . which could best and most rapidly execute the assigned mission with minimum expenditure of explosive power.

Cohen also quotes (1985, p. 12) from a 1972 book by Milovidov and Koslof as follows:

. . . the relationship between politics and war, thoroughly revealed in the writings of Lenin, not only remains valid in the nuclear age, but acquires even greater significance.

Note that Lenin was an avid student of Clausewitz, and took seriously the Clausewitzian link between politics and military action. The current Soviet leadership is still Leninist in this regard. In their view, not even nuclear weapons can change the fundamental linkage between politics and war.[14]

This Clausewitzian-cum-Leninist view is given special emphasis by Byely and his contributors, who made statements such as the following.

The role of economic conditions in modern war has not only grown considerably but has also changed essentially in comparison with the world wars of the past. In a world nuclear war, exclusive importance will be acquired by the stockpiles of nuclear warheads and the means for their delivery to target. . . . Missiles with nuclear warheads are able to paralyse entire industrial regions. Therefore, at the very beginning of the war, after the first nuclear missile exchange, a sharp and radical change may set in in the relation of the combatants' economic potentials. . . . In all probability the war will not end with an exchange of annihilating nuclear missile strikes. Despite the heavy destruction, some part of industrial enterprises and other economic objectives will survive. It is therefore very possible that the remaining enterprises will be engaged both in the production of weapons and in catering to the needs of the population; . . . *Under these conditions decisive importance is acquired not only by the existing industrial potential of the warring coalitions, but also by their viability and mobility; the vulnerability of industry and communications, and the ability to restore industrial production in the course of the war* (1968, pp. 222–23) (emphasis in original).

Byely also states:

Nuclear war . . . should not be thought of as a gigantic technical enterprise alone—as a launching of an enormous number of missiles with nuclear warheads to destroy the vital objectives and manpower of the enemy, or as operations of the armed forces alone. Nuclear war is a complex and many-sided process, which in addition to the operation of

---

[14] In an important sense, of course, Soviet leaders, starting with Lenin, have stood Clausewitz on his head. To them, politics is war conducted by other means. War is the normal state of affairs so long as the world is not yet communist, and politics is simply one manifestation of this war.

the armed forces will involve economic, diplomatic and ideological forms of struggle. They will all serve the political aims of the war and be guided by them (1968, p. 12).

General V. D. Sokolovskiy, who published a series of books on Soviet military thought, stated:

> The Soviet government . . . and their armed forces must be ready primarily for a world war . . . the Armed Forces of the Soviet Union and the other socialist countries must be prepared above all to wage war under conditions of the mass use of nuclear weapons by both belligerent parties. . . . [T]he preparation and waging of just such a war must be regarded as the main task of the theory of military strategy and strategic leadership (quoted by Douglass and Hoeber, 1981, pp. 188–95).

What, then, about the apparent Soviet agreement with Western leaders that a war in which nuclear weapons would be used would be a disaster with no winners? While the Soviet leaders may say such things to an audience of Westerners, they say different things to their own subordinates.

General Milovidov (obviously writing with the approval of his superiors, otherwise he would not have been published) stated:

> There is profound error and harm in the disorienting claims of bourgeois ideologues that there will be no victor in a thermonuclear war.

He stated further:

> This does not mean that nuclear war . . . has ceased to be an instrument of politics, as is claimed by the overwhelming majority of representatives of pacifist, anti-war movements in the bourgeois world. This is a subjective judgment. It expresses merely protest against nuclear war (Milovidov and Koslof, p. 17; quoted by Douglass and Hoeber, 1981).

These excerpts are not simply isolated instances, but are representative of the thinking of Soviet military leaders (and therefore of their civilian superiors). Numerous Western analysts and officials have identified these same themes running throughout Soviet writings on modern warfare.

Richard Pipes, the noted Sovietologist, has written:

> Soviet nuclear strategy is counter*force* oriented. It targets for destruction—at any rate, in the initial strike—not the enemy's cities but his military forces and their command and communications facilities. Its primary aim is to destroy not civilians but soldiers and their leaders, and to undermine not so much the will to resist as the capability to do so.
>
> Soviet theorists regard strategic nuclear forces (organized since 1966 into a separate arm, the Strategic Rocket Forces) to be the decisive branch of the armed services, in the sense that the ultimate outcome of modern war would be settled by nuclear exchanges. But since nuclear war, in

their view, must lead not only to the enemy's defeat but also to his destruction (i.e., his incapacity to offer further resistance), they consider it necessary to make preparations for the follow-up phase, which may entail a prolonged war of attrition. . . . The notion of an extended nuclear war is deeply embedded in Soviet thinking, despite its being dismissed by Western strategists who think of war as a one-two exchange.
. . . the U.S. theory of mutual deterrence postulates that no effective defense can be devised against an all-out nuclear attack: it is this postulate that makes such a war appear totally irrational. In order to make this premise valid, American civilian strategists have argued against a civil-defense program, against the ABM, and against air defenses.
Nothing illustrates better the fundamental differences between the two strategic doctrines than their attitudes to defense against a nuclear attack. The Russians agreed to certain imprecisely defined limitations on ABM after they had initiated a program in this direction, apparently because they were unable to solve the technical problems involved and feared the United States would forge ahead in this field. However, they then proceeded to build a tight ring of anti-aircraft defenses around the country while also developing a serious program of civil defense (1977).

As noted above, we will defer discussion of active and passive defense until later chapters. At this point it is simply worth noting that to the Soviets, these are essential elements in fighting, surviving, and *winning* a war in which nuclear weapons are employed by both sides.

Benjamin S. Lambeth has made a similar evaluation of Soviet views concerning the winnability of nuclear wars.

From every indication that one can gather from its uninterrupted record of force enhancement since the conclusion of SALT I seven years ago [this was published in 1981, but it remains valid today], the Soviet leadership has signalled its unambiguous commitment to the accretion of a credible war-fighting capability in all bands of the conflict spectrum in total disregard of, if not outright contempt for, repeatedly articulated Western security sensitivities. . . . Soviet recognition that nuclear war is a possibility that might some day have to be confronted and dealt with has led to a perceived obligation on the part of the leadership to undertake every feasible measure to mitigate its destructive impact so that the Soviet state might emerge in the least impaired condition possible under the circumstances. . . . What it boils down to essentially is an approach to deterrence based not on acceptance of a mutual suicide pact but on an abiding belief in the plausibility of achieving recognizable victory in strategic nuclear war (1981).

Scrowcroft locates the root of this Soviet belief in the fact that during the years between World War I and World War II, the Soviets did not adopt the views of strategic bombardment common in the United States and Great Britain (outlined in Chapter 2).

Military air forces, including bombers, by and large remained an adjunct to army and naval forces, in at least implicit rejection of the notion of victory through the application solely of aerial bombardment. Thus nuclear weapons have apparently been incorporated into Soviet strategic thought as a part of a combined arms concept, rather than as a distinct revolution overturning traditional concepts and objectives of warfare (1984, p. 74).

Are the Soviets simply wrong about the possibility of fighting and winning a war in which nuclear weapons are used? Should we encourage our arms controllers to continue to try to "educate" the Soviets out of this view? Not only would this be futile, it would be (as I have tried to show in this chapter) completely wrong. As Cohen puts it, the Soviets have set about preparing

> to fight and win a nuclear war, and to survive as a viable society still under communist control. For any American, including the president, to decide for the Russians that they have undertaken this enormous effort (while the Soviet economy has been allowed to suffer greatly) all in vain has to be presumptuous to an extreme. . . . We have been unwilling to look objectively at Soviet efforts to survive nuclear war, in no small way for fear that we might find out that they might be able to survive (1985, p. 91).

Indeed, as Cohen puts it, it is the United States that needs to be educated out of its current views, not the Soviet Union.

> The United States' critical problem has been that it has chosen to opt out of the nuclear age, whereas the Soviets have unhesitatingly accepted it. We have not been willing seriously to contemplate nuclear weapons as war-fighting instruments; the Soviets always have. This fundamental doctrinal disparity has placed NATO in an untenable position (1985, p. 27).

In short, we don't have to convince the Soviets that nuclear war is fightable and winnable. They already believe that. What we must do is convince *ourselves* that it is fightable and winnable. After that, we need to convince the Soviets that we are prepared and willing to fight it *if necessary*, that we intend to keep our military efforts within moral limits, and that we have the will and the ability to penalize them for exceeding moral limits on objectives, targets, and levels of destruction.

Even once we recognize that nuclear war doesn't have to escalate automatically, that it is fightable and winnable in a meaningful sense, there are still some objections to nuclear war-fighting from Chapter 12. We must yet address these.

The first of these objections is that preparing to *fight* a nuclear war, instead of merely threatening a response that would do us no good if we ever had to carry it out, will make deterrence less stable. The current stability, it is argued, depends upon everyone perceiving nuclear war as unwinnable, even by the side striking first; whereas if people perceive it as winnable, they might be tempted to strike first and thereby improve their chances of winning.

The quickest answer to this is that it is too late to stabilize deterrence by convincing everyone that nuclear war is unwinnable. As I have already shown, the Soviets don't believe that. By continuing to argue for unwinnability, and by arming ourselves only with weapons that have no practical military utility but can be used only for immoral purposes, we merely frighten ourselves and provide the Soviets with additional incentives to employ nuclear blackmail on us.

However, from a broader perspective, we want to get away from a deterrence that means the threat of "revenge from the grave", and that amounts to a mutual suicide pact. "Stabilizing" that kind of deterrence is really the last thing we want to do. As I have already argued in Chapter 5, that kind of deterrent threat is probably immoral itself. To use the *destabilizing of deterrence* argument against gaining a war-fighting capability is to argue in favor of retaining an immoral policy.

The second of these remaining objections is that nuclear war is unwinnable since the loser can always destroy the winner before going under. This assertion is not necessarily true. If the Soviets carried out the disarming first strike described above by Cole, it is unlikely that the United States would retain sufficient nuclear striking forces to destroy the Soviet Union. However, there is enough truth in the assertion that we must take it seriously.

As we have already discussed in Chapter 16, conforming to Just War Doctrine means never putting an enemy in a position where he is going down to utter destruction but can still destroy the "winner". That is, while it may be possible for the "loser" to destroy the "winner", that doesn't mean nuclear war is unwinnable. It simply means that the enemy must never be faced with this choice. In particular, it means that in a war between the United States and the Soviet Union, so long as there is a chance the Soviets have any remaining nuclear weapons, we must never put the Soviet leadership in a position where they will inevitably be destroyed. Instead, we must demonstrate the *capability* to destroy them, while making it clear we will refrain from doing so as long as they refrain from indiscriminate or disproportionate attacks against us. This is an important part of the process of keeping the war limited, as discussed above.

The final remaining objection is the one stating that if we prepare to *fight* a nuclear war, nuclear war will become *thinkable*. In a crisis, we might decide to go to war if we believed we could fight it and achieve a meaningful victory.

We must be very clear about what the advocates of this view are saying. They would have us believe that our choices are between having a war-fighting capability and having peace. This is wrong. Our real choices are between having a war-fighting capability and being forced to surrender. As we have already seen, surrender doesn't bring peace. It merely brings a war of the armed against the unarmed, and ultimately may result in a nuclear civil war among people who don't adhere to the Just War Doctrine but who instead seek victory for themselves personally, regardless of the cost to others.

Those who object to our acquiring usable weapons because they might some day be used ought to come clean. Do they have a secret agenda? Would they prefer that we procure only weapons we know to be unusable and make no plans to use them? Would they prefer that in a crisis we have no options but surrender? Is their objection to war-fighting simply a more subtle version of "better red than dead"? As we've already seen in Chapter 10, procuring only unusable weapons means losing all dissuasive effects of the weapons on which we have spent enormous sums of money. In fact, it creates a *moral hazard*, since it might tempt an enemy into aggressive action he would not normally contemplate. Our refusal to make nuclear war thinkable serves only to make it more thinkable for the Soviets. In any case, it would be morally untenable for us either to surrender to tyranny or to prepare to employ unusable weapons.

Those who argue that even limited nuclear war is unthinkable should keep in mind the words of Pope Paul VI, in his "Message for the Observance of a Day of Peace", January 1, 1968.

> [I]t is to be hoped that the exaltation of the idea of peace may not favor the cowardice of those who fear it may be their duty to give their lives for the service of their own country and of their own brothers, when these are engaged in the defense of justice and liberty, and who seek only a flight from their responsibility, from the risks that are necessarily involved in the accomplishment of great duties and generous exploits. Peace is not pacifism; it does not mask a base and slothful concept of life, but it proclaims the highest and most universal values of life: truth, justice, freedom, love.[15]

---

[15] Statements by other popes reinforce this point. Pope Pius XII, in his Christmas Message of December 24, 1948, said: "A people threatened with an unjust aggression, or already its victim, may not remain passively indifferent, if it would think and act as befits a Christian." It should be remembered this is the voice of a man who endured World War

Having demonstrated the falsity of the arguments that nuclear war inherently cannot be kept limited to moral levels of violence, we need to look at the issue of initiating the use of nuclear weapons. As indicated in this and earlier chapters, the United States has adopted a declaratory policy of first use, but not of first strike. The Soviets, by contrast, have adopted a declaratory policy of first strike (although they write instead of "preempting" the United States when we are about to strike them), and they have publicly called for a policy of rejecting first use.

This situation has given rise to a great debate over whether it would be moral for us to "go nuclear" if the Soviets launched a conventional attack. The American Catholic bishops specifically addressed this question, and rejected the NATO first-use policy. They have demanded a "firebreak" between nuclear weapons and war. However, it should be remembered that their rejection was at the lowest of the three levels of authority in the Challenge of Peace pastoral. It was at the level of prudential judgment, not of binding moral principle or of traditional Church application of principle. As such, it deserves only as much weight as is justified by the bishops' professional and technical competence on the subject of nuclear war.

In particular, they judged first use of nuclear weapons to be immoral because it would inevitably lead to ever-greater use and escalation to all-out nuclear war. In short, they made a *slippery slope* objection, not an objection based on fundamental moral principles. This objection is not surprising, considering the "experts" whom the Bishops chose to consult.

As noted in Chapter 12, Mr. McNamara described NATO nuclear doctrine as involving a tight linkage between first use by NATO and escalation to all-out levels. If the Soviets attack conventionally and are winning, NATO will "go nuclear", and will escalate up to and including the level of massive attacks against the Soviet Union.

This situation should not really be described as a slippery slope, that is, one in which we might accidentally slide into all-out nuclear war despite our efforts to avoid it. This strategy, as described by Mr. McNa-

II, and whose other statements showed he was fully aware of the potential horrors of nuclear weapons.

Pope John Paul II, in his World Day of Peace Message of January 1, 1982, stated: "Christians, even as they strive to resist and prevent every form of warfare, have no hesitation in recalling that, in the name of an elementary requirement of justice, peoples have a right and even a duty to protect their existence and freedom by a proportionate means against an unjust aggressor."

Clearly Catholics cannot argue that procuring usable weapons and preparing to use them in defense of important values is contrary to the teachings of the Church. On the contrary, it is not only permitted but demanded by Catholic teachings.

mara, is really a "ski run" on which we embark deliberately. The intent is to frighten the Soviets with the threat that if they attack with such a level of conventional force that we are defeated, we will blow them up completely, even though we ourselves will be blown up in the process. Unfortunately, the primary effect of this declaratory policy is to frighten ourselves, not the Soviets. As we have already seen, they are convinced that they can not only survive a nuclear war, but achieve meaningful victory.[16]

Henry Kissinger commented in 1979 on NATO's declaratory policy of unlimited escalation as follows:

> The European allies should not keep asking us to multiply strategic assurances that we cannot possibly mean, or if we do mean, we should not want to execute because if we execute we risk the destruction of civilization (quoted in Cohen, 1985, p. 29).

This is precisely correct. We should not be assuring our European allies, and trying to convince the Soviets, that if the Soviets attack Western Europe the United States will commit suicide by launching an all-out attack against the Soviet Union. The Soviets don't believe it, but the Europeans (as well as our own citizens) believe it all too much. In short, we should quit promising to start down the "ski run", and instead take the steps needed to avoid the slippery slope, by preparing ourselves to keep a nuclear war limited.

However, the issue of first use may be nothing but a red herring. Can we really expect the Soviets to wait for us to make the decision to "go nuclear"?

Henry Kissinger (1979) has expressed his doubts about the choice being ours as follows:

> Regardless of what we may decide, the Soviets may introduce nuclear weapons first; in fact, if they have not lost their senses, they almost have to use nuclear weapons first (quoted in Cohen, 1985, p. 12).

Bernard Brodie has made a similar argument:

> Can anyone believe, with confidence, that the Soviet Union would challenge us to so deadly a duel and yet leave the choice of weapons entirely to us? Can anyone seriously think that if the Russians launched such an attack, they would not be determined to win it as quickly as possible by

---

[16] Note that from the standpoint of the Soviet leadership, "victory" is a situation in which they remain in power and retain enough of an empire to be worth ruling. Even millions of Soviet lives lost would not be a defeat, so long as they continued to rule the remainder. After all, they have already killed more of their subjects than we would be likely to, especially if they strike first.

offensive action, with whatever weapons were necessary to accomplish that victory? (quoted in Cohen, 1985, p. 12).

This is not to say that the Soviets are guaranteed to open a NATO war with a nuclear strike (there is no other way, of course, in which they could open a war against the United States). Douglass and Hoeber (1981, p. 7) report the following findings from their review of the Soviets' internal literature on nuclear war.

> Should a war in Europe . . . begin with a conventional phase, Soviet operations planning would be conducted with the possible sudden transition to nuclear operations as *the* primary consideration. . . . Therefore the conventional phase is to be designed and conducted with transition to nuclear operations during conventional conflict.
>
> In the Soviet view, the main advantages of an opening conventional phase lie in the fact that it permits the more effective implementation of a surprise nuclear strike if NATO forces already have been alerted and dispersed. Several advantages flowing from an initial conventional phase are explicitly discussed in the Warsaw Pact military literature; all are associated with the problems of beginning a war with a nuclear strike.
>
> In general, the Soviet approach seems to be focused on determining the "most favorable time" to make the transition to nuclear operations. As identified in the Soviet literature, that time appears to be when a Soviet breakthrough first appears imminent (emphasis in original).

Baxter (1986) comes to similar conclusions from his review of the Soviet military literature. He states:

> Soviet tactics, particularly at the lowest levels, do not make the sharp distinction between nuclear and nonnuclear warfare that is traditional in the West. Soviet commanders assume that, if [nuclear weapons] have not been used in battle, their use by one or both sides is imminent, and their forces must be configured for that reality (p. 173).

> Soviet tactics is entirely focused upon war-winning, and if faced with defeat in a conventional war, the Soviet Army would be likely to resort to nuclear weapons regardless of any non-first use doctrine. In this situation, the Soviet Army would not wish to indicate a decision by a change of tactics (p. 249).

Bracken notes that

> Soviet military exercises actually estimate the point that the United States issues orders to use nuclear weapons and then preempt before such an action can take place (1983, p. 47).

He goes on to say that the Soviet Union has made an extensive and successful effort over the past two decades to penetrate NATO defense ministries and communications networks. The Soviets evidently plan to use both espionage and *signals intelligence* to anticipate U.S. release of nuclear weapons authorization and to preempt such a release.

However, we need not depend solely upon the entrail-readings of Sovietologists to learn what the Soviets think of nuclear war. "Viktor Suvarov" (pseudonym for a Soviet officer who escaped to the West, and is under a sentence of death in the Soviet Union), presents an insider's view of how the Soviets think. He characterizes Western thinking about nuclear war as the idea that such a war would grow out of conventional war and would build up slowly. He describes Soviet puzzlement about the true motives of Western leaders, since it was obvious to them that no one could believe such a silly idea. Finally, he goes on to describe what he calls the Soviet "axe theory": that if you know your opponent will start to fight you with his bare hands, then escalate to a knife if that fails, and finally use an axe if the knife isn't enough, the thing to do is not to wait but hit him with your axe right at the outset, and better yet, preempt him by using your axe before he gets in the first blow with his hand. The Soviet concept, as Suvarov puts it, is to hit the enemy by surprise, and with devastating force. He goes on to say that this is the reason the Soviets have put up a missile defense around their capital, instead of around their missiles.

> The best protection for rockets in a war is to use them immediately. Could anyone devise a more effective way of defending them? (1982, p. 162).

In short, the Soviets (despite what they tell the West about "no first use") are in fact planning to "go nuclear" first, in a surprise move, at the time when it is most advantageous to them. Under these circumstances, it is nothing short of foolhardy to concede the nuclear initiative to them by adopting a "no first use" policy ourselves. This doesn't mean we must automatically introduce nuclear weapons at the first sign of hostilities. If, however, we are demonstrably ready to fight and win at the nuclear level, we would provide the Soviets with an incentive *not* to go nuclear themselves and then have a reasonable hope that intrawar deterrence will be successful.[17]

Since escalation to all-out nuclear war is not an inherent feature of either nuclear war or nuclear weapons, but is instead the inevitable (and

---

[17] This assumes, of course, that we face up to the need to increase our conventional forces to a level to match those of the Soviets. Since our forces will be fighting a defensive battle, at least at the outset, they need not outnumber the Soviets' forces. By fighting from prepared positions, even a force that is somewhat inferior can hold off an attacker.

intended) outcome of a policy we have deliberately adopted, the moral issues of first use are different from those addressed by the bishops. The proper moral issue to be addressed is the licitness of threatening escalation to immoral levels, when by properly preparing ourselves we might keep the war limited. It should be evident by this point in the argument that our present policy is immoral, and the most moral policy for us to adopt is the very one rejected by the bishops, namely preparing to *fight* a nuclear war. Unfortunately, the bishops missed the opportunity to provide us with moral instruction on how nuclear weapons *may* be used and instead attempted to judge whether they *should* be used, a judgment which is properly in the province of the statesman.

In this chapter I have argued that nuclear war *can* be kept limited. However, I do not assert that it will be *easy* to keep it limited, nor do I assert that we fully understand how to keep it limited. While our nuclear doctrines and force structure have, over time, improved our warfighting as opposed to our city-busting capability, we still have not really thought through the demands of limited nuclear war, nor procured the equipment needed to fight a nuclear war in a limited way.

From a strictly pragmatic standpoint, it is obvious that we should accelerate the development of our doctrine, and the equipment of our forces, in the direction they have already been tending.

Nye (1986) argues, for instance, that:

> If deterrence should fail, it is important that it be a small failure and that leaders have time to regain their senses rather than [initiate] a preset program for massive slaughter of innocents (p. 108).

And again,

> If war breaks out by accident, the last thing we want is to be programmed for holocaust (p. 110).

Harold Brown, certainly no proponent of nuclear war-fighting, stated in his Annual Report of the Secretary of Defense, FY82,

> . . . I want to emphasize once again two points I have made repeatedly and publicly. First, I remain highly skeptical that escalation of a limited nuclear exchange can be controlled, or that it can be stopped short of an all-out, massive exchange. Second, even given that belief, I am convinced that we must do everything we can to make such escalation control possible, that opting out of this effort and consciously resigning ourselves to the inevitability of such escalation is a serious abdication of the awesome responsibilities nuclear weapons, and the unbelievable damage their uncontrolled use would create, thrust upon us. (1982, p. 40).

Thomas Powers made a similar argument:

> Massive retaliation was one thing; we could then do worse to the Soviets than they could do to us. But how do you credibly threaten an all-out response to *any* attack when the enemy can match us weapon for weapon and city for city? Do you blow up the world if you are attacked with a single nuclear weapon? And if you don't blow up the world, does it follow that you should do nothing? Why invite such a choice? The obvious alternative is to prepare a limited response to limited challenges (1982).

Matthew Murphy drew the obvious conclusions regarding the Catholic bishops' rejection of war-fighting capability, saying that "by opposing nuclear war-fighting capability, the bishops would guarantee that, if deterrence fails, it fails catastrophically (1983)."

Albert Wohlstetter gives a similar argument in his comments on the Challenge of Peace pastoral:

> . . . while [the bishops] sometimes say that we should not threaten to destroy civilians, they say too that we may continue to maintain nuclear weapons—while moving toward permanent verifiable nuclear and general disarmament—*yet we may not meanwhile plan to be able to fight a nuclear war even in response to a nuclear attack.* Before that distant millennial day when all the world disarms totally, verifiably, and irrevocably—at least in nuclear weapons—if we should not intend to attack noncombatants, as the letter says, what alternative is there to deter nuclear attack or coercion? Plainly only to be able to aim at the combatants striking us, or at their equipment, facilities, or direct sources of combat supply. That, however, is what is meant by planning to be able to fight a nuclear war—which the letter rejects (1983, p. 16, emphasis in original).

Those who insist that nuclear war cannot be kept limited, and object to any attempts to keep it limited, are presenting us with a self-fulfilling prophecy. Theirs is just one more of the many attempts to avoid the moral issues of linking the conduct of war with political objectives. It must be rejected just as we reject all the other attempts to avoid the moral issues.

In short, we must not allow ourselves to despair of keeping nuclear war limited. There is ample reason to believe it can be kept limited if we prepare ourselves to keep our actions limited and to penalize the enemy for actions that exceed moral limits. Our first step is to recognize the foolishness of assuming that nuclear war cannot be kept limited, and therefore making no preparations to limit it. We can then start taking some practical measures to keep a nuclear war limited, if we are forced to fight one. In the next several chapters, we will examine some of those measures.

REFERENCES

Baxter, William. *Soviet AirLand Battle Tactics*. Novato, Calif.: Presidio Press, 1986.

Bracken, Paul. *The Command and Control of Nuclear Forces*. New Haven: Yale University Press, 1983.

Brodie, Bernard. "Toward a New Defense for NATO". National Strategy Information Center, New York, 1976. Quoted in Cohen, p. 12.

Bundy, McGeorge, George F. Kennan, Robert S. McNamara, and Gerard Smith. "Nuclear Weapons and the Atlantic Alliance". *Foreign Affairs* (Spring 1982), pp. 753–68.

Byely, B. *Marxism-Leninism on War and Army*. Moscow: Progress Publishers, 1968.

Cohen, Sam. *We CAN Prevent World War III*. Ottawa: Ill.: Jameson Books, 1985.

Cole, Stephen V. "Why SALT FREE is Better Than SALT II". *Conservative Digest* (September 1986), pp. 35–42.

Douglass, Joseph D., Jr., and Amoretta M. Hoeber. *Conventional War and Escalation: The Soviet View*. New York: Crane, Russak & Co., 1981.

Douglass, Joseph D., Jr., and Amoretta M. Hoeber. *Soviet Strategy for Nuclear War*. Stanford, Calif.: Hoover Institution Press, 1979.

Enthoven, Alain C., and K. Wayne Smith. *How Much Is Enough?* New York: Harper & Row, 1971.

Glynn, Patrick. "The Moral Case for the Arms Buildup". In *Nuclear Arms: Ethics, Strategy, Politics,* edited by R. James Woolsey. San Francisco: ICS Press, 1984.

Hart, B. Liddell. *Strategy*. New York: New American Library, 1974.

Kahn, Herman. *On Escalation: Metaphors and Scenarios*. New York: Praeger Publishers, 1965.

Kahn, Herman. *Thinking about the Unthinkable*. New York: Horizon Press, 1962.

Kissinger, Henry. Speech to the Sandia Corporation Colloquium on Tactical Nuclear Weapons. Albuquerque, N.M. October 1965. Quoted in Cohen, p. 12.

Kissinger, Henry. Speech, "NATO—The Next Thirty Years". Brussels, Belgium. September 1, 1979. Quoted in Cohen, p. 29.

Lambeth, Benjamin S. "Soviet Strategic Conduct and the Prospects for Stability". In *The Future of Strategic Deterrence*, by Christopher Bertram. Hamden, Conn.: Archon Books, 1981.

Luttwak, Edward N. *The Pentagon and the Art of War*. New York: Simon & Schuster, 1985 and 1986.

Milovidov, Gen. A. S., and Col. V. G. Koslof, eds. *The Philosophical Heritage of V. I. Lenin and Problems of Contemporary War*. Moscow, 1972.

Murphy, Matthew. "Why Bishops Should Not Take Sides". *Center Journal* (Winter 1983), pp. 158-9.

Nye, Joseph S., Jr. *Nuclear Ethics*. New York: The Free Press, 1986.

Pipes, Richard. "Why the Soviet Union Thinks It Could Fight and Win a Nuclear War". *Commentary* (September 1977), pp. 21-34.

Powers, Thomas. "Choosing a Strategy for World War III". *The Atlantic* (November 1982), pp. 94-95.

Rhodes, Jeffrey P. "Improving the Odds in Ground Attack". *Air Force Magazine* (November 1986), pp. 48-52.

Scowcroft, Brent. "Understanding the U.S. Strategic Arsenal". In *Nuclear Arms: Ethics, Strategy, Politics*, edited by R. James Woolsey. San Francisco: ICS Press, 1984.

Sokolovskiy, V. D. In *Soviet Military Strategy*, edited by Harriet Fast Scott. New York: Crane, Russak & Co., 1968.

Solzhenitsyn, Aleksandr I. *The Gulag Archipelago Three*. New York: Harper & Row, 1978.

Summers, Col. Harry G. *On Strategy*. Novato, Calif.: Presidio Press, 1982.

Sun Tzu, *The Art of War*. Translated by Samuel B. Griffith. Oxford: Oxford University Press, 1963.

Suvarov, Viktor. *Inside the Soviet Army*. New York: Macmillan Co., 1982.

Wohlstetter, Albert. "Bishops, Statesmen, and Other Strategists on the Bombing of Innocents". *Commentary* (June 1983), pp. 15-35.

PART THREE

SOME STEPS TO TAKE

CHAPTER TWENTY-THREE

USABLE WEAPONS

To this point I have argued that nuclear weapons can be used morally, and there is a good chance nuclear war can be kept limited to levels that would be moral. However, there is an important consideration that so far has been treated only implicitly. If nuclear weapons are to be used morally, they must be *usable*. That is, right from the design stage, the warheads themselves and the delivery vehicles must take into account the need to be able to *use* the weapons in a moral manner.

John Garvey, writing in *Commonweal,* stated the issue well. "[I]f your enemy knows that you will absolutely refuse to use a weapon, what you have is no longer a weapon and is therefore useless" (quoted by Wohlstetter, June 1983, p. 26). Our weapons must be such that we would be willing to use them. They must be capable of accomplishing the tasks we may need to carry out, and their effects must be limited to those tasks only.

In subsequent chapters I will discuss specific weapons at greater length. In this chapter I want to illustrate the concept of usability by discussing cases where we either have failed or are failing to take it into account.

The first case is that of the B-1 bomber, canceled by President Jimmy Carter and reinstated by President Ronald Reagan. Mr. Carter's argument against the B-1 was, in part, that intercontinental cruise missiles could deliver warheads more cheaply than a penetrating manned bomber. This cost-effectiveness argument ignored some of the genuine advantages of a manned penetrating bomber. The bomber can be recalled; a missile cannot. The bomber can locate a mobile target that has moved since the bomber took off; the missile goes only where it was sent. The bomber can refrain from hitting a target that has already been destroyed; a second missile sent as "insurance" delivers its warhead anyway. The bomber can decide not to attack if target identification is incomplete or incorrect.[1] The critical point is that a bomber attack is under human control right up to the last minute; human control ends the moment a missile is launched. It may be argued that Soviet air defenses are too strong for a bomber to penetrate, and therefore the bomber is not really usable, but at least this is arguing the right issue. To

---

[1] One of the F-111s that participated in the attack on Libya in the spring of 1986 did just this.

have based the decision on cost-effectiveness was to have used the wrong criterion.

The next case is that of the so-called Midgetman missile. This was proposed by the Scowcroft commission as a solution to the problem of how to make the MX missile invulnerable against a disarming first strike. The Midgetman was to be a small, mobile missile, with a single warhead. It would be mounted on a transporter that would move about continuously on government land. This would keep the Soviets from targeting it, since in the thirty minutes between the launch of their missile and the arrival of the warhead, the Midgetman transporter could move several miles. The transporter would have to survive only a modest overpressure, since it would not be expected to be near ground-zero.[2] To be assured of destroying the Midgetman force, the Soviets would have to barrage the whole area with far more warheads than were carried on the total number of Midgetman missiles. This unfavorable warhead exchange ratio would, in effect, disarm the Soviets.

During 1986 there was a major controversy over whether the Midgetman should be designed to have three warheads instead of one. On one side of the debate were those who said a three-warhead missile would be too large to be mobile. On the other side were those who said that it could still be mobile, and by buying only one-third as many missiles and transporters, we could achieve equivalent deterrence at a considerable saving in cost. They argued the Soviets would still have to barrage the whole area with the same number of warheads, regardless of the number of Midgetman missiles, to assure themselves of destroying them all.

The debate was misdirected. Cost, and Soviet attack doctrine, are really second-order topics. The focus of the debate should have been *usability*. A fact that should be obvious, but is nevertheless often overlooked, is that when we launch a three-warhead missile, we need three targets. If we wish to destroy targets one at a time, we cannot do it with a three-warhead Midgetman. We may wish to conduct what Herman Kahn called a "slow motion" war, in which we give the Soviets time to think after each shot and possibly agree to a truce. Alternatively, we may wish to destroy a single high-value target to penalize the Soviets for violating moral limits on the targets they attack. Or we may wish to use a single warhead for a show of force, for a precision attack on a single target cluster, or for some other reason. If we buy nothing but three-warhead missiles, we shut ourselves out of fighting a war this way.

[2] Overpressure is the excess of bomb blast pressure over atmospheric pressure, a measure of the stress imposed on a target by an explosion.

Thus once again we heard the argument quoted in Enthoven and Smith; roughly: If we don't care how well we do should deterrence fail, then we can have deterrence a lot cheaper. But once again, we should care very much how we do if we are forced to fight a nuclear war. When we procure weapons, we should take into account the idea we may actually have to use them. We should procure only weapons we would be willing and able to use if necessary.

The issue of missile mobility arises in another context as well. In our negotiations on the SALT I treaty (which has of course already expired), we attempted to get the Soviets to agree to ban mobile missiles. They refused to do so, arguing that this issue should be left for a subsequent treaty. The United States then (in Unilateral Statement B) stated that if the Soviets deployed mobile missiles, we could consider that "inconsistent with the objectives of that [SALT I] agreement". In the SALT II treaty (which was never ratified, and which would have expired already even if it had been ratified), the Soviets agreed not to deploy mobile missiles (this portion of SALT II was to have expired in 1981). They have begun to deploy a missile designated by the U.S. Defense Department as the SS-24,[3] which is a rail-mobile missile, and the SS-25, which is a road-mobile missile.

From the Soviet perspective of preparing to fight a war instead of simply preparing a holocaust, mobile missiles make a great deal of sense. Their mobility means they cannot be targeted for a disarming first strike. Barraging the area in which they move produces an unfavorable exchange ratio, since it costs the attacker more warheads than the victim loses. In the case of the Soviet Union, which has a great deal more sparsely-inhabited territory than does the United States, it would probably be horrendously expensive for an attacker to barrage successfully the area used by the missile transporters, even disregarding the unfavorable warhead exchange ratio.

Why, then, was the United States so insistent on limiting mobile missiles? The reason is the arms-control syndrome we have already discussed. Mobile missiles are hard to count. It would be difficult to verify that the Soviets were adhering to the quantitative limits typically found in arms control treaties. Most arms controllers are locked into the logic of MAD: "Nuclear weapons can be used only for the threat of 'vengeance from the grave'; only a few missiles are needed for this threat; accuracy is not needed at all; both numbers and accuracy are destabilizing because they might allow a disarming first strike." Given this logic, they conclude that both sides can be secure if each has only enough mis-

---

[3] We do not know the Soviet designations of many of their missiles. Even in treaty negotiations, Soviet missiles are commonly referred to by their U.S. designations.

siles to destroy the other side's cities. Therefore the arms controller's objectives are to get rid of as many missiles as possible, base the ones that are left in an invulnerable manner, and be sure we can count them. Once we recognized the importance of mobility in protecting our missile force, we attempted to combine the mobility of the MX with countability for arms control, in a so-called racetrack scheme. It turned out to be impossible to combine the two requirements. This led to the Scowcroft Commission and its recommendation of Midgetman.

In 1987, the Reagan administration proposed that MX missiles be based in a *rail garrison* mode. They would be placed on rail-mobile launchers that might be hidden in tunnels or by other means. In a crisis, they would be moved to secret but precisely surveyed locations, so they could be launched with great accuracy. In effect, this proposal abandoned arms control considerations in favor of mobility.

The important point is that had we been looking at *usability* from the beginning, we might well have originally designed the MX missile to be rail-mobile or road-mobile and not made an abortive attempt to keep the Soviets from deploying mobile missiles. In fact, in the 1960s there were well-developed plans to deploy a significant force of Minuteman-I missiles on railroad cars, to prevent the Soviets from targeting them. These plans were canceled by Secretary of Defense Robert McNamara on the grounds they were not cost-effective. Today they might very well be found effective in offsetting the Soviets' enormous advantage in numbers of accurate missile warheads. In the rail-garrison deployment of the MX, we have finally come full circle.

Another class of weapons in which usability is not given sufficient consideration is submarine-launched ballistic missiles. The Polaris nuclear-powered submarine, with its complement of sixteen solid-fueled missiles, was a marvelous technological achievement of the 1960s. The most important characteristic of a nuclear-powered ballistic missile submarine is that it can remain submerged, and therefore concealed, for its entire voyage. The enemy cannot locate it and attack it in a disarming first strike. It is the ideal weapon for "vengeance from the grave".

Unfortunately, such a submarine is not usable for war-fighting. The instant it launches one of its missiles, it reveals its position to enemy reconnaisance satellites or aircraft, and possibly even to over-the-horizon radars. The enemy can then barrage the area around the launch and destroy the submarine.

In the assured-destruction mission, this doesn't matter. The submarine would launch its sixteen missiles in a single salvo, and after that there would be no point in the enemy destroying it. It would no longer present a threat, and destroying it would cost the enemy several warheads. By destroying the submarine's base instead, the enemy can prevent the submarine from reloading with missiles anyway, and at a cost of far fewer warheads.

In a war-fighting mission, however, this matters greatly. If the submarine launches only a single missile, it retains fifteen missiles with three warheads each. To the enemy, it would be worth up to forty-five warheads to destroy the submarine *and its remaining missiles*. The newer Trident submarines, with twenty-four missiles, are even more lucrative targets. After a single missile launch, it would be worth up to sixty-nine warheads for the enemy to destroy one of these submarines.[4]

The ballistic-missile submarine thus poses the same problem as does the multiple-warhead missile, but to a much greater degree. We can't launch a three-warhead missile unless we have three targets. We can't launch the missiles from one of the older Polaris or Poseidon submarines unless we have forty-eight targets. We can't launch the missiles from a Trident submarine unless we have seventy-two targets. If we don't launch all the missiles at once, we reveal to the enemy the location of a lucrative and "soft" target. What this simply means is that our present ballistic-missile submarines are not *usable* in fighting limited nuclear war. The only use to which they can be put is vengeance after it no longer matters. Our present ballistic-missile submarine force is still a technological marvel, but it has no military flexibility.

The issue is not that we shouldn't have built ballistic-missile submarines. Their ability to gain invulnerability through invisibility is an enormous asset. The issue is that before designing them, we should have given more thought to the idea that we might some day need to *use* the weapons they carried. The technical design of our ballistic-missile submarines reflects an inflexible *strategic* doctrine. It reflects a lack of the moral guidance that provides a rational connection between military capability and political objectives. A fleet of ballistic-missile submarines that had the necessary military flexibility might be more expensive, but it would be *usable*.

Another case in which usability is being ignored by many is the cruise missile, despite the inherent usability of the missile itself. From the perspective of someone afflicted with the arms-control syndrome, cruise

---

[4] These figures are based on the assumption that the Soviets would not want an unfavorable warhead exchange ratio. However, if one side has enough warheads to start with, it can afford to accept an unfavorable warhead exchange ratio, because each enemy warhead it destroys means that much less damage it may have to suffer. The side with abundant warheads may be more interested in minimizing damage to itself than in conserving warheads.

missiles are something horrible. They are small; they can be transported easily; they can be concealed prior to launch. All these features make it hard to count them. Thus our arms controllers have attempted to discourage the development and use of cruise missiles, particularly those with intercontinental range (for example, the limitations in the never-ratified SALT II treaty of 600 kilometers range on air-launched cruise missiles).

Horgan notes (1986, p. 76):

> Some experts question the value of trying to limit cruise missiles, arguing that they stabilize relations between the superpowers. In a sense, cruise missiles are the ideal weapon to back up a policy of mutual assured destruction. They are too slow to destroy military targets in a first strike; early-warning technology could spot an attack from the subsonic missiles long before they could reach missile silos deep within the continental United States or USSR. Nor do they tempt a first strike as large, multiwarhead missiles placed in silos do.

Note that even in this analysis, no consideration was given to the usability of cruise missiles for war-fighting, only for MAD. Nevertheless, all the points made are just as valid for the war-fighting application. In addition, the fact that cruise missiles can easily be hidden before launch means they do not invite a preemptive strike.

Horgan further states, however:

> But allowing cruise missiles to proliferate would be "self-defeating", according to Paul Warnke, who directed the Arms Control and Disarmament Agency from 1977 to 1978. "The real difficulty is that you'd never know what the other side had, and since you'd never know whether you had enough, you'd have to keep building them."

Here we see the problem. To someone afflicted with the arms-control syndrome, *enough* is a number to match the other side's number. Since such people have a mindset that refuses to recognize that nuclear weapons can be usable, their only criterion for enough is equality in numbers.

In reality, the problem Warnke describes doesn't exist. Since cruise missiles are not vulnerable before launch, we cannot target Soviet cruise missiles. Therefore the number we need depends not on how many cruise missiles they have, but on how many targets of other kinds they have that we want to hit. Once we have enough cruise missiles for that, it doesn't matter how many cruise missiles they have.

For instance, suppose we counted the number of targets we wanted to hit, took into account the effectiveness of Soviet defenses and possible failures of our own missiles, and concluded that we needed 10,000 singe-warhead cruise missiles. Suppose we then learned somehow that the Soviets had built 20,000 similar missiles. According to Warnke's logic, we would need to build another 10,000 ourselves. But for what? We couldn't target the Soviets' cruise missiles because they would hide them, and we have found only 10,000 other targets worth aiming at. The additional 10,000 missiles would be of no value to us whatsoever. The proper response to learning that the Soviets have built 20,000 cruise missiles is for us to build 20,000 air defense missiles.

In short, the whole debate over cruise missiles is muddled by the failure to take *usability* into account.

Another case in which usability is ignored is the issue of accuracy. This problem arises with both cruise missiles and ballistic missiles.

Given a particular level of technology, cruise missiles can in general be more accurate than ballistic missiles, because it is easier to provide them with terminal guidance. As we have already noted, today ballistic missiles can be very accurate, which implies that cruise missiles could be very accurate indeed. However, there are many who are still locked into the logic of MAD, and oppose building accurate cruise missiles. Horgan describes this objection as follows (1986, p. 78):

> Earle agreed that *limiting accuracy would be stabilizing,* but doubted that such a step could be justified to the military. Limiting the accuracy of missiles, he added, "is like saying no soldier will be able to hit a bull's-eye with his rifle. It just flies in the face of all military training and goals" (emphasis added).

Here the speaker is not only locked into the logic of MAD, but what is worse, he talks as though it were the *military* people who had something wrong with their thinking.

It is only in the logic of MAD that accurate ballistic missiles are destabilizing because they can be used for a disarming first strike. However, even this logic fails to apply to cruise missiles, because they cannot be used for a first strike of any kind.

Nevertheless, we need to look at the idea that accuracy is destabilizing and the damage this idea has done to our ability to *use* the weapons we have built. To begin with, accurate missiles can be used in a disarming first strike only against fixed-based weapons (for example, missiles in silos, aircraft on their bases). Land-mobile weapons are not *easily* destroyed in a disarming first strike, although as pointed out above, it might be done if the attacker has enough missiles to barrage an enormous area with sufficient overpressure. Airborne and seaborne mobile missiles are even less easy to destroy in a disarming first strike. Submarine-launched missiles are currently impossible to destroy in a disarming first strike because of their ability to hide. Thus it is only for arms-control reasons—forces should be few in numbers, countable by the enemy, and invulnerably based—that accuracy is destabilizing. If those afflicted with the arms-control syndrome hadn't imposed the one problem on us, we wouldn't be faced with the other one either.

Nevertheless, the idea that improved accuracy is somehow bad is quite widespread. Even Michael Novak, despite his otherwise excellent analyses of the problems and morality of nuclear war, has fallen victim to this idea. He writes (1983, p. 67):

> Even should the specter of nuclear war be lifted at last from the human race, we recognize the horrors of modern conventional warfare. The power and *terrible accuracy* of rocket-driven conventional arms, launched at great distances, became visible during the last days of World War II. These horrors have been magnified since, as exhibited in the Falkland Islands (emphasis added).

The use of phrase "terrible accuracy" is ironic. The V-2 rockets introduced by Germany late in World War II indeed had "terrible" accuracy. At a range of two hundred miles, only half the warheads fell within eleven miles of their targets. The terror these weapons induced was largely because of their "terrible" accuracy. Had they been accurate weapons, able to hit what they were aimed at, the terror among civilian bystanders would have diminished to nearly zero.

In the Falkland Islands war, several ships were destroyed by one or two highly accurate *smart* weapons each. Such weapons may induce terror among the people (mostly military) right on the target, but they should induce little or no terror among bystanders distant from the target.

It is only inaccurate weapons, particularly those which have been given large warheads to compensate for their inaccuracy, which should inspire terror among innocent bystanders. Thus terror indeed arises from "terrible" accuracy. Highly accurate weapons are not weapons of terror.

Accurate weapons, moreover, are needed to satisfy the Just War criterion of discrimination. Without accuracy, war-fighting is impossible. The attacker ends up terrorizing innocent bystanders, either deliberately or inadvertently.

The concept of *usability* then demands accurate weapons—weapons that can be used discriminatingly and proportionately. Those who are concerned about the terrorizing of innocent bystanders should be particularly concerned that accuracy be a goal of weapon design. As Wohlstetter (June 1983) has put it:

Informed realists in foreign-policy establishments as well as pacifists should oppose aiming to kill bystanders with nuclear or conventional weapons: indiscriminate Western threats paralyze the West, not the East. We have urgent political and military as well as moral grounds for improving our ability to answer an attack on Western military forces with less unintended killing, not to mention deliberate mass slaughter (p. 15).

My own research and that of others has for many years pointed to the need for a much higher priority on improving our ability to hit what we aim at and only what we aim at (p. 19).

Unfortunately, the very people who should be supporting improvements in accuracy to reduce terror and eliminate wanton killing have obstructed these advances. Wohlstetter goes on to say:

Moralists who have chosen to emphasize the shallow paradoxes associated with deterrence by immoral threats against population have been at their worst when they have opposed any attempts to improve the capability to attack targets precisely and discriminately. While they have thought of themselves as aiming their opposition at the dangers of bringing on nuclear mass destruction, they have often stopped research and engineering on ways to destroy military targets without mass destruction; and they have done collateral damage to the development of precise, long-range conventional weapons. . . . They have tried to stop, and have slowed, the development of technologies which can free us from the loose and wishful paradoxes involved in efforts to save the peace with unstable threats to terrorize our own as well as adversary civilians (p. 29).

An excellent example of this obstruction can be found in the Challenge of Peace pastoral. The bishops at one point object to placing nuclear weapons in "forward" locations in Europe, on the grounds that they may be overrun by a Soviet conventional attack, facing NATO with a "use them or lose them" situation. At another point, however, they condemn the introduction of Pershing missiles, which can be placed far enough back that they are not in immediate danger of being overrun, precisely because these missiles are highly accurate even at that longer range. In the bishops' view, the accuracy of these missiles makes them a first-strike threat.

Wohlstetter also emphasizes (December 1983) the importance of usability in allowing us to defend the values for which we might go to war:

. . . extreme inaccuracy . . . made it hard to destroy military targets and at the same time preserve civil society intact. Hard, in other words, to fight a war without destroying the values we are trying to defend. Even with revolutionary technical advances, that will never be easy. But it is absurd to talk—in the way now standard, for example, in the freeze movement—as if any improvement in weaponry increases the weapons' mass destructiveness (p. 19).

Wohlstetter's point here is an excellent one. Those who continue to object to all uses of nuclear weapons, on allegedly moral grounds, are being completely counterproductive. They are preventing us from replacing our unusable weapons with usable ones. If we are to develop weapons that are usable under the Just War Doctrine, we must move from the present intellectual climate, which equates usability with warmongering, to a climate in which a statesman can say, "This weapon is preferable to that one, because if nuclear war breaks out it can actually be used for fighting, not just to commit a massacre. Being equipped with it will thus decrease the likelihood of war, because an enemy will more readily believe we would be willing to use it."

It is interesting that the Reagan administration finally resolved the debate on Midgetman by selecting a single-warhead design, to be carried by an off-road transporter. The reasons offered were that while a two-warhead version "would have reduced total life cycle costs by about 12% and saved an additional 25% in terms of manpower costs", it "would have meant recompeting the propulsion contracts, which would have delayed the program for two years" (quoted in Morrocco, 1987, pp. 20–21). That is, the publicly stated reasons for the decision had nothing to do with usability; they were purely bureaucratic in nature.

How can we introduce *usability* as a criterion for weapon design? To begin with, we must break away from the attitude that takes technology as a given. The American bishops showed they were affected by this attitude when they said in their Challenge of Peace pastoral:

[T]hese criteria demonstrate that we cannot approve of every weapons system . . . advanced in the name of strengthening deterrence. On the contrary, these criteria require continual public scrutiny of what our government proposes to do with the deterrent.

Implicit in this statement is the notion that technologists may propose weapons, and we must then review these weapons for acceptability. Eugene McCarthy was speaking against this notion when he said:

It's rather curious that somewhere along the way we began to talk about strategic weapons. We used to talk about strategy. The weapons were always just tactical. But now, they're strategic weapons. . . . So what you call your strategy, which would be your defense, is a projection of a technology.

From the moral standpoint, our strategy may not be simply a projection of technology. That would be an inversion of the moral order. Technology exists to serve people, not vice versa. Therefore the technology we pursue should reflect the moral purposes for which we plan to use it. This is not to say that we can design weapons that can never be misused. It is demanding too much of a weapon that it have a better-developed conscience than its users. It is to say, however, that once we decide what the moral uses of nuclear weapons are, we should demand that the technology we pursue, and the weapons we procure, be capable of being used morally. The ability to be used morally may, in the long run, be the most important requirement we levy on the weapons-makers. Without that ability, all the others are irrelevant.

REFERENCES

Horgan, John. "The Politics of Peace Pacts". *IEEE Spectrum* (July 1986), pp. 70–80.

Morrocco, John D. "Reagan Will Pursue Rail-Based MX, Full-Scale Midgetman Development". *Aviation Week* (January 5, 1987), pp. 20–21.

Novak, Michael. *Moral Clarity in the Nuclear Age*. Nashville: Thomas Nelson Publishers, 1983.

Wohlstetter, Albert. "Bishops, Statesmen, and Other Strategists on the Bombing of Innocents". *Commentary* (June 1983), pp. 15–35.

Wohlstetter, Albert. Letter to editor. *Commentary* (December 1983), pp. 13–22.

CHAPTER TWENTY-FOUR

THE NEUTRON BOMB

The so-called neutron bomb, or *enhanced radiation warhead*, first came to public attention in 1977, with a *Washington Post* article which announced that the United States planned to produce and deploy such weapons. The preceding development program had not been kept secret; in fact, annual Department of Defense statements to Congress had described plans for development and production of enhanced radiation warheads. However, the public outcry was more than President Jimmy Carter could stand. He canceled plans for production and deployment. Later, President Ronald Reagan ordered production of the warheads, but stated they would be kept in the United States rather than deployed to Europe.

The essential difference between neutron warheads and previously developed nuclear weapons is in the proportion of the different types of energy emitted. In the usual fission warhead, atoms of uranium or plutonium are split in two, releasing energy. About 85 percent of the energy emerges as blast and heat, and about 5 percent as prompt radiation. The remainder is emitted as delayed radiation, and from a military standpoint is detrimental rather than useful. While people can be injured by the prompt radiation from a fission warhead, if they are close enough that the radiation is dangerous, they are probably also inside the lethal radius of the blast and heat.[1]

A fusion weapon, by contrast, combines two atoms of heavy hydrogen (deuterium) into an atom of helium, and emits a neutron. About 80 percent of the energy of fusion emerges as prompt radiation, and only about 20 percent as blast and heat. There is no delayed radiation at all (that is, no fallout). So far, it has proven impossible to build a pure-fusion weapon. All fusion weapons use a fission *trigger* to start the fusion process, and the resulting weapon represents a combination of fusion and fission, with the partition of the energy depending on the relative proportions of each.

---

[1] For instance, for a 20-kiloton burst, blast would be lethal to a person exposed in the open at any range less than about a third of a mile; at that range the person would suffer first-degree burns on exposed skin; but the prompt radiation would be well below 1 REM. This amount of radiation would have no immediate effects and few if any long-term effects.

An enhanced radiation warhead involves a combination of fission and fusion components such that the lethal radius from the radiation is significantly greater than the destructive radius from blast and heat. Thus a neutron bomb, if detonated at the proper altitude instead of on the surface, would kill unshielded people directly below it, but would not cause any physical damage to structures or equipment directly below it. The effective radius for such a weapon is, according to Cohen (1983, p. 51), about 1000 yards or two-thirds of a mile. (Kistiakowsky [1978] presents an authoritative but nontechnical discussion of the technology of enhanced radiation warheads.)

There were two major objections to the introduction of neutron bombs. The first was that they made nuclear war more thinkable. The second was that neutron bombs themselves represented something perverse and immoral.

As an example of the first objection, Archbishop John Quinn of San Francisco stated to the Bishops' Conference in 1978 that an argument

> against development of the neutron warhead is that the introduction of this new and more "manageable" weapon tends to narrow the gap politically and psychologically between conventional war and nuclear war. In other words, it could render more probable the escalation of any war in Europe to the level of nuclear warfare (quoted in Castelli, 1983, p. 32).

We have already encountered, and disposed of, this first objection. Those who object to our acquiring usable weapons evidently want us to spend great sums of money on weapons we know to be unusable or not to buy any weapons whatsoever. The latter is overt unilateral disarmament, the former is merely a more subtle version of it. Nevertheless, it is worth quoting the statements of three presidents who faced the issue of deploying the neutron bomb regarding the effect the neutron bomb would have on lowering the nuclear threshold (all quotes taken from Murphy, 1983).

U.S. Congress, House Committee on International Relations, "Additional Arms Control Impact Statements and Evaluations", 85th Congress, 1st Session, 1977, p. 3 (Ford Administration):

> A decision to cross the nuclear threshold would be the most agonizing decision to be made by any President. These weapons (ER warheads) would not make that decision any easier. But by enhancing deterrence, they could make it less likely that the President would have to face such a decision.

U.S. Congress, Senate and House Committees on Foreign Relations and International Relations, "Fiscal Year 1979 Arms Control Impact

Statements", 95th Congress, 2nd Session, 1978, p. 129 (Carter Administration):

> As to the effect on the threshold, as the President and U.S. Government officials have repeatedly stated, a decision concerning the employment of RB/ER (reduced blast/enhanced radiation weapons) would be treated no less seriously, and no differently than that for any other nuclear weapon. Thus, the deployment of these weapons would not affect the actual nuclear threshold. Moreover, because of the military utility of RB/ER weapons, their deployment could enhance deterrence, reduce the risk of war and, if war should break out, marginally reduce the prospect for escalation and the destructiveness of war.

U.S. Congress, Senate and House Committees on Foreign Relations and International Relations, "Arms Control Impact Statements", 98th Congress, 1st Session, 1983 (Reagan Administration):

> On August 1981, the President announced that ER warheads would be produced and stock-piled on U.S. territory. Any decision to deploy ER warheads would be taken only after close consultation with any country on whose territory they would be based, and then only with the explicit approval of the President.

Thus according to the testimony of the presidents who would actually face the decision to use the neutron bomb, it would not reduce the nuclear threshold below that presently in effect for our existing arsenals, nor make the decision to cross it any easier than it is today. This is as it should be. Making nuclear war thinkable doesn't mean lowering the nuclear threshold. It only means not flinching from the prospect of crossing that threshold *should the need arise.*

However, the most important issue is not whether the neutron bomb makes nuclear war more thinkable, but whether it can be considered moral. Cohen quotes several foreign leaders as responding negatively. Egon Bahr, general secretary of the Social Democratic Party, called the neutron bomb "a symbol for the perversion of human thinking", and added

> It seems to be an idea of [the] latest progress that it is easier to clear away human bodies than to remove the rubble of cities and factories (Cohen, 1983, p. 103).

At the Japanese ceremonies commemorating the bombing of Hiroshima on August 9, 1977, the UN General Assembly President H. Shirley Amerasinghe stated:

> Scientists must realize that although their achievements are dazzling in their brilliance, their products are satanic. The most recent obscenity is

the neutron bomb, a weapon which will destroy human life but spare
human property (Cohen, 1983, p. 104).

The U.S. bishops, in their pastoral letter *Human Life in Our Day*,
wrote of the neutron bomb as follows:

> Nothing more dramatically suggests the anti-life direction of technologi-
> cal warfare than the neutron bomb; one philosopher declares that the
> manner in which it would leave entire cities intact, but totally without
> life, makes it, perhaps, the symbol of our civilization (quoted in O'Con-
> nor, 1981, p. 71).

From a moral perspective, it would be hard to imagine a more egre-
giously wrong interpretation of the significance of the neutron bomb
than that of the bishops. It merely illustrates that when they wrote those
words, they were still in the grip of the notion that nuclear weapons
could be used only against cities, and that the logical target for our nuclear weapons was Soviet cities.

As was made amply clear in statements by several presidents, by several secretaries of defense, and by numerous other officials, the purpose
of the neutron bomb is *not* to annihilate the populations of enemy cities
so we can simply walk in, sweep up the corpses, and occupy the buildings. After all, we are not planning an aggressive war of conquest. Instead, the purpose of the neutron bomb is to kill attacking enemy troops
while avoiding damage to our own cities. The neutron bomb could be
used to destroy enemy units, even tank forces, without damaging
friendly units in the area, and especially without harming innocent bystanders. As Cohen points out, the residents of cities under attack by
Soviet troops could easily survive the use of a neutron bomb by hiding
in radiation shelters below ground. Attacking troops could not take advantage of such shelters, because that would require them to halt their
advance. If the Soviet blitzkrieg could be halted, for instance by Soviet
troops seeking shelter from our neutron weapons, we would then be
well on our way to a truce, and possibly to a withdrawal of their troops.
They could continue their attack only by *not* taking shelter against neutron bombs. Thus so long as the Soviets continued their attack, they
would be vulnerable, while our own people would not be.

Nevertheless, this important point simply got lost in the debate. I recall one student at the University of Dayton asking plaintively during a
discussion of the neutron bomb, "Why not have a weapon which
knocks down buildings but doesn't kill people?" One answer to that is
quite simple. It is only a human being who can decide to stop fighting or
to continue. Mere *things* can't surrender. If your attackers decide to continue fighting, killing them is the only way to protect yourself against

them. More to the point of the neutron bomb, however, is that a weapon that destroys our own cities while leaving the invading troops unscathed is precisely the opposite of what we want. The neutron bomb is an ideal *defensive* weapon, simply because it does destroy the attacking enemy while not harming the dug-in defenders or the innocent bystanders, or their homes.

As Cohen put it (interview with Long, 1981):

> The development of the neutron bomb allows the *return* of civilized warfare, even in a Nuclear Age. The key feature of civilized warfare was the protective wall of the city. All wars were fought beyond the wall by the soldiers, and the civilians remained safe. But in modern times, especially after the population bombing against Germany and Japan during World War II, people seemed to lose hope of ever returning to that kind of limited war. The neutron bomb has made this a real possibility again.

This may be an overly rosy view of medieval warfare. Sieges of cities were grisly things even in those days. However, most of the fighting did in fact occur outside the city walls. Often when the city's army was defeated, the city surrendered. Nevertheless, the neutron bomb does offer the promise of allowing us to keep the war away from the cities and the civilians again, because it does kill invading troops without knocking down our own buildings.

Cohen points out that neutron bombs of our present design might not be all that desirable, since they increase the fraction of energy emitted as radiation from the 5 percent of ordinary fission weapons to only 30 percent. This is an improvement, but still leaves over half the energy coming out as blast and heat. That is, while our current neutron bombs will kill the enemy more effectively while doing a lot less damage to ourselves than would an ordinary fission bomb of the same size, they are still capable of doing a lot of damage to our own people and buildings. We obviously need to improve our neutron weapons to the point where they *can* destroy the exposed enemy while not destroying our own people and our cities and towns. This won't happen as long as people continue to look upon the neutron bomb as an obscene weapon of offense instead of as an ideal weapon of defense.

The moral imperative of improving our neutron weapons, and of deploying them and training our troops to use them, is illustrated by this quote from Cohen:

> After World War II, there were many people who held the leaders of France and England responsible for not preparing their countries to face Hitler. If we ever stumble into World War III after tempting the Soviets to attack by our own failure to prepare sufficiently for our defense, we

will be just as blameworthy as the Neville Chamberlains of the 1930s (interview with Long, 1981).

The neutron bomb is an eminently *usable* weapon, one that can be used in a limited manner, and one that improves our ability to protect ourselves against enemy troops without harming civilians, either ours or theirs. We have a moral obligation to develop and procure these weapons to replace our currently unusable or less-usable tactical nuclear weapons.

REFERENCES

Castelli, Jim. *The Bishops and the Bomb*. New York: Doubleday & Co., 1983.

Cohen, Sam. *The Truth about the Neutron Bomb*. New York: William Morrow and Co., 1983.

Department of the Army. *DA Spotlight*. No. 77–44 (October 1977).

Kistiakowsky, George B. "Enhanced Radiation Warheads, Alias the Neutron Bomb". *Technology Review*. Vol. 80, no. 6 (May 1978), pp. 24–31.

Long, Kevin G. "Samuel T. Cohen, Father of the Neutron Bomb". *The Wanderer* (September 10, 1981).

Murphy, Matthew. "Why Bishops Should Not Take Sides". *Center Journal* (Winter, 1983), pp. 153–162.

O'Connor, John J. *In Defense of Life*. Boston: Daughters of St. Paul, 1981.

CHAPTER TWENTY-FIVE

MISSILE DEFENSE

The current U.S. debate over missile defense revolves around two questions: "Can it work?" and "Should it work?" The first is a technical question and will be considered only briefly here. The second is a moral question, which might more accurately be phrased, "Is it licit to build a system that defends our cities or our military forces against an enemy's nuclear attack?"[1] In this chapter I will focus primarily on this second question.

As we have seen in several earlier chapters, when nuclear weapons were introduced in 1945, many people assumed that their offensive capability would inevitably be overwhelming. Not only would the bomber always get through, but it would always devastate the target. It was taken for granted that there was no defense against nuclear weapons.

In many ways, this is an unhistorical view. From the beginning of recorded history, the pendulum has swung between favoring the offensive and favoring the defensive. At times the offensive is irresistible, while at other times the defensive is impregnable. We saw such a swing of the pendulum between 1918 and 1939, a period of only twenty-one years. During World War I, the most important military fact was the impregnability of defenses. Trenches, barbed wire, and the machine gun halted the offensive in its tracks. Numerous offensives, after unbelievable artillery bombardments of the enemy's defenses and after incredible slaughter of the attackers who moved across open ground, ei-

---

[1] Some of my colleagues, who doubt the technical effectiveness of the approaches to missile defense currently under investigation, have raised another moral question: "Is it licit to spend large amounts of money to deploy a system that has virtually no chance of working?" The short answer to this is, it depends. There might be some cases in which this expenditure could be justified. However, the presumption would be against spending money to deploy a system that has little likelihood of working. Those who wish to deploy the system must bear the burden of proof that the expenditure would be justified from a moral standpoint, as well as from any other standpoint. However, quite often the question is phrased differently: "Is it licit to spend large amounts of money doing research and development to solve a problem that is most likely unsolvable?" Here again, the short answer is, it depends. If the problem is important enough, it may well be worth spending the money to determine whether it's solvable, even if the likelihood of a solution is small. As I try to show in the chapter, the moral justification for missile defense is quite high. Thus, even if the technical problems are extremely difficult, attempting to solve them could very well be justified.

ther faltered completely or halted after capturing only the first line of the enemy's trenches. By 1939 the situation had completely reversed itself. Tanks, aircraft, and self-propelled artillery made the Blitzkrieg irresistable. Only in the vast reaches of the Soviet Union did it finally bog down.

With regard to the effectiveness of defense, it is also worth remembering the history of strategic bombardment, outlined in Chapter 2. In both World Wars I and II, defenses against strategic bombardment turned out to be much more effective than anyone had anticipated beforehand. This may turn out to be the case with missile defenses as well.

In any case, those who argue that strategic defense will never be possible are asserting that something historically unprecedented has taken place: the offensive has gained a permanent advantage that will never be offset. Judging from history this is extremely unlikely. Even if the technical approaches to missile defense that are presently under investigation turn out to be infeasible, it is highly likely that some feasible approaches will eventually be found. Thus we need to address the question, "When effective means of defense are eventually found, will deploying them be a morally good or a morally evil action?"

There are many religious leaders who argue that deploying a defense against ballistic missiles would be a morally evil action. The following citations are taken from Sincere (1986).

In June 1985, the national board of Church Women United, an ecumenical group of lay women, passed a resolution opposing the U.S. Strategic Defense Initiative (SDI), and asked its members to oppose it in letters and calls to their Congresspersons (sic), on the grounds that it "only fuels the escalation of the arms race".

The Canadian Council of Churches urged the government of Canada to "take a strong stand against the Star Wars scheme", and committed its members to do "everything in our power to condemn the expansion of nuclear weapons into space". The council went on to say, "We do not oppose strategic defense because we don't think it would work; *we oppose strategic defense because we believe the world would be a more dangerous place if it did work*". (emphasis added). The council also argued that strategic defense "includes the support of nuclear first-strike and war-fighting options" (p. 5).

In 1985 the General Assembly of the Disciples of Christ issued a statement opposing "the introduction of the Star Wars system (Strategic Defense Initiative) and other new destabilizing systems" (p. 6).

After Sincere published his survey, the United Methodist Bishops in the United States published what amounted to a pastoral letter on nuclear weapons, which included this statement about missile defense.

We therefore commend to all our churches, and to all Christians, the most searching and candid exploration of these disturbing questions concerning the prospects for space-based defense. We are impressed by the doubts of many eminent scientists. We are concerned about the possible offensive implications. We are worried about the consequences for arms reduction. We are appalled at the probable costs. And we remember once again how often the Scriptures warn us against false hopes for peace and security (1986, p. 52).

The Catholic Church has not issued any formal statements on strategic defense. However, Joseph Cardinal Bernardin, who chaired the committee that drafted the Challenge of Peace pastoral, did say:

I wish to express my profound misgivings about projecting the arms race on a new frontier in space, even when the motivation for the proposal has entirely defensible moral intentions. . . . While I understand the motivation behind the SDI, I am very skeptical of its consequences on the arms race (quoted by Sincere, 1986, p. 10).

Clearly, to these religious leaders, strategic defense is evil, and the better it works, the more evil it is. This, then, is the argument I will take up in this chapter. The moral argument against strategic defense takes various forms, including: it militarizes space; it destabilizes deterrence by providing a shield for a first strike; it destabilizes deterrence by making nuclear war appear feasible; it escalates the arms race by providing an incentive to build more offensive missiles; it escalates the arms race by providing another area of competition; since it can't be one-hundred-percent effective we shouldn't have it at all; it won't protect us against bombers, cruise missiles, or terrorism; and it provides a perverse incentive to an attacker to shift the weight of his attack toward cities and away from military targets. These various arguments will be discussed in turn.

The charge that strategic defense militarizes space would be laughable were it not so tragic. Space was long ago militarized. Both the United States and the USSR make extensive use of satellites for military purposes, including reconnaissance, communications, and weather observation.[2] Soviet cosmonauts, from vehicles in orbit, have taken part in Soviet military maneuvers, providing observations from space and

---

[2] During the fighting in Vietnam, the United States used weather satellites to get up-to-date information about cloud cover over targets in North Vietnam, prior to dispatching bombing missions. Several U.S. Congressmen who opposed the war condemned this use of *peaceful* weather satellites for military purposes. Regardless of the merits of their argument, the situation illustrates that even weather satellites have military applications, and thus space has already been militarized.

relaying communications among ground, naval, and air units. The Soviet Union is the only nation to have developed, tested, and deployed a "Fractional Orbital Bombardment System", designed to place nuclear weapons into orbit, then de-orbit them onto targets on the ground. The extent to which the Soviets have already militarized space is indicated by this statement from the U.S. Arms Control and Disarmament Agency:

> In 1984 the Soviet Union conducted about 100 space launches, some 80 of which were purely military in nature. In the same year, by comparison, the U.S. conducted a total of just eleven space missions. All Soviet space launches were conducted by their Strategic Rocket Forces—the same military branch charged with maintaining and commanding the Soviet land-based nuclear arsenal. There is no Soviet equivalent to NASA, America's civilian space agency. The majority of Soviet military satellites have been launched from Plesetsk Missile and Space Test Center, the same site at which nuclear missiles are tested. (The Soviets did not even acknowledge the existence of Plesetsk as a launch site until 1983, by which time they had—since 1966—launched over 800 spacecraft from that site) (1986, p. 9).

However, even if these prior military uses of space had never taken place, the charge of militarization would still be absurd. Ballistic missiles pass through space on their way to their targets. Are we to consider this a "peaceful" use of space, while a system whose sole function is to preserve lives rather than destroy them, a system that can kill only bombs but not people, instead "militarizes" space? To condemn missile defenses while ignoring the militarization of space from ballistic missiles qualifies as straining at a gnat while swallowing a camel. This charge is morally absurd and deserves immediate rejection.

The idea that strategic defense destabilizes deterrence is offered by those still locked into the logic of MAD. We have discussed, and disposed of, this objection in several previous chapters. However, this objection is presented in a somewhat different form in the missile defense debate, and it is worth looking at that argument in detail.

The argument that strategic defense destabilizes deterrence by providing a shield for a first strike is often presented as a reason why we shouldn't build one. It is alleged that we might be tempted to strike first during a crisis, figuring that we would be protected by our defenses. Certain so-called military experts add to this that if we launched a counterforce first strike, our missile defense would be better able to deal with the Soviets' *ragged second strike* than it could with a full-scale Soviet first strike. This, they argue, would increase our incentive to go first in a crisis, thereby increasing the Soviets' incentive to preempt our first strike.[3]

The first thing one needs to say in response to this argument is, "Why aren't the objectors protesting against the existing Soviet ABM system?"[4] Why isn't that system destabilizing? Why do they argue that it would be destabilizing if we built one, but it isn't destabilizing for the Soviets to have one already? Some of the objectors would reply that the Soviets' system isn't very good, therefore it isn't destabilizing. Those who make this reply are inadvertently admitting their belief that if we built one it would work well. However, this is an issue we really needn't get into. The Soviets must have some degree of confidence in their system or they wouldn't be spending as much as they are on it. As usual, those who disparage what the Soviets are doing are implicitly proclaiming their own wisdom and the Soviets' stupidity. In any case, those who raise the objection that missile defense is destabilizing should, as a matter of consistency, be protesting the one missile defense system which already exists, instead of protesting the development of the second.

Beyond the matter of consistency, however, is the issue of whether the existence of a U.S. missile defense system would provide us with an incentive to strike first in a crisis. Those making this objection should recall that at a time when we had what amounted to a one-hundred-percent-effective defense against nuclear weapons—that is, when we had them and the Soviets didn't—we did not launch a first strike despite the occurrence of several crises. Our record on this point is a good one. Those who make this objection are really denying us the right intention required under Just War Doctrine. Moreover, if the USSR had developed the bomb before we did, it is simply incredible that they would not have exploited their advantage. Therefore those who make this objection are also denying the comparative justice of our cause against the Soviet Union. This whole issue is completely false, and is raised only by those who place the United States and the USSR on the same low moral

---

[3] It is curious that many of those who talk about missile defense being more effective against a *ragged second strike* are the same people who are certain that mutual destruction is assured and therefore we don't need to concern ourselves with war-fighting. For instance, the article by McNamara and Bethe makes the "missile defense is more effective against a second strike" argument, while the article McNamara coauthored with Bundy, et. al. makes the "second strike destruction is assured" argument. People like Mr. McNamara are simply working both sides of the argument.

[4] The Soviets are currently spending more on both development and deployment of missile defenses than the United States is, and have been doing so since 1965 (Department of Defense, 1986, p. 46).

plane. Albert Wohlstetter has rejected this argument in the following words:

[I]t is even more absurd and dangerous to suppose that the only way to dissuade the U.S. from unleashing aggression is to help the Soviets threaten our civilians by leaving them defenseless and by leaving us no choices other than capitulation or an uncontrollably destructive offense against Soviet cities that would invite the reciprocal destruction of our own civil society (1983, p. 19).

Beyond the issue of the United States' right intentions and comparative justice, however, there is the question of just what incentives a missile defense does give to a nation. Freeman Dyson, among others, has argued that a counterforce strategy is unstable because during a crisis it provides each side with an incentive to strike first at the other side's offensive missiles. Both sides, fearing a disarming first strike by the other side, have an incentive to launch their missiles. Waiting to see if the crisis can be resolved peacefully may simply mean being destroyed by the other side. This argument falls apart if one's missiles are untargetable (for instance, if they are mobile or are based on submarines). The argument based on crisis-instability is then one more reason to get away from the "use them or lose them" problem by developing less vulnerable offensive missiles. However, it is important to note that *defending* one's own missiles has the same virtue as *hiding* them: it stabilizes a crisis because it eliminates the fear the enemy will launch a disarming first strike. Thus, contrary to the objectors, defending one's own missiles *increases* stability in a crisis.

The argument that strategic defense destabilizes deterrence because it makes nuclear war look feasible is a prime example of MAD thinking. As we have seen in prior chapters, in 1945 defense against nuclear weapons appeared infeasible. Our only defense seemed to be the threat of vengeance from the grave. The thinking was, "since we cannot defend, we must deter". Unfortunately, over the years, this thinking has become perverted to "since we must deter, we dare not defend". The advocates of this view have taken the position that by making nuclear war as horrible as possible, we prevent it from happening. They argue that if we eliminate some of the horror, for instance by defending ourselves, then the chances of having a nuclear war are greater. I have already pointed out the error in this view several times: it assures that if deterrence does fail, it fails in the worst possible way. It puts us in the position of having an unimaginable horror hanging constantly over our heads, held off only by the degree of terror it continually inspires in both us and our enemies.

Missile defense can reduce the severity of the consequences if dissuasion does fail. Since dissuasion is almost bound to fail over a long period of time, maximizing the frightfulness of that failure is a perfect recipe for catastrophe. Over the long run we will be far better off if we reduce the consequences of a failure of dissuasion than if we try to reduce the likelihood of failure by maximizing the horror it would bring.

The logic of MAD is again present in the argument that building a defense provides each side with an incentive to build more offensive missiles. MAD assumes that the only way to be safe is to be able to commit a certain amount of destruction despite anything the enemy does (hence the name "Assured Destruction"). This threat of destruction then deters the enemy. To this MAD logic, anything that reduces the effectiveness of one side's retaliatory-strike capacity must be compensated for by strengthening that side's offensive force.

Unfortunately, those who are locked into the logic of MAD have lost the ability to see that with effective defenses, we no longer *need* to be able to commit a certain amount of destruction in order to be safe. Defenses *replace* the need for assured destruction as a means of safeguarding ourselves. Defenses allow us to *ward off* the enemy's attack, instead of deterring it with the threat of frightful vengeance after we're dead.

But what if only one side has a missile defense? Doesn't the side without one have an incentive to build up its offensive forces, since its safety still depends on being able to commit a certain amount of destruction? Unfortunately for its proponents, this argument has been rendered moot. The Soviet Union already has a missile defense. Nonetheless, it continues to add to its arsenal of offensive missiles. That ever-growing arsenal is not motivated by the desire for deterrence, but by the desire for conquest. Our building a missile defense is not going to increase their desire for conquest. On the contrary, it may discourage that desire by making conquest look less profitable. Hence, while this argument may have some theoretical merit, in the real world in which we must live and make our decisions, a world that contains the real United States and the real USSR, it is completely without merit.

Strangely enough, those who make this argument do not advocate that the United States increase its missile forces in order to compensate for Soviet missile defenses. This again amounts to an admission that they doubt the effectiveness of the Soviet system but believe we could build a missile defense that would be effective.

The argument that missile defense escalates the arms race by providing another area of competition is a strange one. Again, it results from the MAD thinking that telescopes defense into deterrence and confuses devastating the enemy with defending ourselves. We have no interest in dead Russians. On the contrary, we have an interest in live Americans.

If the Soviets *also* get an effective missile defense, this doesn't decrease our security in the least, because once we have such a defense, our security no longer depends upon threatening them with destruction. An arms race in weapons that defend one's own people but are incapable of killing anyone on the enemy's side might be expensive but it is otherwise harmless. It certainly does not lead to the risk of explosion present in races in offensive arms. Escalation in purely defensive weapons might very well turn out to be a good thing. Moreover, such escalation is self-limiting in a way in which escalation in offensive weapons is not. Once we get a defense which is *good enough,* however we define that, we don't need to increase it every time they increase their *defenses.* No matter how many *defensive* missiles they procure, nor how many anti-missile radars they build, our defenses won't be weakened in the least. It is only when they increase their *offensive* capability that our defenses are threatened.

The argument that since missile defense can't be one-hundred-percent effective, we shouldn't have it at all, is morally obtuse at best. It represents a refusal to distinguish between degrees of horror—to recognize that there is a difference between twenty million dead and two hundred million dead. From the standpoint of the 180 million survivors, the first alternative, horrible as it is, would still be better than the second.

Beyond this moral obtuseness, the objection fails to recognize that to dissuade the enemy from attacking, we don't need one-hundred-percent effectiveness. All we need is the ability to convince the enemy that his attack will be thwarted, that it will be unsuccessful, and that he will be taking enormous risks for little gain. If even a less-than-perfect defense is good enough to dissuade the enemy from attacking, then no one gets killed.

This is, after all, the same argument used by the advocates of deterrence through the threat of vengeance. They argue that although the defense provided by deterrence is zero-percent effective (that is, it would save no lives at all during an attack), if we make the threat horrible enough, we won't be attacked, and no one will be killed. The important difference, though, is that in the *deterrence through vengeance* case we are threatening to do something both immoral and futile—kill innocent people on the enemy's side after we're dead; in the *dissuasion through defense* case we are preparing to do something that is both purposeful and moral—preserve our own lives without killing innocent people on the enemy's side.

We would need a defense that is one-hundred-percent effective, or nearly so, only if we were intending to strike first. So long as we retain our current policy of waiting for the enemy to strike, a less-than-perfect defense is still desirable; because if the attack came, we would be better off with the defense than without it.

The arms controllers would consider it a great coup if they could negotiate a 50-percent reduction in the level of Soviet missiles. Yet we can achieve the same result, unilaterally, by deploying a missile defense which is 50-percent effective. Moreover, we wouldn't have to worry about Soviet cheating, about different understandings of treaty terms, or about any of the other things that plague our attempts to negotiate arms reductions without letting the Soviets flimflam us. Missile defense is a way to achieve arms control without regard to what the Soviets do.

In addition, one of the benefits of even a less-than-perfect defense is that it increases the likelihood of maintaining continuity of government and the capability to prosecute a war instead of merely taking vengeance on the enemy. Thus even should dissuasion fail, a missile defense could still contribute to reducing the damage done, both to us and to the enemy.

The arguments about one-hundred-percent effectiveness are, at best, simply a distraction. They exemplify the old saying, "The best is the enemy of the good". If these arguments had been accepted in the past, neither the antiaircraft gun nor the interceptor aircraft would have been developed. Instead of demanding one-hundred-percent effectiveness, and giving up because we can never attain it, we should today be deploying a system that will give us at least as much protection as the Soviet's system currently gives them, and we should then work to improve it.

The argument that missile defense wouldn't protect us against bomber and cruise-missile attacks is correct but misses the point. During the 1960s the advocates of cost-effectiveness dismantled our defenses against bombers on the grounds that they were useless since they couldn't defend us against missile attacks. They argued that so long as the missiles were going to get a free ride, there was no point in spending money to keep the bombers from getting a free ride.

Now many of those very same people are turning the argument around. Because we have let our antibomber defenses decay, they urge us not to build antimissile defenses. They say there's no point in defending ourselves against missiles when the bombers will get a free ride anyway. But what this really amounts to is an argument for rebuilding the air defenses we allowed to decay over the past two decades, as well as building missile defenses. We need to counter the cruise-missile threat as well as the ballistic-missile threat. The charge that one type of defense won't deal with both threats is simply an attempt to confuse the issue. We need to build both kinds of defenses.

The argument that missile defense wouldn't protect us against terror-
ists is likewise an attempt to confuse the issue. We might, in the extreme, lose a city or two to nuclear terrorism. But even if at some point
in the future terrorist groups acquired a handful of nuclear weapons,
they would still not be able to deliver the weight of attack that the Soviet Union can deliver *right now*. The Palestine Liberation Organization
(PLO) might some day be able to wound us grievously, but it would be
only a wound—not a fatal blow to us as a nation. The Soviet Union can
today destroy us as a nation. To argue that we shouldn't defend ourselves against the Soviet Union because we would still be vulnerable to
the PLO is to confuse seriously the relative magnitude of the two
threats.[5]

The argument that missile defenses provide a perverse incentive to
attack cities is presented by Kavka (1984, p. 134):

> Critics of this [President Reagan's] proposal have claimed that such a sys-
> tem would be enormously expensive, would not work well enough,
> would itself be vulnerable to attack, could be counteracted by the other
> side's building more missiles, and might conceivably tempt the other
> side to strike first before the system was completed. They are probably
> right about much of this. But, unless such systems are perfect (that is, 100
> percent reliable) shields, there is yet another powerful strategic and
> moral reason against building them: they provide increased incentive for
> each side to select the other's cities instead of its missile bases as its pri-
> mary targets.

Kavka's argument goes as follows. The nation with the less-than-
perfect shield has a reduced incentive to target the other's missiles, since
the shield will take care of some of them (that is, the counterforce and
damage-limiting mission is in part taken over by the shield); therefore,
it can switch its missiles to cities to do more damage. The nation without the shield will be less willing to target the enemy's missiles, since
they will be defended; it will instead switch its missiles to the cities, to
increase the damage done despite the defenses. If both sides have
shields, the effects reinforce each other.[6]

[5] Even a moderately effective missile defense would have a high capability of protecting us against terrorist ICBMs. A Khadaffy with a handful of missiles might try blowing
up New York as a means of escalating after we responded to a terrorist attack (as we did
by our air strike against Libya in 1986). It wouldn't even be necessary that his missiles be
nuclear-armed; a few tons of high explosives delivered on New York or Washington by
ICBM would be an effective terrorist attack. When thinking of missile defense, we
shouldn't focus solely on the Soviet Union as the possible attacker. It would be worth
having a defense against people like Khadaffy.

[6] Note this same logic would imply that cruise missiles and mobile ballistic missiles, as
well as submarine-launched missiles, all of which are harder to target than are silo-

This argument is typical of those who are so locked into the convoluted logic of MAD they have forgotten why MAD was invented in the first place. It may well be that missile defenses will be more effective in defending missile silos than in defending cities.[7] But why should that cause the enemy to weight his attack against cities? What does the attacker gain by devastating cities in a first strike? By doing so, he has increased the number of surviving missiles on the victim's side. Moreover, he has used up some of his striking power, thus reducing the number of counterforce targets for the attack victim and in turn increasing the number of weapons available for vengeance on the attacker's own cities. In short, by such a move the attacker weakens his own intrawar deterrent posture, weakens his own bargaining position, and increases the risk of a revenge strike against his own cities. Only an irrational attacker would behave in this fashion, and an irrational attacker cannot be dissuaded anyway. The only thing effective against an irrational attacker is a defensive shield.

This objection is rooted in the notion discussed above, that to deter attack the defender must be able to carry out a certain amount of destruction even after being attacked. The people making this objection, however, have forgotten the reason for the original idea, and take it for granted that *even in a first strike* the attacker will wish to do as much damage to the victim's *cities and population* as possible. There is no reason to believe this is the case. On the contrary, there is every reason to believe that a nation making a first strike would try to *minimize the damage to itself* by weighting its attack against the victim's offensive forces. If the attacker does not have sufficient forces to succeed in disarming the victim, despite the victim's defensive shield, it is more likely *not to attack at all* than it is to make the irrational move of devastating the victim's cities while leaving the victim's missile forces intact. In short, the defensive shield, far from providing an incentive to weight the attack toward cities, is more likely to discourage attacks on cities, and perhaps discourage any attacks at all.

Disposing of these false objections to strategic defense is not the full story, however. The real problem is the one discussed in Chapters 1 and 3: the telescoping of defense and deterrence; the confusion of devastat-

---

launched missiles, should be aimed primarily at enemy cities. This despite the fact that the extreme accuracy of cruise missiles suits them very well for precise attacks on military targets.

[7] This is certainly true of terminal defenses. However, defenses that destroy the attacking missiles in midcourse or during boost phase will be equally effective in defending both cities and missile silos. In fact, at those phases of the attacking missile's flight, the intended target not only need not be known, but cannot be known to the defender.

ing the enemy with preserving ourselves. We have so long been used to thinking that our only defense is the threat to devastate, that when the opportunity for a real defense is presented, too many people think of it only in terms appropriate for devastation. Consider the following extract from a letter to the editor in *Ohio Peace and Justice Calendar* (1986), p. 3.

> Strategic Defense Initiatives (S.D.I. or "Star Wars") delegates the authority to fire nuclear activated lazer [sic] beams *to computers*. Since the time to distinguish between a real attack and a false alarm is about three minutes, there is no time for our elected officials to become involved. Computers will decide to fire or not to fire. Let's not delegate to computers humanity's existence. The super complicated star wars computers have to work right the first time without ever having been tested in operation. Impossible? Based on all our many experiences with faulty computers, which have had lots of testing, I believe it is impossible (emphasis in original).

This statement is correct on one point. The short time available to fire a defensive weapon after detecting a possible missile launch does indeed mean that much of the system will have to be automated. It probably will be impossible to give the president the chance to make the decision whether or not to activate the defenses. But so what? Suppose the defensive system does zap an empty spot in space, through some kind of error. What harm has been done? None at all. Activating the defense system *does not* mean killing people; it *does not* mean blowing up cities; it *does not* mean going to war.[8] None of the defensive techniques proposed so far has any capability to harm anyone on the ground.[9]

---

[8] In fact, we will probably *want* to fire our defensive weapons from time to time during peace to increase both our confidence *and that of the Soviets* that our system does work. And the Soviets will undoubtedly want to do the same with their system.

[9] Some of the opponents of missile defense have stopped arguing that it can't work, and are instead arguing that it will work all too well; that in fact it can be used to *replace* ICBMs by burning cities from space with high-powered lasers. The article by Herzenberg (1986) is typical of this line of argument. It is gratifying that opponents of missile defense have recognized their earlier denials of technical feasibility were mistaken. That they continue to oppose missile defense, but on opposite grounds, indicates that their objection is ideological rather than technical. Since the technology of missile defense is still in its infancy, it is pointless to debate whether it can be used to replace ICBMs. Suffice it to say that the moral objections to destroying cities apply equally to lasers and ICBMs. It is also worth noting that even if space-based lasers eventually achieve the ability to punch through the atmosphere and burn targets on the ground, the laser beam is a narrow, pinpoint weapon. It would have to start fires one at a time, at different points in a city, while a nuclear explosion starts fires everywhere at once. Using a laser offensively would allow the city residents time for evacuation. Furthermore, a laser doesn't produce any radioactive fallout or radiation casualties. Finally, it is worth noting that the Herzen-

Why, then, do people react to a purely *defensive* system with the horror that ought to be reserved for the immoral act of using multimegaton weapons on whole cities? It is largely because of the telescoping of defense and deterrence, the confusion of preserving ourselves with devastating the enemy. *It is crucial that we get over this kind of thinking.* It is crucial that we learn again to distinguish between preserving ourselves, with a defensive shield, and devastating the enemy.

There is another thing we have to get over, and that is the demagogic use of the word *nuclear.* Note its presence in the quote above. It is used there purely as a scare word. The "bomb-pumped X-ray laser" that some people have proposed as a possible defensive system would utilize a nuclear explosion to generate a high-intensity beam of X-rays. These X-rays would then destroy the delicate electronic circuits in an attacking missile. It is important to note that the explosion itself would have no direct effects on people or things on the ground. The beam of X-rays would not even be strong enough to do any gross physical damage to the missile, but would depend solely on creating microscopic damage in transistors and other circuit elements. The beam of X-rays could not possibly reach the ground to injure anyone. *Even if such a weapon were fired by mistake in peacetime, no harm would be done.*[10] Yet the calculated and deliberate use of the word *nuclear* in the quote is intended to imply that firing such a weapon immediately leads to the end of the world, that allowing an automatic system to fire it is simply computerizing our doom. We need to free ourselves of the attitudes that allow demagogues to manipulate the public with the calculated use of the word *nuclear.*[11]

---

berg article still raises the spectre of *nuclear winter,* even though the nuclear-winter hypothesis was disproven in articles published months before hers appeared. (See Thompson and Schneider [1986] for a nontechnical analysis, with references to the technical literature.) This emphasizes again the ideological nature of the opposition to missile defense.

[10] Note that the explosive yield of a bomb-pumped laser would be too low to produce an electromagnetic impulse (EMP) or any significant blast-damage on the ground beneath it, even if it were detonated high in the atmosphere rather than in space. There would be some radioactive fallout from the explosion, but it makes little sense to worry about this in the context of an enemy attack that would produce far more fallout if not successfully countered by a missile defense. Nevertheless, one of the problems with a bomb-pumped laser is that under the existing test ban treaties it cannot be tested in peacetime, at least not in the atmosphere or space. Such testing would also create the moral problems discussed in Chapter 27. Hence even if we overcome the demagogic use of the word *nuclear,* there are valid reasons for preferring a non-nuclear missile defense.

[11] In reality, a bomb-pumped X-ray laser could not be based in space. Such a weapon destroys itself when it is fired. Therefore an effective enemy tactic would be to send a single antisatellite (ASAT) missile against each orbiting laser. We would then find our-

There is another nuclear approach to missile defense that might also be worth investigating. This is the use of a neutron bomb for terminal defense. The high neutron flux generated by such an explosion would cause the nuclear material in the attacking warhead to "slump" or even melt, and would prevent the warhead from detonating. Here again, the word *nuclear* does nothing but obfuscate the issue. It can't be argued that using a neutron bomb in this way would breach the nuclear threshold, since it would be used only after the enemy had launched nuclear weapons against us. The defensive warhead would need to be detonated at high altitude to be effective against an incoming warhead, so the blast and radiation would not harm anyone on the ground. As a terminal defense weapon, it would be detonated only over our own territory, so even firing it by mistake would not pose a threat to another country. And yet, the mere fact that it is called nuclear is enough to cause many people to condemn it.[12]

It may be, of course, that neither the bomb-pumped laser nor the neutron bomb will work, at least not well enough to be effective weapons against enemy missiles. The point is that we should be willing to investigate them, just in case they might work, and not be "deterred" by the demagogic use of the word *nuclear*.

Reviving the distinction between defending ourselves and devastating the enemy is important from a moral standpoint. The confusion of the two has, over the past forty years, led to the moral problems described in chapters 1 through 11. The only way we can bring an end to those problems is to make the distinction real again by building a *defense that defends,* as soon as the technology is available.

The American Catholic bishops made a statement in their Challenge of Peace pastoral that has not been given the prominence it deserves. They stated:

> We affirm a nation's right to defend itself, its citizens, and its values. Security is the right of all, but that right, like everything else, must be subject to divine law and the limits defined by that law. *We must find means of*

---

selves with the dilemma of seeing the ASAT missile destroy our laser, or destroying the laser ourselves to kill the ASAT missile. As a result of this, not even Dr. Edward Teller, one of the foremost proponents of the bomb-pumped X-ray laser, proposes putting them in orbit. Hence the letter quoted not only uses the word *nuclear* in a demagogic manner, but also completely misrepresents the U.S. research program for missile defense.

[12] It is worth noting that many of the same people who oppose the neutron bomb because "it kills people but doesn't damage things" also oppose missile defense, even though that only damages things, but doesn't kill people. However, it is perhaps too much to expect consistency from this group. Despite their lack of consistency, the use of neutron bombs for missile defense is certain to upset them.

defending peoples that do not depend upon the threat of annihilation (1983, no. 221, emphasis added).

This is precisely what missile defense is intended to offer: a means of defending our people that doesn't depend upon the threat to annihilate another country, either before or after ours has been annihilated. Bishops and other religious leaders should be encouraging the development of missile defense systems instead of condemning them for specious reasons. After all, as President Reagan said in his March 24, 1983 speech in which he advocated missile defense:

> Would it not be better to save lives than to avenge them? Are we not capable of demonstrating our peaceful intentions by applying all our abilities and our ingenuity to achieving a truly lasting stability? I think we are—indeed, we must.

This is not just a technical issue, it is a moral one. Preserving ourselves is morally superior to devastating the enemy. We should be working diligently to find ways to preserve ourselves, instead of denying that it can be done or saying that it would be immoral to do it.

REFERENCES

Bundy, McGeorge, George F. Kennan, Robert S. McNamara, and Gerard Smith. "The President's Choice: Star Wars or Arms Control". *Foreign Affairs* (Winter 1984–1985), pp. 264–278.

Department of Defense. *Soviet Military Power, 1986.* Washington, D.C.: U.S. Government Printing Office, 1986.

Dyson, Freeman. *Weapons and Hope.* New York: Harper & Row, 1984.

Gentry, Tom. Letter to the editor. *Ohio Justice and Peace Calendar* (Summer edition 1986), published by American Friends Service Committee (reprinted from the *Akron Beacon Journal*).

Herzenberg, Caroline. "How Star Wars Could Come to Earth". *New Scientist* (October 9, 1986), p. 62.

Kavka, Gregory S. "Nuclear Deterrence: Some Moral Perplexities". In *The Security Gamble,* edited by Douglas MacLean. Totowa, N.J.: Rowman & Allanheld, 1984.

McNamara, Robert S., and Hans A. Bethe. "Reducing the Risk of Nuclear War". *The Atlantic Monthly* (July 1985), pp. 43–51.

Sincere, Richard E., Jr. "What the Churches Are Saying about 'Star Wars' ". *This World* (Spring/Summer 1986), pp. 3–11.

Thompson, Starley L., and Stephen H. Schneider. "Nuclear Winter Reappraised". *Foreign Affairs* (Summer 1986), pp. 981–1005.

The United Methodist Council of Bishops. *In Defense of Creation.* Nashville: Graded Press, 1986.

U.S. Arms Control and Disarmament Agency. "The Soviet Propaganda Campaign Against the U.S. Strategic Defense Initiative". *ACDA Publication 122.* Washington, D.C.: August 1986.

Wohlstetter, Albert. "Bishops, Statesmen, and Other Strategists on the Bombing of Innocents". *Commentary* (June 1983), pp. 15–35.

CHAPTER TWENTY-SIX

COMMAND AND CONTROL

In Chapter 19 we observed that a nation that failed to provide itself with the Command and Control (C & C) system necessary to conduct a limited nuclear war might be incapable of satisfying the Just War criterion of competent authority. Therefore it is important to consider how well the United States is prepared to maintain control by properly constituted authority over a limited nuclear war and to see what steps we should take to improve our capability.

In the early 1960s, the U.S. C & C system was totally inadequate. Enthoven and Smith write:

> Perhaps the most critical vulnerability problem, however, lay in the U.S high-level command structure, which was located in a comparatively small number of points on or near Strategic Air Command (SAC) bases or major cities, all of which were themselves prime targets for enemy attacks.[1] Most of the facilities were soft, and most of the communication links were vulnerable. A well-designed Soviet attack would probably have begun by destroying all these points in a closely coordinated missile volley. A successful attack would have deprived our forces of their authorized commands to proceed to targets. In all likelihood, if all U.S. forces obeyed their orders, our ICBM's would have remained on the ground to be destroyed by follow-up Soviet bombers, and our air-borne bombers and our Polaris submarines would have returned to bases already destroyed by Soviet ICBM's (1971, p. 166–167).

Thus C & C can be at least as important as the weapons themselves, the delivery vehicles, and the training of the crews who will operate them. Steinbruner (1981–82, pp. 21–22) notes:

> None of the popular measures of relative U.S. and Soviet strategic capability—delivery vehicles, warheads, equivalent megatonnage, lethal area coverage, hard target potential, or post-attack force balances—takes command performance into account, even though it is undeniably a critical element of actual capability.

---

[1] Note the assumption that our cities are inevitably on the enemy's target list. This assumption pervades Enthoven and Smith's book, even though it was written well after Mr. McNamara's "No-cities" speech. This assumption is consonant with the MAD doctrine later adopted by Mr. McNamara, however.

Ford points out that an inadequate U.S. C & C system might lead to the moral hazard of inviting attack in a crisis:

> If the Soviets . . . began to fear a U.S. attack . . . the vulnerability of our command system would give them another option besides waiting to be destroyed; a first strike that would have some chance of crippling a major part of the U.S. nuclear war machine. This kind of move, which would be too risky to contemplate under normal circumstances, could surface as the prime Soviet military option in a desperate situation (1985, p. 47).

Ford also points out the particular problem of terminating a war:

> No provision for a surviving hot line has been made, yet the current U.S. strategy of controlled escalation presumes that a nuclear war can some-how be terminated on terms favorable to the United States. Some form of contact with the Soviets, and some kind of negotiations, will have to take place. But who will be able to represent the United States? How will they communicate with the other side? Whom will they talk to? Without a reliable means to carry out high-speed negotiations, a strategy of con-trolled escalation has a rather fundamental problem. "The United States has no business having a war-fighting policy if we have no ability to call them off", one official said. "How do you call off a war? How do you accept the Soviet surrender? Or give them ours?" (1985, pp. 165–66).

Ford goes on to point out that if we plan to strike first, we need good intelligence beforehand about where the targets are, but we don't need much in the way of C & C. If we plan to fire every weapon we have in retaliation, we don't need much in the way of intelligence information, and we need only enough C & C to deliver the *shoot everything now* or-der. However, if we plan to fight a nuclear war, then we need good intelligence and an elaborate C & C system which can survive enemy attack.

Thus if we intend to fight a nuclear war, as opposed to committing a nuclear atrocity, by keeping our use of weapons within the bounds of discrimination and proportion, and if we intend to enforce these bounds by penalizing the Soviets for exceeding them, then we need good C & C as well as good intelligence.

Some of these criticisms of our C & C system are no longer as valid as they were when they were written. Since 1981, a concerted attempt has been made to improve our C & C system. Nevertheless, many of the critical flaws that Enthoven and Smith pointed out as existing in the early 1960s (1971) still exist and are not being addressed by the current improvements in the system.

Why is the U.S C & C system so inadequate, when the Soviets have apparently managed to deploy a much better one? Ford claims that the current system was never designed as an entity, ascribing the problem to bureaucratic infighting in the Pentagon and to perverse incentives faced by military officers trying to enhance their careers (1985). (Promotions go to officers who work with weapons and troops, not to communications specialists.) However, while these conditions are real, they are only symptoms, not causes. The fundamental problem is that the United States has never seriously tried to develop a strategy for fighting a nuclear war. Those who have addressed the problem have done so only on a tactical level: if we strike first, which targets do we hit? if in retaliation, then which targets? The linkage between national objectives and military action has been largely absent.

The reason this linkage has been missing, and therefore the fundamental reason our C & C system is in terrible shape, is that our political leaders have never made up their minds what kind of orders they want to be able to transmit so that the military could build a system capable of transmitting them. If the political leaders had done that, all the other problems, such as low priority for procurement of better C & C systems and lack of promotions for communications specialists, would have been solved in short order. But the political leaders have never given the military a clear-cut directive regarding the kind of C & C system they want. As a result, they have never had any criteria, any bottom line, by which they could judge whether the C & C bureaucracy was doing its job well or not.

Part of the problem, of course, is the national attitude that says that if we ever have to use nuclear weapons, all meaningful national objectives have been forsaken anyway. If this is true, then there is no need to think about what to do afterwards. As Enthoven and Smith have observed (1971), if we don't care what happens once deterrence fails, we can save money by not preparing for that eventuality. In particular, we don't need to think about what kind of C & C system we need, and we don't need to spend money on a good one.

Moreover, any president who speaks publicly about what kind of a war we should prepare to fight is accused of "planning to fight a nuclear war", as though that were synonymous with "trying to get us into a nuclear war". As a result, our political leaders have been unwilling to say, "We want the ability to command and control a war in which nuclear weapons will be used in a discriminating fashion against legitimate targets." That is, they have been unwilling to demand the C & C system needed to fight a nuclear war.[2]

---

[2] Note that so long as our C & C system is unhardened and vulnerable, it can be portrayed as increasing rather than decreasing the danger to us—that is, the moral hazard of inviting an attack, mentioned in the chapter. Conversely, an attempt to harden the C & C

What should a C & C system be capable of doing? On the basis of the preceding chapters, we can outline the requirements. To some extent, we can distinguish between C & C for strategic and for tactical purposes.

The first requirement for strategic C & C is that the National Command Authority (NCA) be capable of discerning when we are being attacked and what kind of strategic attack is being made upon us. In particular, the NCA must be able to distinguish between attacks on legitimate military targets and attacks on innocent bystanders. Even in the case of attacks on legitimate military targets (discriminating attacks), the NCA must be able to determine whether those exceed the bounds of proportion.

The second requirement for strategic C & C is that the NCA be able to give orders to our strategic forces (bombers, cruise missiles, submarine-launched missiles, silo-launched missiles, and mobile missiles) regarding what kinds of targets are to be attacked, and what kinds of things are off limits (even if only temporarily). Moreover, the NCA must be able to do this *despite* enemy attempts to destroy the C & C system.

The third requirement for strategic C & C is that the NCA be able to receive reports from our strategic forces regarding their current status and capabilities and the extent to which they have carried out their previous orders.[3] That is, there must be communications from the forces back to the NCA, not just the ability to transmit orders to the forces.

The fourth requirement for strategic C & C is that this capability be *enduring*. It must survive not only an initial attack, but continuing attacks, during the weeks and months a limited strategic nuclear war might last. These attacks may be not only warheads delivered by missiles or bombers, but attacks on communications nodes made by Soviet Special Forces (*spetsnaz*) units infiltrated into the country or by infiltrating troops of Soviet allies (for example, Cuba or Nicaragua) or even by domestic Soviet sympathizers. It may not be possible to construct a system that can survive without repairs. To meet this requirement, it may be necessary to reconstitute the system from time to time after war has broken out. Thus part of the peacetime preparations must include provisions for repair or rebuilding, including training sufficient specialists and stockpiling spare parts or replacement equipment. The issue here is

system can be opposed as "trying to make nuclear war possible". Moreover, some people are not above working both sides of the argument.

[3] The need for wartime intelligence-gathering is obvious but is beyond the scope of this discussion. Suffice it to say that information gathered by reconnaisance and intelligence sources must be able to be transmitted to the NCA.

not the *technical* one of designing and constructing a system capable of enduring (difficult though that will be), but of adopting the *attitude* that says we intend to maintain control over our forces and will take the steps necessary to assure that we can do so.[4]

The fifth requirement is to meet the problem raised by Ford's anonymous source: to be able to communicate and negotiate with the Soviets. The requirement to accept or give a surrender is probably irrelevant. If the war is not kept under control, there will be nothing left on either side to give or accept a surrender. If the war is kept under control, however, (as discussed in several preceding chapters) neither side is going to be pushed to the point of surrender. Thus the C & C system for dealing with the Soviets must meet not merely the requirement of giving or accepting a surrender, but the far harder requirement of negotiating the end of hostilities. We must design into our C & C system the ability to communicate not only with our own forces but with the Soviets, and the communication capability must be capable of rapid transmission of lengthy and detailed messages.[5]

The requirements for tactical C & C are somewhat different from those for strategic C & C. The strategic C & C must be capable of transmitting orders from the NCA to the people who actually launch the weapons. While this chain involves several links, it is not nearly as long as the chain needed for tactical C & C. Thus the tactical C & C must make provisions for a longer chain and for greater flexibility in both directions.

The first requirement for tactical C & C is that the NCA be able to communicate to the theater commanders the objectives for which the war is being fought. It is these objectives that define the limits commanders must observe in selecting targets for nuclear weapons and in selecting weapons to be used on those targets.[6] These objectives also

---

[4] Bracken takes for granted that the second, third and fourth requirements will not be met (1983). He stresses at several points in his book the idea that once nuclear war breaks out, our C & C system will be fragmented into discrete "islands" within which internal communication is possible, but which cannot communicate with each other. He offers no proof of this. It is simply one of the assumptions of his analysis.

[5] One possible technical solution is to put several satellites in synchronous orbit, 22,000 miles above the earth, and inform the Soviets these are intended as a backup for the *hot line*. We should test this alternative link periodically, and make sure the Soviets know we are using it for nothing else, thereby eliminating any incentive on their part to destroy it. Note that we may also wish to be able to open communications with Soviet military and political leaders *below* the level of their NCA, with the intent of encouraging *palace revolts* or *secessions*. Hence these satellites (or whatever other technical means we select) must be capable of coupling into the Soviets' existing military and civil communications systems.

[6] As noted earlier, this does not mean the President imitates Lyndon Johnson and personally reviews every target list, but that he imitates Abraham Lincoln and advises the

define the ends toward which the commanders will shape their strategy, but this is true even of war without nuclear weapons.

The second requirement for tactical C & C is that theater commanders be able to report back to the NCA about what the enemy is doing. This is particularly important if Soviet targets *outside* the theater are being held hostage for Soviet good behavior *within* the theater, as described in Chapter 22. Theater commanders in Europe, for instance, should not be given the responsibility for *enforcing* Just War bounds by striking targets in the Soviet Union that are not related to the ongoing fighting in the theater. This risks spillover of the tactical war to the strategic level, and may leave the Soviets uncertain about why specific targets were hit. Instead, these *enforcement* strikes should be made under the control of the NCA and their purpose communicated to the Soviets through the strategic C & C. The actual strikes may be made by forces assigned to the theater commander and acting on orders relayed through him by the NCA, but the decision to strike, and the choice of targets, are not properly within the competence of the theater commander.

The third requirement for tactical C & C is that the theater commanders and all their subordinate commanders be linked together well enough so that subordinate commanders do not have to be given autonomy in use of nuclear weapons. Many critics of the idea of nuclear warfighting postulate a mechanism for escalation in which subordinate commanders lose touch with higher authority; under such circumstances they are granted authority to employ the nuclear weapons in their possession at their discretion, since the alternative, of denying them that authority, inevitably means their defeat. According to the argument, these subordinate commanders would then use their nuclear weapons in an indiscriminate and disproportionate manner. I have already argued, in Chapter 22, that this doomsday mechanism is not as automatic as its proponents suppose. Nevertheless, tactical C & C should be designed to minimize the chances of this mechanism operating. C & C must provide means by which subordinate commanders can stay in touch with their superiors.

The fourth requirement for tactical C & C is that subordinate commanders should be able to report to those higher levels having authority for release of nuclear weapons: just where their units are, where enemy units threatening them are located, and where there are innocent bystanders who must be avoided by nuclear strikes.[7] It is only through the

---

commanders of what he wants, replacing them if they don't conform. The President is responsible for managing the war, but must avoid micromanaging it.

[7] The existence of C & C able to do this does not, of course, mean that subordinate commanders will make use of it. This is a matter of discipline rather than of the technical

ability to locate targets precisely that we can hope to keep nuclear weapons sized to the targets. When the targets are not located precisely, only two alternatives are available: either use a bigger weapon to compensate for the uncertainty, with the possibility of unintended damage to friendly troops and innocent bystanders, or refrain from using nuclear weapons altogether, thereby increasing the likelihood of enemy victory.

The fifth requirement for tactical C & C is similar to one imposed on strategic C & C: it must be capable of *enduring*. However, the problems are somewhat different. Strategic C & C needs to be global in coverage. It depends heavily on satellites, land-lines and undersea cables, switching centers, and high-powered transmitters, which may be attacked directly by the enemy. Tactical C & C is less dependent upon such targetable facilities. Instead, it is more vulnerable to enemy countermeasures such as jamming. Despite the differences in the problems, however, the requirements are the same. The system must continue to operate, at a level sufficient to permit control of the war, despite the enemy's efforts to disrupt it.

For both strategic and tactical C & C, the starting point in the design is therefore not technological but instead is political and strategic. The first question must be, "What do we want to be able to transmit?" Only then can we ask, "What equipment will allow us to transmit it?" Any C & C design that takes the technology as the starting point will almost inevitably put us right back in the spot we are now, of finding ourselves unable to carry out the communications needed to command and control a limited nuclear war.

To some extent, the C & C problem is independent of communications hardware. For instance, one way to overcome possible communications difficulties is to develop a common doctrine by which units at all levels of command, and in all the armed services, know what kinds of targets are legitimate for nuclear weapons and what kinds are not, and which responses to enemy actions are considered acceptable and which are not. Each unit then knows what to expect of other friendly units, and what will be expected of it, even when it is out of communication with those other units.[8] Although doctrine cannot be a complete substi-

---

capability of C & C systems. It is incumbent upon commanders at all levels to pass down the budget of permitted damage to innocent bystanders, based on the objectives set by the NCA, and to see that their subordinate commanders do not exceed it.

[8] Note that this doctrine cannot be kept secret. It will be written in training manuals, taught in service schools, and practiced on maneuvers. We must expect that the enemy will know it and will try to exploit it. Thus the doctrine developers must think through several steps, for example, "What will the enemy do if he knows we're going to do this?"

tute for communications, it can be of considerable help in coordinating the actions of friendly units when communications are disrupted. Moreover, suitable doctrine will have to be developed anyway, so that separate units can coordinate their activities on the nuclear battlefield. It will be important to recognize from the beginning that this doctrine should cover what to do when communications are disrupted.

In summary, improving our C & C is not a technical problem. It will not be solved simply by hardening C & C facilities, buying duplicate networks, or increasing the number of promotions for communications officers. It can be solved only by our elected leaders, and then only if they take seriously their oaths of office and their responsibilities for *defending* the United States. These leaders must not only decide what kinds of orders they might *need* and *be willing* to give, they must also demand a C & C system that would be capable of transmitting those orders, despite the best efforts of the enemy to prevent those orders from being transmitted.

REFERENCES

Bracken, Paul. *The Command and Control of Nuclear Forces*. New Haven: Yale University Press, 1983.
Enthoven, Alain C., and K. Wayne Smith. *How Much Is Enough?* New York: Harper & Row, 1971.
Ford, Daniel. *The Button*. New York: Simon & Schuster, 1985.
Steinbruner, John D. "Nuclear Decapitation". *Foreign Policy* (Winter 1981–82), pp. 16–28.

CHAPTER TWENTY-SEVEN

NUCLEAR WEAPONS TESTING

In their Challenge of Peace pastoral, the American Catholic bishops urged an end to nuclear weapons testing:

> In this same spirit [of working for arms control], we urge negotiations to halt the testing, production and deployment of new nuclear weapons systems (1983, no. 204).

However, this was not the first time the Catholic Church had spoken against nuclear testing. In his Christmas message of 1955, Pope Pius XII included a statement opposing the testing of H-bombs.

Opposition to nuclear testing also appears in other religious bodies, and within the Catholic Church, on the part of others besides bishops. Shevtchuk reported that:

> Since summer 1985, the Reagan Administration has been asked by Protestant, Jewish, and Catholic leaders to join the current Soviet moratorium. Catholics making that plea include the Conference of Major Superiors of Men, the Leadership Conference of Women Religious, and at least eight bishops. Cardinal Bernardin, chairman of the committee that wrote the war and peace pastoral, also called July 2 for an immediate ban on nuclear testing (1986, p. 4).

Davidson, in his survey of positions by major religious bodies in the United States, found that every one had issued a formal statement calling for a comprehensive test ban, for a freeze on development and testing of nuclear weapons, or both (1983, Appendix B).

If religious leaders are going to oppose nuclear testing in their capacities as religious leaders, rather than in their capacities as private citizens, they must be able to make the case that nuclear testing is in some way immoral. If they do not or cannot make that case, then they are overstepping their legitimate bounds. They are using their position as religious leaders to sanctify one side in a partisan debate. What, then, are the moral grounds for opposing nuclear testing?

Before 1963, there were ample moral grounds for opposing atmospheric tests of nuclear weapons. The fallout from such tests spread throughout the world. Those of us who were alive then still carry in our bones the residue of nuclear tests.[1] Paul Ramsey argued that the damage

---

[1] The half-life of Strontium-90 is about thirty years.

done by fallout could be justified, under Just War criteria, if the benefit from testing was great enough (1968, p. 158). However, the evidence since then indicates that atmospheric testing was not necessary. Underground testing has proven to be adequate for most needs of the then-established nuclear powers.[2] Hence we can conclude that atmospheric testing was probably immoral.

However, atmospheric testing has not been an issue for the United States since the signing of the Limited Test Ban Treaty in 1963. Since then, all U.S. nuclear tests have been conducted underground. On only a few occasions have the nuclear tests *vented* radioactive materials to the surface, and in no case have these materials gone beyond the boundaries of the United States at detectable levels.[3]

Why, then, do religious leaders oppose nuclear testing? Why do they consider testing to be a moral issue rather than a political or prudential one?

The arguments offered by the opponents of testing really involve two distinct issues. First, some see a ban on testing as a backdoor method of getting rid of nuclear weapons entirely. Second, some see continued testing as increasing the danger of annihilation from nuclear weapons.

Those who propose a test ban as a backdoor approach to nuclear disarmament argue that if nuclear-armed nations quit testing their weapons, as time passes, those weapons will become unreliable. They reason that the leaders of those nations will then lose confidence in the weapons they have in their inventory. This, they argue, will decrease the chances of a nuclear war. In a crisis, because we lack confidence in our weapons, we will make more efforts to find a peaceful solution.

There is a more than accidental similarity between this argument and the argument that says we shouldn't build usable weapons because in a crisis we might be tempted to use them. This argument, like its cousin, is nothing but another attempt to avoid the hard questions of how to use nuclear weapons morally. And like all the other attempts to avoid the moral issues, it leads to worse moral problems than the ones it attempts to avoid.

It is a mistake to believe that lack of confidence in one's weapons will affect both sides equally. The Soviets are in an inherently better position to blackmail us as long as they can *appear* to have confidence in their weapons. We may lack confidence in our own weapons because we

[2] France, India, and China have since then conducted atmospheric tests of nuclear weapons.

[3] By contrast, the Soviet Union has had a large number of incidents in which underground tests vented radioactive materials that were detected beyond its borders. This is a serious violation of the Limited Test Ban Treaty.

haven't tested them recently, but we won't have the same lack of confidence in the Soviets' weapons.

In fact, our uncertainty about the unreliability of Soviet weapons may be completely justified. The Soviets may well have reequipped their missiles and bombers with newly manufactured weapons built according to a design they have great confidence in, because they had tested it thoroughly before the ban. Thus the lack of confidence arising from a comprehensive test ban could be a very one-sided thing.[4]

Note that this argument against the efficacy of a test ban is really the same argument that the advocates of unilateral disarmament make to assure us we would be safe even if we disarmed. The argument goes that no amount of calculation by the Soviets would be enough to convince them that they could get away with an attack, because they could *never be sure* that we hadn't hidden a few weapons away that we could use in retaliation.

By the same token, *we* could never be sure the Soviets' weapons *wouldn't* work. This uncertainty might inhibit us from resisting their demands, despite the fact that some of our weapons might work if we used them in a counterattack. After all, even if a few of ours still worked, that wouldn't defend us or bring back the dead. Therefore, those who argue for nuclear disarmament on the grounds that a residual Soviet fear that we are cheating will still protect us, should be equally willing to accept the argument that even if the Soviets haven't tested their weapons recently, we will still have a residual fear that Soviet weapons might work. They should then cease trying to get nuclear disarmament through the backdoor method of a test ban.

The argument that nuclear testing increases the threat of annihilation arises not so much from an attempt to avoid the moral issues as from confusion about why we continue to test. The objection is often expressed in words such as, "Why do we need to continue testing? We have enough weapons now to blow up the whole world. What do we need more for?"

This objection exhibits confusion between *testing new designs* and *producing additional weapons*. In reality, there is no connection between the two. Because the Kennedy administration made a unilateral decision not to produce any more weapons-grade uranium, we are currently in the position of mining old weapons to get the nuclear material for new

---

[4] Note that if we also reequip our forces with newly produced versions of old weapons, this whole argument against testing falls apart. All that a test ban achieves, then, is a freeze on weapon design. As I argue in this chapter, from a moral standpoint, that is the last thing we want.

ones. Thus when we produce new weapons, we do not add to our total stockpile. The new ones are produced at the expense of weapons from our stockpile. As just one example of the consequences of this one-sided restraint, President Jimmy Carter personally made the decision to reduce the planned explosive yield of the warheads on the MX missile from the level of over 400 kilotons each, which the Air Force wanted, to just over 300 kilotons, because we were short of weapons-grade uranium.

Thus the testing issue has nothing to do with *how many* weapons we have in our inventory, but with the *kinds* of weapons. Here is where another type of confusion arises.

The argument that continued testing brings us closer to annihilation is a cousin to the argument, already discussed in Chapter 22, that making weapons more accurate makes them more terrifying. Both arguments are wrong. They arise from the assumption that the only possible use for nuclear weapons is to blow up cities and kill civilians, and that therefore any improvements in nuclear weapons must make them more effective at this horrible task. But just as making weapons more accurate makes them less dangerous to innocent bystanders because they can be aimed more precisely at military targets, continued testing takes us farther from annihilation because it means our weapons can be controlled more precisely.

One of the most important points is that we do not want to blow up the whole world, or even any significant part of it. We need the *kinds* of weapons that will allow us to defeat an enemy *without* blowing up the whole world.

Continued nuclear testing has in fact allowed us to improve our ability to fight a nuclear war instead of merely being able to commit a nuclear atrocity. As Adelman notes (1984/1985, p. 253), by 1985 modernization of weapons had brought us to one-fourth fewer weapons than we had in our inventory in 1967, and 75 percent less megatonnage than in 1960. That is, because of nuclear testing, we are *less able* to blow up the world than we were two decades ago. He adds, "Modernization has of late concentrated on making nuclear weapons smaller, safer, more reliable, and more survivable."

The beneficial results of nuclear testing are described in more detail by Frank J. Gaffney, Deputy Assistant Secretary for Nuclear Forces and Arms Control Policy:

> While we are actively investigating technologies that could one day make us less dependent on offensive nuclear arms for our security, the United States and our friends and allies will rely for the foreseeable future on nu-

clear weapons to deter Soviet aggression. And as long as that reliance
continues, nuclear testing will be required.

Nuclear testing is essential for the safety and security of our warheads
and weapon systems. It also is essential if we are to maintain their reliabil-
ity and effectiveness as well as their capability to perform their military
missions, if required, with as little collateral damage as possible. Finally,
and perhaps most important for the stability of deterrence, nuclear testing is required to ensure that the weapon systems, themselves, are survivable. As the Soviets are well aware, nuclear testing also permits us to
respond to their unprecedented buildup of offensive nuclear weapons and
strategic defense efforts over the last 15 years (1986).

General John L. Pickett, Director of the Defense Nuclear Agency,
provided additional information on the value of testing our weapons
(reported by Ulsamer (1987, p. 92). He stated that with a single exception (the Mark-11 warhead), every major new nuclear weapon program over the past twenty-one years "had produced unexpected results
when exposed to a full-scale test underground. Some of these failures
have been catastrophic." He adds that these surprising failures came despite extensive computer analysis and extensive above-ground testing
of the non-nuclear portions of the system. The General reported that
during exposure of an experimental reentry vehicle to an underground
nuclear explosion,

> a major portion of the heatshield [was] blown away as a result of the radi-
> ation energy that was deposited in the system [by the explosion]. I want
> to emphasize that this damage was caused [exclusively] by radiation.
> This failure, if undetected, could have compromised the force if the Sovi-
> ets were to deploy a comprehensive ABM system (Ulsamer, 1987, p.
> 92).

This latter point is important, since the existing Soviet ABM system
utilizes large nuclear warheads as its *kill mechanism*. A reentry vehicle
that is vulnerable to the radiation from such a warhead would fail when
used.

The virtually uniform finding that, despite the best efforts of our
weapons designers, our warheads and reentry vehicles still present us
with surprises when subjected to underground nuclear testing, emphasizes the fact that without such testing we could have no confidence in
our weapons.

Some of the objectors to continued testing recognize that testing allows us to develop weapons in which we have confidence. They bring
up the argument we have considered before, that making weapons
more usable increases the chances they will be used. If we don't test
smaller and more accurate weapons, they argue, we will be more reluc-

tant to use the large and less accurate weapons in our inventory. However, making nuclear weapons less frightful through testing may or may not mean they are more likely to be used. It does mean that if they are ever used, they will be *less frightful*. Refusing to improve them means that if they are ever used, they will be *more frightful*.

The point is ultimately a simple one. We may need to defend important moral values against the threats of a nuclear-armed enemy. We must carry out that defense without betraying the moral values we are defending. To do that, we must have *usable* weapons. The only way we can design those weapons, and continue to have confidence in them after they are deployed, is through nuclear testing.

We need to develop lower-yield weapons, so they will do less damage to things other than the targets we intend to destroy. We need to develop weapons that can be delivered more accurately, so they don't destroy things other than the targets at which they are aimed. We need to develop weapons that are safer, in the sense that they are less prone to accidents. We need to develop weapons that are more controllable, in the sense that they will detonate only where and when we want them to. Only through testing can we achieve these goals.

One of the strangest sights of the past three decades has been the parallel efforts of Western religious leaders and leaders of the Soviet Union to get us to quit testing nuclear weapons.[5] To some extent, this is a recent development. As Father Conway notes, when Pope Pius XII opposed H-bomb testing in 1955, he was *not* joining in the then-current Communist campaign against U.S. and British nuclear testing (1957, p. 489). He proposed an indivisible, three-part package that included: (1) an end to testing, (2) renunciation of all use of nuclear weapons, and (3) an inspection system capable of enforcing items 1 and 2. Such an international agreement, which would amount to complete nuclear disarmament, would not be subject to the moral problems we have discussed above.[6]

More recent pleas by religious leaders, such as those referred to by Shevtchuk, have not been as carefully devised as the plan by Pius XII.

---

[5] It is worth noting that the leaders of the Russian Orthodox Church have not spoken out against Soviet nuclear testing in the way in which religious leaders of other nations, as well as the Russian Orthodox leaders themselves, have spoken out against U.S. nuclear testing. Those religious leaders who still have the freedom to criticize their own nations should give this fact some careful thought. There *is* a moral difference between the United States and the USSR, and defending that difference is justified, even to the extent of using nuclear weapons in a discriminating and proportionate manner.

[6] We now know that achieving item 3 would be far more difficult than Pius XII imagined it would be. This does not, however, denigrate the careful balance of his proposed *package deal*.

They have simply asked for a ban on testing, without regard to the effects on our ability to defend ourselves against a nuclear-armed aggressor. In fact, the religious leaders Shevtchuk lists have not demanded a negotiated and inspected test ban. They have instead demanded that the United States agree to join in a Soviet moratorium on nuclear testing, which, as of this writing, had been in effect for about 17 months. The result would be for us to halt testing while we negotiated with the Soviets about how a comprehensive ban was to be monitored and enforced. There would be no monitoring or enforcement system operating while the negotiations were taking place. Moreover, the Soviets could filibuster indefinitely during the negotiations, keeping us from testing with no assurance that they weren't testing surreptitiously or getting ready to test on a large scale.

It is worthwhile to recall the last time we joined in such an uninspected moratorium with the Soviets. In 1958 we agreed to a testing moratorium in tandem with negotiations on a test ban. During this moratorium, our testing facilities were allowed to decay and many of our best nuclear weapons specialists, seeing no opportunity to ply their trade, left our weapons laboratories and found jobs in nonweapons activities. In 1961, the Soviets broke the moratorium with the biggest series of nuclear tests ever conducted by any nation, including the two biggest explosions ever set off by human beings.

It was obvious at the time that the Soviets had been preparing this test series in secret for months prior to its start, all the while pretending to be complying with the moratorium. However, several high-level defectors from the Soviet Union have since asserted that even before the moratorium had started the politburo had decided that if we accepted the moratorium, they would resume testing after they had gained the maximum advantage from the moratorium.

We were caught completely by surprise when the Soviets broke the moratorium. Our intelligence agencies had no indication the Soviets were preparing the enormous series of tests they set off, one after the other. Moreover, our own ability to test had atrophied almost completely. It took us six months to put together a few tests, and we did not even come close to matching the extent and variety of Soviet tests.

When the Soviets broke the moratorium, there was the usual pressure from a variety of people, including not only religious leaders but the Soviet peace campaigners as well, to conclude a test ban treaty. The result was the 1963 atmospheric test ban, mentioned above.

One of the results of the test ban treaty, signed so hastily after the Soviets broke their own moratorium, is described by Douglass and Hoeber (1979). In their survey of Soviet literature on nuclear war they note the importance which the Soviets place on electromagnetic pulse (EMP) from large, high-altitude nuclear explosions. The Soviets make frequent reference to this effect as a means of disrupting communications and destroying the electronics in ballistic missiles before the missiles are launched. Douglass and Hoeber then state:

> This effect was apparently noted quite early by the Soviets; they appear to have used their 1961–1962 atmospheric test series, with which they broke the nuclear test moratorium entered into in 1958, to collect considerable high-altitude experimental data. This series also included explosions with yields of 25 and over 50 megatons. (The Soviets have subsequently stated that they have these yields in their active inventory.) *Following the conclusion of the test series, the Soviets moved quickly to agree to the partial test ban treaty, thus prohibiting further testing in the atmosphere and outer space* . . . (1979, p. 79, emphasis added).

As I indicated above, atmospheric nuclear tests are probably immoral, because of the fallout they distribute over the earth without sufficient gain to justify this damage. Therefore we should have agreed to ban them, regardless of any other consequences. We cannot argue that we should be allowed to do something immoral, just to learn what the Soviets learned through their series of immoral tests. The fact remains, however, that the Soviets have for over twenty years been in possession of detailed knowledge about the effects of high-altitude nuclear explosions, for disrupting communications and for *blinding* antimissile radars, knowledge that we have not yet matched. They obtained this knowledge in a series of tests that they planned carefully while they were allegedly observing a moratorium. As soon as they gained the knowledge, they moved to shut us out of it by calling for a test ban treaty.

There is an old saying: "Fool me once, shame on you. Fool me twice, shame on me." We have been down this road once before. We would be utter fools to agree to another uninspected moratorium on nuclear testing. This is particularly true since there is not the same *moral* objection to underground testing that there is to atmospheric testing. On the contrary, there are strong *moral* reasons to continue to increase the usability of our weapons through testing.

Nonetheless, previous Soviet duplicity regarding test moratoria should make us wary. What did they discover *this time* that they want to keep us from learning? In an article on the technology of detecting nuclear tests, Zorpette describes a seismic array located in Norway, then notes that in the summer of 1985 the array detected a .25 kiloton nuclear bomb tested at Semipalatinsk (1986, p. 65). The article presents this information to assure us that we could detect even minor Soviet violations of a comprehensive test ban. But the information should lead us to ask other questions, in view of past Soviet behavior. What was the purpose of testing that quarter-kiloton device? To develop a warhead the Soviets can use safely in close proximity to their own troops? To develop the trigger for a mostly-fusion (that is, very low blast) neutron warhead? And if the latter, is it intended for tactical use against ground troops? For terminal defense against ballistic missile warheads? For both? Or was the test for some other purpose? In short, the fact the Soviets conducted this "interesting" test and then began such a vigorous campaign to get us to stop testing, ought to raise a warning flag.

Does this mean we should never agree to any kind of test ban treaty with the USSR? Not at all. As I indicated above, atmospheric nuclear testing was probably immoral. Once we realized this, we should have stopped it regardless of what the Soviets did. Getting them to agree to stop their testing was a pure bonus, for which we should be grateful.

Beyond this, there are limits to the size of weapons we need. We would probably have no moral use for a 100-megaton weapon, let alone a 1000-megaton weapon.[7] However, such a weapon would serve the Soviet Union admirably for blackmail purposes. It is not in our interest to see the Soviets develop such a weapon. Therefore the Limited Test Ban Treaty, which places a ceiling of 150 kilotons on underground tests, is in our interest. It evenhandedly prohibits either side from testing such enormous weapons, but inevitably tilts in our favor, since we have no use for such weapons, while they do. Thus despite the problems of verifying the 150-kiloton limit, the Limited Test Ban Treaty serves our interests.

The opponents of further testing argue that once a ceiling on yield is negotiated, the only avenue for improvement is qualitative improvement. They then want to close off that avenue as well. But this is precisely wrong. Qualitative improvement is exactly what we want, to enable us to deploy weapons we could use with confidence, and in good conscience, if the need arose. It is in the interest only of the Soviet Union to have us armed with weapons in which we have no confidence, or about which we have moral qualms, or which frighten us more than they do the Soviets.

[7] There is some indication that a high-altitude burst of a large warhead, in the 100-megaton range or larger, would disrupt electrical and electronic networks over a large area, without causing any blast- or radiation damage on the ground. This might be precisely what we need to disrupt the Soviet leadership's apparatus of control, without killing any innocent people in the Soviet Union. However, atmospheric testing would probably be needed to confirm this. So long as we lack confidence that we could reliably generate such an effect without killing people on the ground, we could not justify developing such enormous weapons or keeping them in our inventory.

But, it might be argued, won't continued testing allow the Soviets to develop more usable weapons as well? Wouldn't a test ban, which freezes present weapon designs, be better than letting them improve their weapons? In response, I say, let us hope they do develop better weapons. It is in our interest for them to abandon the monstrous weapons they now deploy and to shift to morally usable weapons. That would make easier our task of keeping nuclear war within moral limits. Cohen has stated the testing issues admirably:

> If stopping nuclear testing, which has been an official U.S. policy for the past quarter century, deprives us, or our key allies, of obtaining highly discriminate warheads that pose no threat of the nuclear doomsday so widely heralded these days, why is this an ingrained virtue and a boon to our security? Or if stopping testing precluded possibilities for defensive nuclear warheads that could substantially reduce the damage to our country in the event of nuclear attack, how can this be construed as reducing the risk of war and improving our security? (1985, p. 70).

Far from being immoral, underground nuclear testing, within the limits set by the Limited Test Ban Treaty, is a moral imperative. We *must* have nuclear weapons we would be willing to use if the need arose, rather than weapons that, in a crisis, we were unwilling to use. To get these weapons, we need to continue testing. Religious leaders would do better to focus their protests on Soviet violations of existing test ban treaties rather than trying to get us to sign a treaty that would freeze us into a generation of weapons whose use is morally questionable.

REFERENCES

Adelman, Kenneth L. "Arms Control with and without Agreements". *Foreign Affairs* (Winter 1984/1985), pp. 240–263.
Cohen, Sam. *We CAN Prevent World War III.* Ottawa, Ill.: Jameson Books, 1985.
Conway, Father Edward A. "Pius XII on H-bomb Tests". *The Catholic Mind* (November-December 1957), pp. 487–497.
Davidson, Donald W., Chaplain (Major), U.S. Army. *Nuclear Weapons and the American Churches.* Boulder, Colo.: Westview Press, 1983.
Douglass, James D., Jr., and Amoretta M. Hoeber. *Soviet Strategy for Nuclear War.* Stanford, Calif.: Hoover Institution Press, 1979.

Gaffney, Frank J. Presentation to NATO officials, quoted in *Air Force Policy Letter for Commanders*. Washington, D.C.: August 1, 1986.

Ramsey, Paul. *The Just War*. New York: Charles Scribner's Sons, 1968.

Shevtchuk, Liz. "Efforts to Halt Nuclear Weapons Tests". *Catholic Telegraph* (July 25, 1986), p. 4.

Ulsamer, Edgar. "Three Battle Arenas: A Situation Report". *Air Force Magazine* (February 1987), pp. 91–95.

Zorpette, Glenn. "Monitoring the Tests". *IEEE Spectrum* (July 1986), pp. 57–66.

CHAPTER TWENTY-EIGHT

CIVIL DEFENSE

Clayton Cramer has written a fable which (paraphrased somewhat) goes as follows (1985, p. 46).

You are going on a picnic with four friends, and are loading up your car. You open the trunk to put in the picnic supplies, and your friends suddenly voice expressions of horror: they observe in your trunk a spare tire and a jack.

One says, "It doesn't matter if you have a spare, If we have a flat, it'll be a blowout. We'll go off the road and all die anyway. So why bother?"

The second says, angrily, "Being prepared with a spare shows you support the *concept* of flat tires."

The third says, in a gentler voice, "People who are prepared to survive flat tires have no incentive to drive carefully. Is that fair to other drivers?"

The fourth says, "Why did you spend money on the jack and the spare? Instead you could have bought more beer."

Then they all walk off, leaving you standing there open-mouthed.

These arguments, while silly, are parallel to those offered by opponents of civil defense:

1. No one will survive anyway, so why bother?
2. Civil defense preparations means we support the concept of having nuclear wars.
3. If we have civil defense, our leaders will be more willing to get us into a nuclear war.
4. We should spend the money on _____ instead (fill in the blank with your favorite project).

Objection 1 is a purely practical objection. The rest, in one way or another, touch on moral issues. I will discuss the practical objection briefly, but the moral issues are the more important ones.

In Chapter 22 I argued that use of nuclear weapons not only *must* but *can* be controlled and kept limited. But even if use is limited, is civil defense hopeless? Will we all die anyway in a nuclear attack?[1]

---

[1] In Chapter 22 I quoted a description of a purely counterforce attack against the United States, which spared our cities but disarmed us. Critics of the idea of limited nuclear war object that even such a purely counterforce strike would result in massive casualties in our cities from radioactive fallout. When it is pointed out that these casualties could be avoided by fairly simply fallout shelters, the critics respond that the shelters would not protect against the blast and firestorms resulting from attacks on cities. Once

The destruction at Hiroshima and at Nagasaki has been depicted numerous times. We have all seen pictures showing a seemingly endless vista of buildings flattened and burned out by the atomic bombings of August 1945. Moreover, since the bomb at Hiroshima was dropped from a single plane rather than a formation, there was no warning, no sounding of the air raid sirens. In the main, the people did not take to even such shelters as they had. Therefore it may come as a surprise to learn that at Hiroshima, 73 percent of the population *survived*. At Nagasaki, 78 percent survived. Only one day after the attack at Hiroshima, both electric power and streetcar service had been restored throughout most of the city. Within thirty days, industrial production in both cities had been restored to 75 percent of the preattack levels (Keegan, 1986, pt. III). That is, despite the enormous destruction brought about by the two atomic bombs, it simply wasn't the case that everyone died, nor that recovery was impossible.

It may be objected, of course, that in another war, the nuclear weapons used may be much larger than those used at Hiroshima and Nagasaki. Moreover, it may be argued, those two cities received aid from other cities. In another war, the other cities may be blown up too, and unable to provide aid.

That's true. Those things *may* happen if nuclear weapons are ever used in war again. But there is no certainty they *will* happen. They also *may not* happen. Instead, it might happen that a lot of people die who could have lived if there had been adequate provisions made to protect them.

How much would be adequate? What would it take to provide protection against blast, fires, and fallout?

One model of *adequacy* might be the Soviet Union. The Soviets take civil defense seriously.[2] The Department of Defense reported in 1985:

> The Soviets also have created an elaborate system of emergency relocation facilities, many of which are bunkered, designed to ensure the survival of Party and State control through the protection of high-level Party, government, and military leaders. These facilities are equipped with hardened communications equipment and would serve as alternate command and control posts for the top leadership in wartime. In addition, managers and factory personnel of critical industries would be

---

more, these critics are not above working both sides of the argument. As I show in this chapter, there is reason to believe that even blast shelters could be effective in saving lives, and such shelters would be even more effective against fallout in the event of a no-cities attack.

[2] Keegan claims to have documented, from Soviet sources, a $10 billion annual budget for civil defense (1986, part II).

evacuated with critical machinery out of urban areas and away from immediate battle areas to emergency locations to facilitate their continued operation. All these measures are designed to provide uninterrupted functioning of the various elements of Soviet strategic leadership and the national economy in wartime, including nuclear war (p. 19).

Baxter observes that:

Soviet belief that a future war will be a war of survival fought with nuclear weapons as well as conventional weapons finds expression in several practical ways. It explains Soviet preoccupation with civil defense, which many in the United States view as illogical. As long as it holds this belief, the USSR will continue to seek means of reducing the relative degree of destruction that it may suffer (1986, p. 17).

Many commentators have argued that even as elaborate as the Soviet civil defense program is, it could not provide a high level of protection for the average Soviet citizen. Despite the numerous shelters, and despite the fact that civil defense training is mandatory for all Soviet citizens, it is argued that many would still die in a nuclear attack. This argument may be correct, but misses the point. The Soviet civil defense system is not intended to provide protection for the average Soviet citizen. Its intent is to provide protection for the leadership, to provide continuity of government and survival for the *nomenklatura*.[3] As Pipes observes:

. . . the Soviet Union does not regard civil defense to be exclusively for the protection of ordinary civilians. Its chief function seems to be to protect what in Russia are known as the "cadres", that is, the political and military leaders as well as industrial managers and skilled workers— those who could reestablish the political and economic system once the war was over. Judging by Soviet definitions, civil defense has as much to do with the proper functioning of the country during and immediately after the war as with holding down casualties. Its organization . . . seems to be a kind of shadow government charged with responsibility for administering the country under extreme stresses of nuclear war and its immediate aftermath (1979).

Moreover, the Soviet civil defense preparations go beyond blast shelters. The Soviets have provided for underground storage of food, machines, and spare parts, to tide them over until farms and factories can be put to work again (Keegan, 1986, part II):

The Central Intelligence Agency (CIA), which has a history of playing down the extent and effectiveness of Soviet civil defense measures,

---

[3] Strictly speaking, *nomenklatura* is the list of Soviet positions which may be held only by party members. Figuratively, it can be used for the leadership of the Soviet Union.

still rates them as quite effective. The Congressional Office of Technology Assessment summarized CIA evaluations as follows:

> The CIA study found that a worst case attack could kill or injure well over 100 million people,[4] but many leaders would survive; with a few days for evacuation and shelter, casualties could be reduced by more than 50 percent; and with a week for preattack planning, "Soviet civil defenses could reduce casualties to the low tens of millions" (1979, p. 57).

The Soviets have invested an enormous amount of money, time and effort in their civil defense system, and they appear satisfied that the system has a good chance of carrying out the function they assign to it. To assert they are wrong, that their civil defense wouldn't work if put to the test, takes a great deal of arrogance. Nevertheless, the objectives of the Soviet civil defense system are different from those we would want for an American civil defense system. Therefore it is probably not a good model for us. A better model for the United States might be the Swiss civil defense system. Dyson provides a description of the Swiss requirements for bomb shelters (1984):

> According to Swiss law, every new house or public building must have a bomb shelter. . . . The law has been enforced for thirty years, and during that time the construction of new homes, suburbs, schools, shops, and factories has never stopped. As a result, a high percentage of the Swiss population has immediate access to a shelter (p. 85).

He describes one shelter he saw under construction:

> Swiss building codes, even for ordinary construction, are far more stringent than American codes. Every part of the house was made of reinforced concrete and looked as if it was built to last five hundred years. The shelter looked as if it was built to last five thousand years, like a pharoah's grave (p. 88).

As with the Soviets, Swiss civil defense preparations go beyond blast shelters. The Swiss have built underground hospitals, fully stocked and supplied, which are not used but are kept in operating status by military reservists who are assigned to spend their annual active duty tours at them (Keegan, 1986, part II). Dyson states that according to Swiss estimates, their shelters will reduce by more than three-fourths the lethal

---

[4] Note that this assumes the United States makes direct attacks on cities, with the intent of causing massive civilian casualties. If the United States conducts a nuclear war in accordance with the Just War Doctrine, the Soviet civil defense program could be extremely effective in saving the lives of civilians whose deaths would otherwise occur in attacks on legitimate military objectives. To the extent that we could induce the Soviets to follow the Just War Doctrine, an equivalent U.S. civil-defense program would be extremely effective in saving the lives of Americans.

blast area of a nuclear weapon (1984, p. 66). Swiss civil defense expenditures come to about one-tenth of the Swiss annual military budget.

Both the Soviets and the Swiss are convinced that civil defense measures such as shelters can work. They may be wrong. But if they are right, should there be a nuclear war, many of their people will survive who would otherwise die. From a purely pragmatic standpoint, it is foolish to accept the self-fulfilling prophecy that "in a nuclear war we'd all die anyway".

However, the moral issues as usual outweigh the pragmatic ones. What about the remainder of the objections to civil defense?

The objection that by adopting civil defense measures we are accepting the concept of nuclear war is really a strange argument. Cramer notes that those who make this argument don't argue that wearing a seat belt means you approve of the concept of auto accidents, nor that getting a polio immunization for your children means you approve of the concept of polio, nor that buying medical insurance means you approve of the concept of huge medical bills. The objectors seem to recognize that in these cases, the misfortune in question might occur, and it makes sense to take steps to reduce the damage as much as possible.

Nevertheless, people who wouldn't think of objecting to seat belts, or even to spare tires, raise this objection to civil defense. For instance, several hospitals, run by Catholic orders of nuns, have publicly refused to participate in the government's planning for evacuation and treatment of victims of nuclear attack. They have done so on the grounds that by participating in civil defense planning, they would be approving the idea of nuclear war.

This objection is really a variant of one we have discussed before, that civil defense measures make nuclear war thinkable. This variant is invalid, just as are the others we have already discussed. To the Soviets, nuclear war is already thinkable, and they have made extensive preparations to fight and survive it. Since we may actually be faced with the prospect of nuclear war, we must think about it, and make preparations for it. As discussed in earlier chapters, that preparation means finding ways to fight it morally. But preparation also means finding ways to survive it, since it would be immoral to fight a war we have no hope of winning. Trying to keep nuclear war unthinkable is just another way of avoiding the moral issues. Whether we like it or not, nuclear war is thinkable, and we must think about how to survive it. Should nuclear war come, this argument against civil defense will appear rather hollow.

Consider those nuns who have refused to take part in civil-defense planning. What would they do if we suffered a nuclear attack? It is utterly unthinkable that in those circumstances they would actually refuse to treat the victims. One's immediate reaction is to say that *of course* they would open their hospitals to the victims and would cooperate with the government's efforts to provide medical treatment for the victims. But because they refuse to take part in planning ahead of time, they may not have the right kinds or quantities of supplies on hand. In addition, there will be delay and confusion arising from changes in the orders of civil-defense officials and ambulance drivers in order to divert to those hospitals some victims who were originally planned to be sent elsewhere. The inevitable result of these nuns' present attitude is that if we undergo a nuclear attack, people are going to die whom they might have saved. This is a high price to pay for someone's refusal to face up to the issues of fighting a nuclear war morally.

But then we reach the third objection, which in effect states that civil defense preparations make nuclear war more likely. We have encountered this objection before, too. It is the same logic which says that if we make nuclear war horrible enough it won't happen, and which then requires us to threaten to commit immoral actions in retaliation against an attacker. It is the same logic which says that if we acquire usable weapons, in a crisis we may be tempted to use them. It is the same logic which says that if we develop defenses against nuclear attack, we are more likely to resist than to seek "peaceful" ways of resolving a dispute.

Those who make this objection have an obligation to be honest with the rest of us. In a crisis, would they prefer that we surrender rather than resist? Would they prefer that we fold up in the face of a nuclear threat? Would they prefer that we cave in to nuclear blackmail? Do they want us to surrender piecemeal to the communists' well-developed *salami-slice* tactics? Do they really want us to create a moral hazard by tempting an aggressor?

Furthermore, what do those who make this objection have to say about Soviet civil defense? Do Soviet preparations increase the risk of war? If so, why are they not protesting the world's biggest civil defense program, instead of protesting against our attempts to start one? If Soviet civil defense measures do not increase the risk of war, then why should ours?

Ultimately, the problem is the inverse chauvinism of those who make this objection. They take the attitude that "My country is always wrong". They simply refuse to face the facts about the world in which we live—facts, which were presented at length in Chapter 15, on the comparative justice of the U.S. and Soviet causes.

The simple facts of history are that it is the Soviet Union which is an expansionist power, not the United States. It is the Soviet Union which seeks to dominate each new set of neighbors it acquires as it absorbs the old ones, not the United States. It is the Soviet Union which is a threat to peace, not the United States. To argue that U.S. civil defense measures increase the risk of war because they might cause our leaders to be more belligerent is to stand reality on its head. To the extent that civil defense measures make our resistance to aggression more credible to the Soviets, they actually reduce the risk of war. Moreover, they reduce the Soviets' temptations to test our will or to attempt nuclear blackmail against us.

A variant of this objection states that even though we have peaceful intentions, the Soviets might perceive our civil defense program as preparation for an attack, and launch a preemptive strike. Therefore we must refrain from arousing their suspicions. We can reject this form of the objection as well. After all, why doesn't this same logic apply to the Soviets' civil defense measures? Why shouldn't we perceive their program as preparation for an attack, given their history of aggression? Given such perceptions, wouldn't our own civil defense program be more moral than launching a preemptive strike ourselves? If the Soviets see us preparing to survive, they may be less tempted to launch the attack that this logic says we should assume they must be planning. Given the actual history of U.S. and Soviet behavior, U.S. civil defense is thus a nonthreatening, nonlethal deterrent.

We come, then, to the final objection, that the money would be better spent on other things. Those who raise this objection are not really demanding reduced government expenditures. They invariably want the money redirected to their favorite purposes. Moreover, as Cramer points out, their objections might be more impressive if they weren't so hostile to *private* civil defense efforts as well.

Before we can decide whether the money would be better spent on civil defense or on health, education, and welfare, we need to ask, how much would civil defense cost? The Federal Emergency Management Agency has stated:

> An optimum civil defense capability would seek to maximize population survival in the event of an attack and would, in addition, provide an improved basis for eventual postattack recovery. Such a program, modeled after the Swiss program to develop blast shelter for each citizen, *would be extremely costly,* requiring a sustained *annual budget of approximately $9 billion—roughly $38.00 for every man, woman and child in the United States.* This is probably infeasible (1983, p. 18) (emphasis added).

This statement is itself incredible, not to mention incredibly defeatist. The United States spends more than $30 billion annually on tobacco products, and more than $50 billion annually on alcoholic beverages.

Annual expenditures on jewelry and watches come to more than $21 billion (U.S. Bureau of the Census, 1986, pp. 422, 739). To argue that we cannot spend $9 billion annually on civil defense is utterly absurd. We don't need to divert money from health, education, and welfare to civil defense. What we spend on booze and cigarettes is nine times what an optimum civil defense program would cost.

In summary, we can reject completely all the arguments against civil defense. The pragmatic argument alone, that civil-defense preparations will assure that we don't "all die anyway" in a nuclear war, is sufficient justification for civil defense. The objections on allegedly moral grounds are also invalid. Making civil defense preparations does not mean we want to have a nuclear war, nor (given the actual behavior of the United States and the Soviet Union) can it be taken to mean that *we* are the ones who are threatening to start a nuclear war. Finally, we can afford adequate civil defense without shortchanging any other activities of our government, even those of much lower priority than preparing to survive a nuclear attack. Civil defense, then, is a nonthreatening way of preparing to survive a nuclear war we may have to fight.

Far from being a morally dubious activity, civil defense is a moral imperative. Since nuclear war may be forced upon us, we must be prepared to survive it rather than betray the values that the Soviet Union has effectively suppressed elsewhere in the world.

REFERENCES

Baxter, William. *Soviet AirLand Battle Tactics.* Novato, Calif.: Presidio Press, 1986.

Cramer, Clayton. "Spare Tires Cause Flats!" *Reason* (February 1985), p. 46.

Department of Defense. *Soviet Military Power 1985.* Washington, D.C.: Superintendent of Documents, 1985.

Dyson, Freeman. *Weapons and Hope.* New York: Harper & Row, 1984.

Federal Emergency Management Agency. "Report for the Senate and House Committees on Armed Services on National Civil Defense Program". July 3, 1983.

Keegan, George J., General (Ret.), U.S. Air Force. "Civil Defense Revisited", *American Defense* (May–June 1986) part I, (July–August 1986) part II, (September–October 1986) part III.

Office of Technology Assessment. *The Effects of Nuclear War.* Washington, D.C.: U.S. Government Printing Office, May 1979.

Pipes, Richard. "Why the Soviet Union Thinks It Could Fight and Win a Nuclear War". *Commentary* (July 1979).

U.S. Bureau of the Census. *Statistical Abstract of the United States: 1986* (106th edition). Washington, D.C.: Government Printing Office, 107th edition, 1987.

CHAPTER TWENTY-NINE

THE MORAL PROBLEMS WON'T GO AWAY

In 1960, Father John Courtney Murray wrote that there were three possible starting points for analyzing the problem of war in an age of nuclear weapons ("Theology", 1960). The first of these was the enormous physical destruction that these weapons are capable of producing. However, he said, looking only at this consideration was likely to lead to the view that war had become a "moral absurdity"; one might be led to nuclear pacifism. The second starting point was the enormous threat that communism poses to life, liberty, and the Western and Christian traditions. Looking only at this consideration, he said, might lead to advocating a "holy war", or to the position that "since the adversary is completely unprincipled", we may use any means that seem necessary to victory. The third starting point was the existence of the United Nations, which by its charter is committed to peaceful settlement of disputes. He argued that looking only at this consideration would be a mistake, since the UN's decisions "are natively apt to sanction injustice as well as justice".

He argued that if we limited ourselves to any one of these starting points, we would fail to find our way to "an integral and morally defensible position on the problem of war". However, he said, all these positions do reflect reality, and we must take them all into account.

Today, more than a quarter of a century later, how do these possible starting points for analysis of modern warfare look?

Today hardly anyone would argue seriously that the existence of the United Nations has ended the validity of warfare as a means of defending oneself against aggression. There are people who have, over the past four decades, invested their careers and reputations in touting the United Nations as "our last, best hope for peace". However, by now they resemble the chickens I used to see running and flapping their wings after my father had cut off their heads—all reflex, no reason. Most people have come to recognize what Father Murray was prophetic enough to see: the United Nations defers to raw power, not to justice.

The second starting point is today no more likely to be taken than the third. It is now intellectually unacceptable to speak of the evils of communism. Consider the reactions, the criticisms of a *Cold War mentality,* that followed President Reagan's description of the Soviet Union as an "evil empire". As Joseph Sobran wrote, this phrase contains two words: a noun and an adjective. Which is it the objectors don't like, the noun or the adjective? In reality, it is neither the noun nor the adjective that bothers the objectors. What really bothers them is that Mr. Reagan violated the unspoken rule that one must not tell the truth about the Soviet Union and communism.[1] The reason the objectors offer is the same one Father Murray gave for not concentrating solely on the evil nature of communism: someone might decide to wage a holy war. However, Father Murray didn't say we must ignore the evils of communism, let alone deny them. He merely said we must not look at them only. Today the danger is not that people will look at them only, but that people will not look at them at all.

While Father Murray's second and third starting points are currently unthinkable because unfashionable, the first is widely used, and has led to the precise problem he foresaw.

Father Richard McSorley's article "It's a Sin to Build a Nuclear Weapon" (1976) is a perfect example of what Father Murray meant. Over 50 percent of the article is devoted to a description of the physical effects of detonating a twenty-megaton bomb over Manhattan.[2] Father McSorley then leaps from the horror of that explosion to the conclusion that the use of any nuclear weapons, regardless of size or target, is immoral, and therefore building one is a sin. There is no argumentation, no reasoning, no moral analysis, to justify this leap. There are none of the nuances or the ambiguity so beloved of Catholic theologians nowadays. There are only appeals to emotion and rhetorical questions such as: "Can we imagine Jesus pushing the button that would release nuclear weapons on millions of people?"

This rhetorical question should be analyzed in the light of Catholic doctrine, to illustrate how focusing solely on the destruction caused by nuclear weapons leads to incorrect moral conclusions about war. We must remember that Jesus never repudiated so much as one word of the Old Testament. On the contrary, He stated clearly that He had come to

---

[1] As the French writer Raymond Aron once put it: "Detente means the Communists may continue to tell lies about us, but we may not tell the truth about them."

[2] Note that the explosion is portrayed as being in Manhattan, not in, say, Moscow or Leningrad. One wonders if Father McSorley is intentionally appealing more to our fears of what might be done to us than to our moral revulsion at what we might do to others. The proper Christian attitude is to be concerned that *our* use of nuclear weapons not be sinful. To call *our* ownership of them sinful through fear of what the enemy might do to *us* is hypocritical.

fulfill the Law, not to abolish it. He also emphasized His oneness with His Father. In the Old Testament, God *ordered* the Israelites to put to the sword some of their (and His) enemies, not even sparing women, children, and livestock.[3] This is the same God Whom the Old Testament records as wiping out Sodom and Gomorrah with fire and brimstone. To assert that Jesus objected to these actions of His Father is not merely contrary to Catholic doctrine, it is blasphemy. Finally, according to Catholic doctrine, Jesus will ultimately condemn unrepentant sinners to something far more horrible than death in a nuclear explosion. Our inability to imagine Jesus "pushing the button" reflects more the limits of our imaginations than it does any limits on Jesus' capabilities.

McSorley of course is not alone in beginning his analysis with the horrors of a nuclear explosion. Kenny (1985), despite his excellent analysis of the intentions of the would-be deterrer, ultimately falls into the same trap of utilizing this starting point. He does not condemn any use of nuclear weapons as sinful. He recognizes that *we* could fight a nuclear war justly. However, he urges that we should not attempt to do so, but should instead surrender when threatened with nuclear attack, because of what the Soviets would do to us as they fought unjustly. He argues that it is better to live in Warsaw under the Soviets than in Hiroshima under the bomb. It apparently doesn't register with him that forty years later the inhabitants of Hiroshima are free and prosperous under the *umbrella* of the bomb, while the inhabitants of Warsaw are neither free nor prosperous and are *still* under the Soviets.

Unfortunately, this tendency to look at nuclear war from only one starting point is not limited to individual scholars, priests, or bishops. It crept into the Catholic bishops' Challenge of Peace pastoral (1983, no. 129):

> Papal teaching has consistently addressed the folly and danger of the arms race; but the new perception of it which is now held by the general public is due in large measure to the work of scientists and physicians who have described for citizens the concrete human consequences of a nuclear war.

As Mangieri notes (1983, p. 5), papal teaching concerned itself with *prudential* issues: the medical consequences of a nuclear war represented a good reason not to have one. The bishops have elevated this to a *moral* issue and have conferred upon the medical profession the status of moral leaders.[4]

---

[3] For example, Deut. 20:16–18.

[4] One wonders if the bishops would be as willing to accept the moral leadership of members of the medical profession on the issue of abortion as they are on the issue of nuclear war.

Spaeth, in commenting on the Challenge of Peace pastoral, makes a similar observation:

Pacifism among today's Catholic bishops differs from the strict ideology that has moved other pacifists to reject all violence and to insist upon total and unilateral disarmament. These bishops appear to have embraced pacifism as a response to the dangers of nuclear arms instead of as an *a priori* acceptance of immutable Christian principles (1982, p. 9).

That is, the bishops have made the first of Father Murray's catalog of mistakes: starting their analysis from the horrors of nuclear war.

However, the fact the pacifism of the American bishops may be rooted more in fear than in Christian principles doesn't mean that trying to root it in Christian principles would be any better. This is the mistake G. E. M. Anscombe warned against (1961, pp. 52–53). She describes what she calls a false image of Christianity. "According to this image, Christianity is an ideal and beautiful religion, impracticable except for a few rare characters". She then says the problem with this false image is that it leads to high-sounding principles that are obviously impossible to keep in practice. For instance, this false view of Christianity makes counsels, such as turning the other cheek, into precepts. It then concludes that since the precepts cannot be kept, Christianity is an impractical religion. Holders of this view, Anscombe says, believe "absolute pacifism is an ideal; unable to follow that, and committed to 'compromise with evil', one must go the whole hog and wage war *a outrance.*" She goes on to say:

The truth about Christianity is that it is a severe and practicable religion, not a beautifully ideal but impracticable one. Its moral precepts . . . are those of the Old Testament; and its God is the God of Israel (1961, pp. 53–54).

She then concludes:

. . . pacifism teaches people to make no distinction between the shedding of innocent blood and the shedding of any human blood. And in this way pacifism has corrupted enormous numbers of people who will not act according to its tenets. They become convinced that a number of things are wicked which are not; hence, seeing no way of avoiding "wickedness", they set no limits to it (1961, p. 56).

This false view of Christianity is clearly present in the words of Victor Gollancz (1959, in the "Notes for the American Edition"):

Politics, everyone knows, is the art of the possible. Christ demanded, almost everyone thinks (whatever some may profess), the impossible.

The theme of this book is simply that, unless the impossibilism of Christ is substituted for the possibilism of politics, the world must destroy itself. In the nuclear age, the wages of sin is [*sic*] universal death.

The inevitable result of asserting that Christianity demands what is in fact impossible is just as Anscombe described it. When people recognize that it is impossible, they set no limits on the possible. Consider the following quotes regarding use of atomic bombs against Japan (all from Walzer, 1977, p. 265):

Harry S. Truman: "Let us not become so preoccupied with weapons that we lose sight of the fact that war itself is the real villain."

Arthur Compton, a scientific adviser to the U.S. government during World War II: "When one thinks of the mounted archers of Ghengiz Khan . . . the Thirty Years War . . . the millions of Chinese who died during the Japanese invasion . . . the mass destruction of western Russia. . . . One realizes that in whatever manner it is fought, war is precisely what General Sherman called it."

James Byrnes, Secretary of State in 1945: ". . . war remains what General Sherman said it was."

This attitude did not end with the conclusion of World War II. Tucker quotes General Omar Bradley as stating, in rebuttal to objections that mass bombing was immoral, that "war itself is immoral", and that in retaliation for attacks on our cities, it would be both moral and militarily useful to attack enemy cities (1960, p. 59, note 52). Tucker also quotes a statement made by George Kennan, the former ambassador to the Soviet Union and prominent Sovietologist, during the hearings on J. Robert Oppenheimer.

. . . in responding to the question of whether he had opposed the hydrogen bomb on moral grounds, George Kennan declared: ". . . I didn't consider that. After all, we are dealing with weapons here, and when you are dealing with weapons you are dealing with things to kill people, and I don't think the considerations of morality are relevant" (1960, p. 77, n. 70).

Clearly what Anscombe describes as a false view, that morality in general, and Christianity in particular, demand pacifism, and that morality is therefore irrelevant to practical considerations, has permeated the leadership of our nation for the past several decades. However, a statement that was even more frightening to me, since it came from a fellow military professional, is this extract from the biography of Charles "Chuck" Yeager, who describes a mission he was ordered to fly during World War II:

> Our seventy-five Mustangs were assigned an area of fifty miles by fifty miles inside Germany and ordered to strafe anything that moved. The object was to demoralize the German population. . . . We weren't asked how we felt zapping people. It was a miserable, dirty mission, but we all took off on time and did it. . . . *By definition, war is immoral; there is no such thing as a clean war. Once armies are engaged, war is total. We were ordered to commit an atrocity, pure and simple,* but the brass who approved this action probably felt justified because wartime Germany wasn't easily divided between "innocent civilians" and its military machine. . . . In war, the military will seldom hesitate to hit civilians if they are in the way. . . . I'm certainly not proud of that particular strafing mission against civilians. But it is there, on the record and in my memory (1985, p. 63, emphasis added).

The people of the United States, especially those in the military services, deserve better of their moral leaders than a statement that "Any use of nuclear weapons is immoral." The likely result of that, as Anscombe warns, is to lead decent people like Chuck Yeager to conclude that once war is forced on us, there are no limits, and therefore they can licitly participate in something they recognize as an atrocity.

The Just War Doctrine is not the exclusive property of Christians, let alone of Catholics. Many people have reached the same conclusions by other routes, such as Natural Law. Nevertheless, Christians in general, and Catholics in particular, have a special relationship to the Doctrine, since it was developed under their auspices. Not only Augustine and Thomas Aquinas, but Martin Luther, and the English Puritan William Ames, contributed to its development. This relationship is still relevant even in the age of nuclear weapons.

Abraham Lincoln has been accused of putting the Constitution in mothballs—denial of habeas corpus, seizure of property without compensation, abuse of executive authority—while waging a war to preserve the Constitution. Christians must not allow a false image of Christianity to lead them to put their Christianity in mothballs while they defend Christian values and the societies in which these values are (however imperfectly) embodied. As the Second Vatican Council said in the *Pastoral Constitution on the Church in the Modern World* (1965, no. 79) "Neither does the mere fact that war has unhappily begun mean that all is fair between the warring parties."

Catholic tradition, of course, has always held this position. Not all is fair in war. However, some things *are* fair in war, including killing in self-defense and in defense of the victims of injustice. Just as Jesus will one day distinguish between the guilty and the innocent, we are expected to do the same in war, even though the worst of our acts against the guilty pale by comparison with His. The Just War Doctrine was intended to delineate the difference between *fair* and *unfair* in war. But except for the attempt by Father John Ford to analyze obliteration bombing in World War II, the Catholic Church as such made little attempt to apply Just War Doctrine either to World War II or to the use of nuclear weapons since 1945.[5]

This failure to apply Just War Doctrine meant that initially the Church did not criticize the widespread view that since war is immoral anyway, anything goes once it has broken out. More recently, the failure to apply Just War Doctrine has meant that the Church does not criticize the growing tendency toward nuclear pacifism, and even total pacifism, among misinformed Catholics.

John Courtney Murray addressed this failure to apply Just War Doctrine:

> I think that the tendency to query the uses of the Catholic [Just War] doctrine on war initially arises from the fact that it has for so long not been used by Catholics. That is, it has not been made the basis for a sound critique of public policies and as a means for the formation of a right public opinion. . . . I think it is time to say that the traditional doctrine was irrelevant during World War II. This is no argument against the traditional doctrine. The ten commandments do not lose their imperative by reason of the fact that they are violated (quoted in O'Connor, 1981, p. 64).

The primary duty of all Christians, but especially Catholics, with regard to war in today's world, becomes the critique of public policies from a Just War perspective.[6] In particular, it is our duty to demand that our defense department take Just War Doctrine into account when its officials plan to defend us. It is past time for Christians to stop putting Christianity into mothballs while we prepare to defend it.

---

[5] As someone put it, during World War II the Catholic bishops would have been more upset had American aircraft been dropping contraceptives on Japanese civilians than they were that the aircraft were dropping bombs on them. (I believe this comment was made by prominent Catholic pacifist Gordon Zahn, but I have been unable to trace the reference.)

[6] This obligation falls on the Christian peace churches, who do not accept even as much war as Just War Doctrine would allow, just as much as it falls on those who have held and taught the Doctrine. Even from the perspective of the peace churches, pulling nuclear war back within the limits of Just War Doctrine would represent an improvement over today's situation.

Protestant theologian Paul Ramsey argued that we should be preparing to fight a war, if necessary, instead of preparing a holocaust.

> It is the responsibility of defense establishments to find the way to relate means of violence rationally to the ends of policy, and not fight all the war—or many of the plans of war—they are capable of fighting today (1968, p. 196).

Thirty years ago, Thomas E. Murray, as a member of the U.S. Atomic Energy Commission, argued for developing nuclear weapons that could be used for fighting a just war, not committing a nuclear atrocity:

> There are issues . . . which may have to be settled by arms. Broadly, they are issues of justice, the classical issues of war. They are always limited issues. And war is the legal institution available as a last resort for their settlement. In its political and moral meaning war is man's ultimately resolute declaration of his fixed and firm purpose—that he will have peace indeed but only with justice. . . . Our central problem therefore is to deter limited aggressions and to retaliate by effective but limited force, if deterrence fails (1957, p. 395).

Perhaps the best-stated moral argument for learning how to fight a limited nuclear war is that made by Father John Courtney Murray, over a quarter of a century ago.

> The facts assert that today this *ultima ratio* takes the form of nuclear force, whose use remains possible and may prove to be necessary, lest a free field be granted to brutal violence and lack of conscience. The [Just War] doctrine then asserts that the use of nuclear force must be limited, the principle of limitation being the exigencies of legitimate defense against injustice. Thus the terms of the public debate are set in two words, "limited war". . . . [T]here are those who say that the limitation of nuclear war . . . is today impossible. . . . In the face of this position, the traditional doctrine simply asserts again, "The problem today is limited war". But notice that the assertion is on a higher plane than that of sheer fact. It is a moral proposition, or better, a moral imperative. In other words, since limited nuclear war may be a necessity, it must be made a possibility. . . . To say that the possibility of limited nuclear war cannot be created by intelligence and energy, under the direction of a moral imperative, is to succumb to some sort of determinism in human affairs (1960, pp. 270–271).

The challenge we face hasn't changed in the thirty years since the two Murrays first expressed it: to find moral ways to use nuclear weapons to defend ourselves against aggression. The alternative is to concede the use of nuclear weapons to only those who recognize no morality. By doing that we would abandon all that is decent in the world to the dubious mercies of the Hitlers, the Stalins, the Pol Pots, the Idi Amins of history. That would be immoral in itself. It would fly in the face of the consistent teachings of the Church from Augustine to John Paul II.

Since the two Murrays wrote, we have drifted toward nuclear warfighting, and away from simply planning a holocaust. However, there have been no consistent rules, no guiding moral principles, behind this drift. Instead, this unsteady trend has arisen from accidents of technology (more accurate guidance systems meant we could use smaller warheads, thereby conserving scarce nuclear material) and from an inarticulate but nonetheless real horror of actually doing what our weapons were designed to be capable of doing.

We have a lot of lost time to make up. We can only pray that we will be granted the additional time necessary. We must begin by rejecting both defeatism ("It cant be done!") and moral obtuseness ("It shouldn't be done!"). Then we must undertake the hard tasks we have neglected in all the years since Hiroshima, those of learning how to use nuclear weapons morally, and of building weapons we can use in good conscience should the need arise.

REFERENCES

Anscombe, G. E. M. "War and Murder". In *Nuclear Weapons: A Catholic Response,* edited by Walter Stein. New York: Sheed and Ward, 1961.

Gollancz, Victor. *The Devil's Repertoire.* Garden City: Doubleday & Co., 1959.

Kenny, Anthony. *The Logic of Deterrence.* Chicago: University of Chicago Press, 1985.

Mangieri, Thomas P. *Nuclear War, Peace, and Catholicism.* Front Royal, Va: Christendom Publications, 1983.

McSorley, Father Richard T. "It's a Sin to Build a Nuclear Weapon". *U.S. Catholic* (October 1976), pp. 12–13.

Murray, John Courtney. "Theology and Modern War". In *Morality and Modern Warfare,* edited by William J. Nagle. Baltimore: Helicon Press, 1960.

Murray, John Courtney. *We Hold These Truths.* New York: Sheed and Ward, 1960.

Murray, Thomas E. "Rational Nuclear Armament". *The Catholic Mind* (September–October 1957), pp. 387–397.

O'Connor, John J. *In Defense of Life*. Boston: Daughters of St. Paul, 1981.

Ramsey, Paul. *The Just War*. New York: Charles Scribner's Sons, 1968.

Spaeth, Robert L. "Disarmament and the Catholic Bishops". *This World* (Summer 1982).

Tucker, Robert W. *The Just War*. Baltimore: Johns Hopkins University Press, 1960.

Walzer, Michael. *Just and Unjust Wars*. New York: Basic Books, 1977.

Yeager, Chuck, and Leo Janos. *Yeager*. New York: Bantam Books, 1985.